Advance Praise for *Among the Ancients*

Among the Ancients is a gift for people from all walks of life. It is a guidebook not only to beautiful, sacred places, but also to reconnecting to the reverence for our beautiful planet we call home. May we all work together to respect, restore and protect our wild places, for what we do to the Earth, we do to ourselves.

—*Julia Butterfly Hill, activist and author of* The Legacy of Luna

This is a guide that could change your life, or at least the way you see America. In lucid, elegant prose, Joan Maloof takes you on ecological, spiritual, and aesthetic tramps through the very best that remains of the eastern forest that existed before humans had much say over the landscape. Maps and directions to ancient forest preserves in twenty-six states let you make your own pilgrimage.

Among the Ancients laments all we've lost through centuries of plunderous logging, and critiques the narrow, "production" viewpoint of all too many modern foresters. But it's never heavy-handed and is ultimately uplifting, celebrating the wonder and beauty still available to those willing to hike a bit, and to let Maloof expand their sensibilities.

—*Tom Horton, winner of the John Burroughs Medal for Nature Writing*

An ode to lost old-growth forests everywhere, and a celebration of those few that remain. Joan Maloof simultaneously writes with the precision of a scientist and the passion of a poet. *Among the Ancients* will have you looking at all forests—young and old—with a new eye.

—*Gary K. Meffe, co-author,* Principles of Conservation Biology

With her beautiful book *Among the Ancients*, Joan Maloof has again done a great service for the forests, wildlife, and people of the eastern United States. In the noble tradition of naturalists John Muir, E. Lucy Braun, Mary Byrd Davis, and others, Maloof vividly describes and strongly champions surviving remnants of the great forests that once blanketed the East. Take the literary journey with her, and you will find yourself enthralled.

—*John Davis, former edito*

D1608166

Among the Ancients

RAMSEY'S DRAFT, VIRGINIA

Among the Ancients

ADVENTURES IN THE
EASTERN OLD-GROWTH FORESTS

Joan Maloof

Ruka Press
Washington, DC

First edition published 2011 by Ruka Press, PO Box 1409, Washington, DC 20013

All photographs used in the book are by Joan and Rick Maloof, except those for Virginia, which are by David McDaniel. Used by permission.

The map data is from OpenStreetMap and copyright OpenStreetMap contributors, under the Creative Commons Attribution-ShareAlike 2.0 license. See: http://www.openstreetmap.com and http://creativecommons.org/licenses/by-sa/2.0.

The tree illustrations used on the map pages are by USDA-NRCS PLANTS Database / Britton, N.L., and A. Brown. 1913. *An Illustrated Flora of the Northern United States, Canada and the British Possessions.* Copyright free.

Directions to the parks are by the author and are offered without warranty. Travel data, such as park hours and access, were accurate at the time of the author's visits but are subject to change. Contact the author at *www.amongtheancients.com.*

Library of Congress Control Number: 2010942749

ISBN 978-0-9830111-0-1

10 9 8 7 6 5 4 3 2 1

Printed in the United States of America

Design by Sensical Design & Communication

*For everyone who has had the experience
of being in an old-growth forest,
and especially for those who have
shared these trails with me.*

SHE WAS NO longer that woman with blue eyes
who once had echoed through the poet's poems,
no longer the wide couch's scent and island,
nor yonder man's possession any longer.

She was already loosened like long hair,
and given far and wide like fallen rain,
shared like a limitless supply.

She was already root.

—Rainer Maria Rilke

Table of Contents

🌳

Among the Ancients

AREA OF VIRGIN FOREST
1620

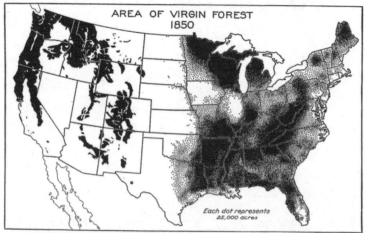

AREA OF VIRGIN FOREST
1850

Each dot represents
25,000 acres

AREA OF VIRGIN FOREST
1920

Each dot represents
25,000 acres

Preface

I WROTE A SMALL book about trees. One of the chapters in that book described visiting an old-growth forest in Maryland. The book was well received, and I got many heartfelt e-mails and letters, but nearly all of my readers wanted to know the same thing: *how to get to that old-growth forest.*

I knew how they felt because it had taken me, too, a long time to find directions to an old-growth forest in the East. For many years I didn't even bother asking for directions, because when I inquired about ancient, uncut forests in the East I was told there were none left. Like many other tree lovers, I visited the redwood and the sequoia groves in the West, and although they were a wondrous consolation, they were not an image of what my home ground ever was, or could be.

I had read the accounts written by early explorers describing the majestic and diverse eastern forests stretching from the Atlantic Ocean to the Mississippi River. I had seen the photographs of the unbelievably large white oaks, bald cypress, longleaf pines, tulip poplars, and hemlocks—most of them taken either just before or just after the trees were cut. I longed to experience what the eastern forest was like in its original state.

Not until the 1990s did the first stories of eastern old growth reach me.

In that decade, a dedicated group of forest lovers started publishing their findings: there *was* old growth in the East. Although the estimates of *how much* were depressingly low—less than *one half of one percent* of the great eastern forest was still old growth—the fact that it existed at all brought joy to my heart. The remaining fragments were scattered far and wide, but they existed, and I could see them.

Most residents of the eastern United States never get to see an old-growth forest. They think perhaps the forests are too far away, or they lack directions. Like the forests, the directions are scattered far and wide.

In order to write this book, I visited one old-growth forest in each state east of the Mississippi River—twenty-six states in all. The forests are all open to the public, and in these pages I tell you how to get there and what you will find when you arrive. Some of the forests are pristine; some are in distress. Some are an easy drive, others a difficult hike or paddle. Some are vast; others cover just a few acres. I hope the book will be an enjoyable adventure even if you never leave your couch. But if, like my earlier readers, you are eager to experience the ancients for yourself, this book can guide you to them.

IF YOU HAVE read this far and you are still not sure what an old-growth forest is, there is no need to be ashamed. It is a difficult concept to pin down, and I would wager that more tree fiber has already been used to print various definitions of old growth than currently exists in old-growth forests in the East. There is no single definition for it. When someone at the United Nations Forestry Division went looking for definitions, he found ninety-eight of them. So we won't get involved in that debate.

For our purposes, we will be content with the notion that old-growth forests are places that have been left alone for a very long time. This usually results in large, old trees, but in some marginal environments, such as mountaintops, even the ancient trees are small. When forests are left alone, the natural cycles of life and death are easy to witness. The structure of a forest changes with age, and as the structure of an ancient forest develops, the plant and animal communities become more diverse and complex. Even the soil changes as a forest ages. The reason definitions are so difficult is that *every forest is different*.

We will have to see for ourselves what old growth really is. On our journey, we will see numerous examples of old-growth attributes. We are going to the forests with the biggest trees we can find, and we are going to experience how full of life they are. But we are also going to look at the forests from the human perspective. We will discover who had the dream, who drew the line, who said "no" to the loggers.

Although state boundaries are human-made political divisions and do not closely reflect the various forest bioregions, I have organized the book by state to show that, no matter where you live in the East, there is an old-growth forest you can reach in a day. These are not excursions to the trackless wilderness; these are places almost anyone can go.

These are true stories. You may use them individually, as guides for places you'd like to visit, or take the whole journey with me from beginning to end. The astute reader will note that, as a result of organizing the chapters geographically, they are not in the order in which I visited the forests. If you would like to know the dates of my visits, I have included them in the reference notes, along with the Latin names of the species I discuss.

Some might wonder why I would want to share these places, why I would want to make it easier to find them. Besides the human instinct to share the best the world has to offer, I believe that, as more of us visit these places, more of us will understand what our landscape used to be, and more of us will make the effort to protect the ancient forests that remain. I want to see even more people out there on the shady paths, so more voices will speak out for the trees and the creatures that live among them.

Forests change—even old-growth forests. On my journeys, I found myself hoping that we humans could change too, change in a way that would allow ancient trees to be a more common part of our landscape and make it even easier to walk among them.

Moody Forest Natural Area, Georgia

SOUTHERN FORESTS

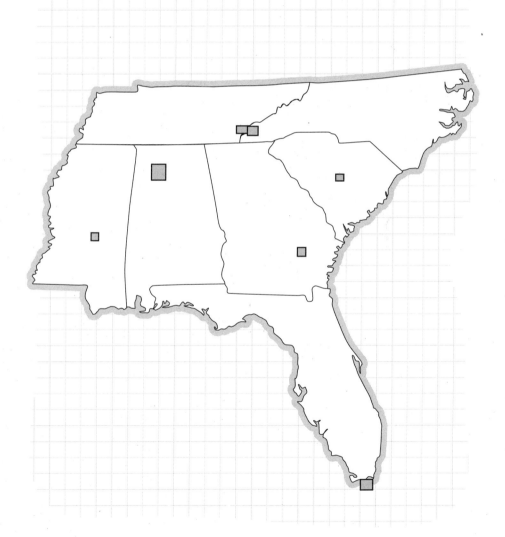

ALABAMA

★
Birmingham

Thompson Creek
trailhead

SIPSEY
WILDERNESS

60

195

Tulip poplar

Double Springs

TRAVEL DIRECTIONS

Northwestern part of state, Winston County. Closest town: Double Springs.
From Double Springs, go north on Route 195 for 9.4 miles. You will see a sign
for the Sipsey River Picnic Grounds; make a right there (my map indicates
that this is Route 60, but it was not marked as such). Continue straight on
this road; do not make the next right toward the picnic area. After about three
miles, the road changes from hard surface to gravel; keep going. After another
three miles or so, you will pass a church and shortly after that the road will "T."
Make a right at the T onto Forest Service Road 203. Make the first right off of
FS 203, following the signs to Thompson Creek trailhead. In about four miles,
you will cross a narrow wooden bridge and the road ends. This is where trail
206 begins.

To get to the Tree, take trail 206 to trail 209 to East Bee Branch. The
Sipsey Wilderness Hiking Club has a very helpful website with trail maps at
www.sipseywilderness.org.

Alabama

SIPSEY WILDERNESS, WILLIAM B. BANKHEAD NATIONAL FOREST

The Tree...Being still and paying attention

AH, SIPSEY. I would like every forester to see Sipsey Wilderness. Many foresters I talk to seem to think that without their management the forests would be unhealthy—full of weedy species, insects, and dying trees. But here, where the forest is unmanaged, there are big, beautiful trees of all kinds: pine, beech, sweet gum, hemlock, hickory, oak, and tulip poplar. This forest is not shaped by any human plan, and yet it is vibrant, healthy, alive. This is the real thing, the true old growth, the original forest for all to see.

I am not alone in my admiration of Alabama's old growth. An early natural history explorer of this region, Phillip Henry Gosse, described the forest he found here in 1838:

> There is an inexpressible grandeur in these primeval forests. Many of the trees are of immense magnitude, and their trunks rise like pillars from the soft and damp soil, shooting upward in columnal magesty [sic]....The number of young saplings that at first sprang up together prevented the throwing forth of side-shoots; each struggled upward toward the light of heaven, each striving for mastery over its fellows, for the possession of space and the light which could be obtained right upward. To this end all the vegetative energy was

directed; the sap was not wasted in lateral buds, or if such peeped forth, they withered for lack of light. But as all were engaged in the same struggle, the desired object still removed as the summits of the aspiring trees pushed upward; till the weaker, being left behind, died out one by one, and the mighty winners of the race at length found themselves comparatively few in number, and divided by vacant spaces sufficiently wide to allow the expansion of lateral branches, and the formation of verdant crowns of interwoven foliage.

This is the forest I was walking through alone, in the early morning, with a pack on my back. Although individual trees had come and gone since Gosse's time, the forest as a whole had changed very little. "To walk alone in the forest," wrote Gosse, "is a high gratification. The perfect stillness and utter solitude, unbroken, commonly, by even ordinary woodland sounds and sights, tranquillize and sober the mind....The devout spirit is drawn upward in such a scene...."

Despite the weight on my back, my steps through the Sipsey Wilderness were light.

I HAD READ about the Tree on the big tree websites, and I planned to visit it on my hike. The trail to the Tree is unmarked and starts more than four miles from the closest parking area. A simple fork in the path puts you on a very rough, very narrow trail. There will be some things you have to crawl under and some things you have to climb over. You will be tired already, from the long hike you have been on just to get to this trail (not to mention the long drive from anywhere). I had maps, but I still wasn't completely sure I was on the right trail. In the middle of nowhere, a sweaty guy appeared from behind a huge boulder. He was moving quickly down the trail, but I stopped him to ask if I was where I thought I was.

"Is this East Bee Branch?" I asked.

"You going to see the big tree?" he replied.

I wondered how he knew. "Yes, do you have any advice?"

He thought for a second, then shrugged his shoulders. "Just go for it." And he quickly disappeared down the trail. He was obviously one of those trying to get to the Tree and back in one day. Not easy to do. You must be in excellent physical condition to get there and back before darkness falls.

I continued up the trail not knowing what I would find. Would I recognize the Tree when I saw it? Looking for a single, certain big tree in a sea of trees can be a challenge. You start wondering: Could this be the Tree? Maybe that's the Tree? But in Sipsey, there was no doubt.

A mile farther up the trail, I looked up and was overcome by a rush of recognition: the Tree! I approached it and touched it. I circled it. How to describe it? *Ginormous* was recently added to the Merriam-Webster dictionary, but perhaps *behemoth* would work as well—though I didn't really like either of those terms for this tree. There is no English word for something so large and so old that you want to pay it homage, something that has survived when everything around it has perished. This tulip poplar was already growing here when the native people called the species by a different name: sipsey.

When I pulled my attention from the Tree, I saw that I was in a circular canyon. The trail went no further because there was nowhere else to go. Technically this should be called a box canyon, but the word *box* was way too square for this place, which was so very round. All around me the smooth, dripping, rock walls rose up in a large arc that enclosed a jumble of big boulders and a small assortment of trees; there was just enough room for the trail to enter and the stream to exit. Although I had been hiking uphill, once I arrived I felt as though I were in a circular depression. There was another forest above, growing atop the smooth rock walls, and some of the trees in the canyon did not even reach up to the roots of the trees growing along the rim. If the Earth had a navel, I would swear I was in it. And, as if the result of some sort of geomancy, the Tree rose from the center point of the navel.

There is only one spot in the canyon that is large enough and level enough for a human to sleep comfortably. I took the pack from my back and set it there. Then I loosened the straps holding my camp pad and spread it on the ground. Camping is not recommended in this ecologically sensitive area, but I was enthralled, and I had no intention of leaving. Just a single human, being gentle and careful, I gave myself permission to sleep with my beloved.

Normally, fresh cold water poured over these rock walls. I tried to imagine how marvelous it would be to be encompassed by that circle of water, with the sound ricocheting off the walls in all directions and moist vapor baptizing everything. But my pilgrimage brought me here at the end of a long, dry summer. Only drops were coming off the walls now. But what wonderful drops! Slow, relaxing, quiet drops all the way around. Plants usually hidden behind the water had their roots in the damp mud and their flowers in the sunshine. A honeybee was visiting tiny *Heuchera* flowers, and a young five-lined skink ran under my knees. As I was marveling at this place, at this feeling, I heard a young man's voice call out:

"I found it! I found it, and it's really f—in' big!"

He was with three friends, and they had come here to see the Tree, too. We took turns taking pictures of each other next to it. They told me they had tried to find it last year, but they ended up at *West* Bee Branch by mistake. While we were visiting, another pair of backpackers arrived. They didn't say anything to anyone—just walked the circumference of the circle and left. The young ones left too, after a while, and I was alone in the canyon again.

The sun was low, and the air was getting cool already. I knew it would be a chilly night, so I sought out the last bit of sunlight to warm me for as long as possible. The last rays of sun in that navel were shining on the base of the Tree. And there, from its base, a root undulated across the ground like a giant anaconda. I accepted the invitation, set my bottom on the root, and leaned my back and head against the massive trunk. I closed my eyes against the warm sun.

I was sitting, just being. Present moment, beautiful moment.

I have friends who have gone on silent Buddhist retreats to cultivate inner stillness and to practice being in the present moment. Their practice is mostly indoors, but I prefer to practice here—at the foot of this tree, lulled by the dripping walls. Some would call it meditation: being aware of the life force, being aware of my creatureness, just being in beauty. Beauty. The real old growth is so very beautiful. Just surrounding yourself with that beauty feeds the soul. Something in our culture seems to have forgotten the importance of natural beauty.

WHEN THE SUN finally dropped beneath the ridgeline, I went back over to my pack and my pad. I put on extra layers of clothes and pulled out my sleeping bag. I made myself a bed on the small level spot and watched, just watched, as the colors faded and the sky darkened. From where I lay, I was able to see the Tree, sacred omphalos. I listened to the water dripping off the rock walls and the tree crickets as they began calling. Yes, this was indeed beauty.

I drifted off to sleep, and when I opened my eyes again, I could see stars in the small bits of sky between the branches of the hemlock tree I was sleeping beneath. It was clear and cold. The sky was black, and the stars seemed brighter than usual. It was too cold for the crickets now, but a large owl flew into the canyon, and his deep, melodious hooting echoed off the rock walls.

Normally if I wake in the night I want to return to sleep right away, but here, in this magically perfect bowl, I remembered the poet Rumi's advice: *don't go back to sleep.* I opened my eyes wide, tilted my head back toward the stars, and tried to *pay attention,* to fully experience the love I was feeling in this place, for this place. When I felt it without question, as one hears the tone of a bell, I practiced expanding my love for this place until it encompassed the entire globe of the Earth. All the forests, all the birds, all the insects, even all the misguided humans were included in my swollen heart. It is easy to know when a bell's tone starts, but it is impossible to say when it stops.

This is what a forest can give us. That night will stay with me as long as I live.

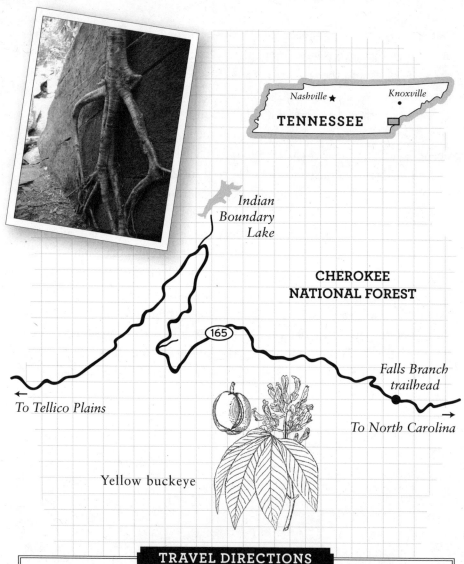

Nashville ★   Knoxville •

TENNESSEE

*Indian
Boundary
Lake*

**CHEROKEE
NATIONAL FOREST**

165

←
To Tellico Plains

*Falls Branch
trailhead*

→
To North Carolina

Yellow buckeye

TRAVEL DIRECTIONS

Southeastern part of state, Monroe County. Closest town: Tellico Plains. From Tellico Plains, take Tennessee 165 east (Cherohala Skyway). When you get to the well-marked turn for Indian Boundary Lake, reset your trip odometer but do not turn. In about eight miles, you will cross a bridge. Park in the first lot to the left after the bridge (this is 8.5 miles from the Indian Boundary Lake turn). The lot is not marked, but it has parking spaces for many cars and is bordered by a low rock wall with an opening. The opening is where the trail begins. A short way down the trail, you will see a sign for trail 87; follow it until it crosses a rocky stream (a bit more than a mile). You will hear the waterfall.

8

Tennessee

FALLS BRANCH, CHEROKEE NATIONAL FOREST

Muir's footsteps...Yellow buckeye...A waterfall...Floating

I CHECKED MY TRUCK'S ODOMETER frequently and followed the directions I had written down to find the trail into the forest. It is an obscure trail, the type you have to know about to find. There are no signs on the road for it. But what a road! This was the same route that naturalist and writer John Muir walked in 1867, and I will give his description, which still holds today:

> Such an ocean of wooded, waving, swelling mountain beauty and grandeur is not to be described. Countless forest-clad hills, side by side in rows and groups, seemed to be enjoying the rich sunshine and remaining motionless only because they were so eagerly absorbing it. All were united by curves and slopes of inimitable softness and beauty. Oh, these forest gardens of our Father! What perfection, what divinity, in their architecture! What simplicity and mysterious complexity of detail! Who shall read the teaching of these sylvan pages, the glad brotherhood of rills that sing in the valleys?

Although from a distance the scenery here looked the same as it did in Muir's time, vast changes have occurred since he walked through. Muir was looking out across thousands of acres of old-growth forest, but serious logging followed closely on his heels. A person stopping at this overlook midway between Muir's visit and mine would have seen thousands of acres of clear-cut stubble: stumps, splintered trees, and understory plants left to bake in the sun. Today this land is all part of the Cherokee National Forest. The sign at the overlook on the Cherohala Skyway tells the story:

> Between 1900 and 1930 all the forest you see before you was privately owned and commercially logged. Every tree that could be used for saw timber, railroad ties, fence posts, pulp wood for paper products or bark for tanning was removed by timber companies whose sole interest was profit. The result was ecological destruction. The huge amount of cut wood left over fueled catastrophic fires never before seen in the entire Southern Appalachian Mountains. Soils which took thousands of years to form were washed away in a matter of years and with no forest canopy to retain the rainwater, the valleys below were subjected to disastrous flooding.
>
> Appalled by this rampant environmental destruction, the people of the United States pleaded for the protection of their dwindling forests and their resources. Their efforts were rewarded with the passage of the Weeks Law in 1911, which authorized the acquisition of this and other private lands and the creation of national forests in the Eastern United States. From the beginning, as it still is today, the primary purpose of the Forest Service has been to restore the forest canopy, protect the watershed, and maintain and enrich the ecological diversity of all that you see before you.

Although it's a great sign, I'm skeptical. If the managers of a national forest were asked to state in one sentence their primary purpose, would they use the words "restore," "protect," or "enrich"? I'm guessing they would say something about a "management plan," and frequently that management plan includes logging.

There are some small areas in our national forests, usually less than ten percent, which have been protected from logging—they are the designated wilderness areas. One of these, Citco Creek Wilderness, is where I was headed. As the sign at the overlook states, most of the area surrounding this wilderness was logged, but the massive fires resulting from all the logging slash destroyed the railway used for logging, and as a result a few patches of original forest escaped destruction. I would hike through one of those patches—the ravine surrounding Falls Branch.

It was only eight o'clock in the morning, but already it was blisteringly hot. I locked my truck and stepped off the asphalt into the cool shade of the forest. This was a summer-morning forest with the high buzzing sound of the cicadas in the trees and the low buzzing sound of the bumblebees on the white snakeroot flowers. I was surprised to see that the largest trees were buckeyes. No doubt these bumblebees, or their kin, gathered nectar from the yellow flowers of the buckeyes earlier that summer. In this forest, I was seeing more bumblebees and more wildflowers than in other forests that time of year. I wondered if the early blooming buckeye trees gave the bee colonies a good early start. Then later, when the wildflowers bloom, there would be plenty of pollinators, and therefore more seeds, and more wild-flowers the next year.

The buckeye is a species I don't get to see very often, and I had never before seen it as the dominant tree in a canopy. The buckeye has leaflets attached to a central point on a petiole—like fat green fingers attached at the palm. The fruit is a large nut, and inside the husk is a very large, shiny, brown seed with a tan oval marking on it. When part of the husk is removed, the seed is supposed to resemble the eye of a male whitetail deer, hence the name "buckeye." Like human babies, sometimes these seeds come in twos or threes, but most often there is just one. Native people in North America ate the seeds after roasting, peeling, soaking, boiling, and mashing them.

The range of yellow buckeyes is quite small. They are trees of the Appalachian hills, but they don't go very far north (just barely into Pennsylvania) or very far south (just barely into Georgia). I was pleased to be in the midst of them. The first place I ever saw natural, unplanted buckeye trees was in West Virginia. I was hiking through a forest and the large nuts on the ground alerted me to their presence. When I inquired about the West Virginia trees a number of years later, I learned that the hillside where I saw them had been logged. I asked the owner about the yellow buckeyes, if they had been logged out too, but he wasn't even sure what they looked like. "They're not a very big tree, are they?" he asked.

Well, the biggest one we know of is in the Smoky Mountains of Tennessee; it is 136 feet tall, and the trunk is 19 feet in circumference. That's a big tree! Buckeyes are choosy—within their restricted range, they only grow in the best soils—but once established they can live for more than three hundred years.

As remarkable as it may seem, according to the Forest Service *Silvics Manual,* "no information is available as to the age at which yellow buckeye trees begin bearing seeds, the number of seeds produced by individual trees, the conditions favoring seed production, or the frequency of seed years." We do know that once an old-growth forest containing buckeyes is clearcut, no buckeyes will return for the first fifteen years. In forty years, there will be only buckeye saplings. So if you cut your buckeye trees, you will not see them as large trees again in your lifetime. We are losing them before we even understand them, and buckeye wood is not even very useful. Chances are those trunks will be used for pulp to make paper, maybe the type you write on, or maybe the type in your bathroom on the little roll.

Most of the forest lands in the East are privately owned. I wonder how many landowners who sign logging contracts even know what species they have. Often the contracts are for such generous amounts of money that the overwhelmed forest owners are willing to let the loggers do almost anything. I think this is the point at which we lose control of our own land. I urge anyone about to sign a logging contract to consider removing five or ten or fifty acres, whatever you can afford, from the logging plan. Watch that reserved corner age, watch how beautiful it becomes, compare it to the logged areas. Let your own senses tell you what is best for your land.

I would love to see more "ecological foresters" offer their services, and more landowners take advantage of those services. Those foresters do not try to manage anything or put anything under contract; they merely educate the owners about what they have. Call it a second opinion.

I WAS WALKING in the shade of a buckeye canopy. You can't do that in many places. It was a joyous feeling. Out there in the real world (the unreal world?), people were dying from the heat, but under this leafy canopy I was comfortable. The trail rambled downhill for a few miles, under the buckeyes and the oaks, through the rhododendron thickets, over the old mossy roots, finally ending at a waterfall. When I reached the waterfall, I was overwhelmed by how large and intense and absolutely lovely it was—a wide wall of rock with streams that split and rejoined in endless patterns. I hadn't seen anyone else on the trail, and I was the only one at the falls. I hadn't spoken to another human yet that day. The sound of the waterfall, and perhaps the energized airflow it creates, had put me into a meditative state. I sat for a long while following the journey of the water from the lip, down through the various paths on the rock face, and finally to the reunion of the streams in the pool below.

I wonder why, of all the ways my life could have gone, it is these untrammeled forests that have claimed me. The poet Rainer Maria Rilke says that what you are called to is also calling you. Is it the trees that want their story to be told? Or is it this beauty, this stunning beauty of our planet that does not want to be forgotten? Perhaps what I'm searching for is beauty, and I just keep finding it over and over again in these old-growth forests. These places of beauty and life are the seeds of hope. We have erased the beauty from many places, but not all. Here it still exists. And the Earth can still heal, the way we, as individuals and as a species, can heal. The seeds of hope are here. The seeds are beautiful.

William Douglas, former Supreme Court justice and naturalist, passed this way, too, and sat in a place very similar, if not the very same. He said:

> After a while the roar of the water is lost to consciousness. One seems transported to a wilderness far, far away. This is a woodland as it was before man came to value a forest in terms of board feet. This is a forest filled with so many wonders, one man could never know them all, even if he saw it every season and examined it from the spores of the fungi of the forest floor to the tops of the wild black cherries. This is a place for sheer wonder, a place for worship.

I sat for so long by the waterfall that my skin got cold. If I were going to be here much longer, I would have needed to put on a long-sleeved shirt. This was a good place to be on a hot summer day.

*   *   *

BACK IN "CIVILIZATION," it was too hot to sleep in my truck, so I rented a small air-conditioned cabin with a pool. At sunset I floated on my back, just watching the clouds move across the sky. A roughly dressed man in his late thirties, the only other person around, walked into view with a drink in his hand and plopped down in one of the white plastic chairs. "Mind if I join you?"

Well, a little tiny bit I did, but what could I say? Turns out he spent this 103°F day putting down black asphalt and then spraying it with toxic sealer. Me? I spent it walking in the woods by myself a long way from home. The conversation was beginning to remind me of one that John Muir had when he traveled through Tennessee. Muir would knock on doors inquiring about a room for the night. If he couldn't find a house, or if he was turned down, he slept outside. One night he knocked at the door of a blacksmith and his wife. Muir describes the blacksmith as "bare-breasted, sweaty, begrimed"; no doubt he had been working hard all day at the hot forge. Over dinner the blacksmith had this conversation with Muir:

"Young man, what are you doing down here?" I replied that I was looking at plants. "Plants? What kind of plants?" I said, "Oh all kinds; grass, weeds, flowers, trees, mosses, ferns,—almost everything that grows is interesting to me."

"Well, young man," he queried, "you mean to say that you are not employed by the government on some private business?" "No," I said, "I am not employed by anyone except just myself. I love all kinds of plants, and I came down here to these Southern States to get acquainted with as many of them as possible."

"You look like a strong-minded man," he replied, "and surely you are able to do something better than wander over the country and look at weeds and blossoms. These are hard times, and real work is required of every man that is able."

I imagined the road worker was thinking something like that about me, but I just floated on my back and looked up at the clouds and thought: there is nothing better.

NORTH CAROLINA

• Asheville

Basswood

*Joyce
Kilmer
Memorial
Forest*

1134

129

**NANTAHALA
NATIONAL FOREST**

143

← *To Tennessee*

Robbinsville

TRAVEL DIRECTIONS

Western part of state, Graham County. Closest
town: Robbinsville. From Robbinsville, take
Route 143 west. In about twelve miles, turn right
onto SR 1134 (Joyce Kilmer Road). Go two miles
and turn left into the forest. It is well marked.

If coming from Tellico Plains, Tennessee,
take Route 165, which becomes Route 143 after
you cross the North Carolina border. In a few
more miles, you will see signs directing you to
the forest. There is a forest service campground
very close to the forest.

North Carolina

Joyce Kilmer Memorial Forest

Burials...Children...Tulip poplar trees...Ravenel's Woods

M Y APPROACH TO the trailhead at Joyce Kilmer Memorial Forest felt like the final steps of a long pilgrimage. This was the first eastern old-growth forest I planned a special trip to visit. The idea for this book had not even been born yet, but it was spring and I was being drawn toward the forest. I had had enough of the academic life, with its computers, books, and grading; I wanted towering trees and clear streams tumbling over cracked rocks. I wanted ferns and moss and trillium—and maybe even bears. I longed to wander through the forest breathing, touching, listening. I wanted to sit, perhaps sleep, under the rare towering giants.

I loaded all my supplies into my little pickup truck. The forest, although a twelve-hour drive from my house, was less than two hours from my father's house. I planned to visit with him for a few days before I spent time with the trees.

But my father was not well and my two-day visit with him turned into a week. My hiking boots went unworn, the mattress in my truck unused. The time scale of an old-growth forest is nothing like our own, I told myself. The Joyce Kilmer forest would have to wait.

*   *   *

I DIDN'T GET to the Joyce Kilmer forest that year, or the next year when I tried again. On my third visit to Dad's, I didn't even bother bringing my boots. I flew down and rented a car. Dad was in a hospital bed in his living room. He knew who I was, but I wasn't sure he remembered my name and I didn't want to ask him. I no longer had to worry about him forgetting his medications or burning down the house; he couldn't get out of bed.

AT DAD'S FUNERAL, my daughter took the opportunity to ask about *my* arrangements. I didn't have a good answer for her. It's not that I am trying to avoid the issue; it's just that what I prefer used to be the easiest, oldest way of dealing with a body, but in this era, in this place, it has become the most difficult. I want to be buried in the ground, preferably healthy ground full of microorganisms. No embalming of the body, no vault, and, if possible, not even a casket. (How many trees are cut for those anyway?) Just wrap me in linen, or burlap, and put me in a hole in the ground where I will feed the soil organisms, and in time the trees, and eventually the birds (with nuts and berries from the trees). Perhaps a natural stone for a marker, no inscription necessary.

As William Faulkner describes a woodland grave in his novel *The Bear:*

> ...not held fast in earth but free in earth and not in earth but of earth, myriad yet undiffused of every myriad part, leaf and twig and particle, air and sun and rain and dew and night, acorn oak and leaf and acorn again, dark and dawn and dark and dawn again in their immutable progression and, being myriad, one.

But what a burden I would put on my daughter if I told her that.

"Just do what's easiest honey," I answered.

THESE DAYS, EASIEST is to send the nutrients into the sky with flames. But some people are using death to save forests. The current natural-burial movement was started in England. There they have an Association of

Natural Burial Grounds, which has developed approved procedures and standards. Members of the association even lobby government agencies to change existing regulations so natural burial will be easier. The first natural-burial site in the United Kingdom was opened in 1993, and just thirteen years later there were 215 natural-burial grounds there. Some of them are operated for profit, but many of them are nonprofit organizations. Around the world people are trying to protect forests, and making them burial sites is one way to do so. In an effort to let one forest return to old growth, a group of friends in Wales joined together to buy eight acres of formerly logged forest. This is their vision:

> As time passes, the burial ground will become a more diverse nature reserve, where the bereaved experience the peace of the trees as they remember those they have lost. The unobtrusive graves, marked by natural stone, wooden memorials and specifically planted trees, will, over decades, fade into the forest background without becoming lost. By being buried in this way, we can continue even after death to help preserve the wonder of life in all its diversity. It is never too late to contribute to the environment.

It is the intention of the original investors that the land never be sold, the bodies never be moved, and the trees never again be cut. This small forest is not only for burials; besides being a haven for wildlife, it is also open to anyone who would just like to take a walk in the woods.

In the United States, the natural-burial movement is much younger and much smaller. Here it is usually called "green burial." The first green-burial cemetery site in the United States opened in 1998. By 2006 six states had them, and by 2009 a dozen states had green-burial sites. Land trusts and other conservation organizations are beginning to pay attention and to consider offering green burials as a way to both preserve natural land and to provide a service for their members.

DAD REQUESTED CREMATION. He wasn't a very green guy anyway. He was one of those who thought that Rachel Carson, responsible for the banning of DDT, should have minded her own business. You can imagine that he was somewhat conflicted about my view of the world. I accepted his choice. We should all have choices. I prefer an end for my body that will be part of the Earth's recovery process. I dedicate this flesh to beauty and diversity. But make it as easy for yourself as possible. Life is for the living.

AND HERE I was living it. I was finally, finally here! And there really were towering trees and clear streams tumbling over cracked rocks, and ferns and moss and trillium and rhododendron. Perhaps if my trip hadn't been delayed for years, this writing project would not have had the time to germinate and take root in me as it did.

The moist grove was absolutely lovely, but I was not the only one here. The parking lot was humming with motorcycles, cars, and people. Just as I started up the trail, a group of fifteen children of assorted ages, accompanied by chaperones, started up the trail, too. Some visitors might have been disappointed by all the people, but after visiting many empty old-growth forests I was pleased to see this one being appreciated. As we entered the forest, a girl at the end of the string of children, who appeared to be about eleven years old, said to the adult accompanying her: "This is just like I remembered it in my dreams."

I was looking at every little thing, as usual, and the children got ahead of me on the trail. Later I passed them when they stopped for a water break.

"This is *fun*," I heard one little girl say.

"Look, we're halfway up the side of a mountain already!" said another child.

One of the chaperones addressed me as I walked by: "Excuse me, ma'am, we're almost to the forest, right?"

What do you think you're standing in? I wanted to say, but I held my tongue and reassured him that he was almost there.

Ahead there was a plaque dedicating the forest to the poet Joyce Kilmer, "until time shall be no more." Kilmer is famous for his *Tree* poem, which many school children, including me, were required to memorize: "I think that I shall never see/A poem lovely as a tree..." Unfortunately, Kilmer never got to see his forest. He was killed in World War I. I assume it was this plaque the chaperone was heading for.

The loop trail was not long, but it contained the most remarkable collection of giant tulip poplar trees I had ever seen. Although the trees were

easy to see from the trail, everyone seemed drawn to walk right up to touch
them. The result was that each massive tree had a small path to its base. I
worried that these trees were being loved to death—many feet compacting
the soil and damaging the roots. Even though I know better, I, too, was
drawn to the base of more than one. There is an inexplicable energy shared
between humans and trees when physical contact is made. It is possible to
feel it with small trees, too, but in my experience, the older the tree, the
stronger the feeling.

I am using words like "gigantic" and "massive," but when scientists
compare forests they use the measure of "basal area," the area covered
by the trees' trunks. The same researchers who measured and documented the Joyce Kilmer Memorial Forest also measured another forest, Ravenel's Woods, described as "a virgin hemlock forest near Highlands, North

Carolina." The local people called it the Primeval Forest. Bob Zahner, a friend and forester who visited the forest as a young boy, tells its story in his book, *The Mountain at the End of the Trail.*

The Primeval Forest originally "belonged" to the Cherokee Indians, but in 1819 a treaty took a vast area of land away from the Cherokee and gave title to the state of North Carolina. From the 1840s to the 1860s, the state awarded land grants to various white settlers. In the 1880s, the Ravenel family began to buy up land all around Highlands, including the Primeval Forest. Their son, Prioleau, continued to buy land when he came of age, and eventually he owned more than fifteen hundred acres. By 1913, most of the other private forest lands in North Carolina were a chopped-down mess, but the Primeval Forest remained intact.

Around this time, the federal government began buying forest land to create the national forests. The Primeval Forest was considered for purchase, but Prioleau Ravenel did not want to sell. Perhaps he had an emotional attachment to his forest. He generously let others use it and study it. In 1939, researchers from Duke University and the University of Nevada documented the impressive old-growth forest, but there were no land trusts or Nature Conservancies then, and Ravenel did nothing to protect the forest beyond his lifetime.

He remarried late in life, and when he died, in 1940 at the age of seventy-two, the land became the property of his second wife, Beatrice. They lived in Charleston then, and she was not interested in spending time in the forest at Highlands. After Prioleau Ravenel's death, she moved to Florida. In 1942, just after the U.S. became involved in World War II, the Powell Lumber Company approached Beatrice Ravenel and urged her to sell her timber for the sake of the war effort. (There were soon to be many military contracts for pulp and timber products.) Beatrice was never going back to Highlands, and she never really cared about that forest anyway. She sold it.

Citizens and scientists alike were outraged by the deal that had been made hundreds of miles away, but all energy and resources were going toward the war effort. Fathers and sons of Highlands' citizens were headed off to war. No federal money was being spent on forests now. The loss of the precious forest seemed a *fait accompli.*

Ironically, the wood was never used for military contracts. Logging began in 1946, after the war was over. Zahner visited the site with the chief forester for the mill just before logging operations started. I will let Zahner tell it:

> He told me that although he recognized the intrinsic value of preserving such an ancient forest, his company could not cancel the logging contract....Their chief forester explained to me, a naive young man about to embark on a career in forestry myself, that Champion had preserved enough forest in other locations, and that the Primeval Forest here "will grow back" in time. I believe it was on that day that I understood the difference between a conservation ethic and a business ethic.
>
> I have since learned much from that statement, "the forest will grow back," a golden rule of forestry still used today to cover the many ills of clearcutting....Certainly, trees grow back, and in a few hundred years we may have the outward appearance of a forest. However, we now know that a thousand years or more is required for the biota of such an ancient forest community to be restored in all of its diversity, integrity, and beauty.

When I compared the data for the Joyce Kilmer forest and Ravenel's Woods, I was shocked to see that the average basal area of the trees in Ravenel's Woods was greater than the average for those in the Joyce Kilmer forest. It was difficult for me to imagine a collection of trees in the East with girths larger than those I had witnessed in the Joyce Kilmer forest.

Zahner eventually left his tenured professorship in forestry at the University of Michigan to have more time to live close to the land, to spend time with his family, and to battle clear-cutting and advocate for old growth. He worked tirelessly to protect forests and to educate others. Perhaps he was always trying to make up for missing the opportunity to save the Primeval Forest.

I SAT AMONG the massive trees to write, and the echo of children's laughter could be heard throughout the forest. I was thinking about my father: *Dad, your generation is leaving us; my generation is next; but today this wonderful forest is filled with the cheerful noise of the next generation. And that is as it should be.*

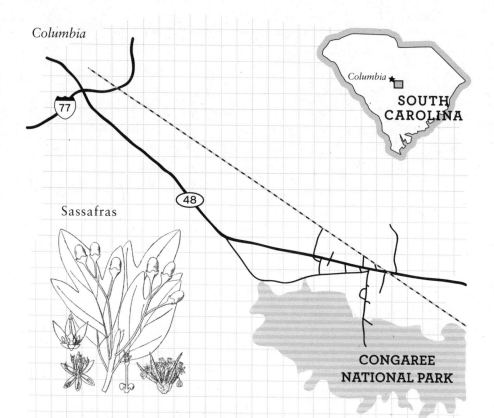

Columbia

SOUTH CAROLINA

Columbia

77

Sassafras

48

CONGAREE
NATIONAL PARK

TRAVEL DIRECTIONS

Central part of state, Richland County.
Closest town: Columbia. From the city of
Columbia, or Interstate 77 just south of
town, take Route 48 (Bluff Road) south.
You will see signs on Route 48 directing
you to the park, which is nineteen miles
from Columbia and about fifteen miles
from I-77 (exit 5).

There are two primitive camping
areas in the park and many nice hotels
in Columbia. The visitor center is open
every day from 8:30 a.m. to 5 p.m. The
first section of the trail is a wheelchair-
accessible boardwalk. If the weather has
been very rainy for very long, call ahead
to check on conditions: (803) 776-4396.

South Carolina

Congaree National Park

Rain...A floodplain forest...Woodpeckers

CHANCE OF RAIN: 100 percent. It had been the driest summer on record in the eastern United States. In forest after forest, I had been greeted by cheerful blue skies, and I felt lucky. But as the months went by with no soaking rains, even the trees seemed a bit tired of perfect weather. Some leaves couldn't hold on—they turned brown and fell before they had a chance to feel autumn's cool air. By the end of October, I was no longer hoping for clear skies. I was hoping for rain. On the day I visited Congaree I was not disappointed.

I pulled into the parking area very early in the morning as a gentle, pittering rain was starting. I was prepared with head-to-toe rain gear: jacket, pants, and waterproof boots. I pulled it all on in the drizzle and headed for the trail. But after only a few steps I turned and went back to the car—not to avoid the rain, but because I wanted to *hear* the rain. I wanted to experience the forest with all my senses, and my hood was interfering. I grabbed an old umbrella out of the trunk.

Setting out again with my umbrella overhead, I started down the sturdy boardwalk that began just steps from the parking lot at the visitor center. Being first on the trail, the early morning drizzle, and the tall, tall trees all put a happy spring in my step. Wet leaves of all kinds were flattened on

the boardwalk, and as I walked I recognized old friends. If I had dropped through a wormhole to this spot, I would have known I was in the South. Here were my friends the sweet gum and sassafras, and oaks of all kinds: the sharp narrow leaves of the southern red oaks contrasted with the wide scalloped edges of the swamp chestnut oaks. Of course, there were beech and black gum, too. My list could go on and on and on—there were more than seventy different species here—and what I loved was how they shared the space with each other. The bald cypress were up to seven hundred years old. The only evergreens were the giant, widely spaced southern pines, the loblolly pines. These few loblollies came from very lucky seeds that happened to land on a small piece of sunny forest floor and then held their ground—for centuries. Some of the loblollies are more than two hundred years old, and they are proudly holding their own among the oaks, maples, and hickories.

In a work plan for the large publicly owned forest near my Maryland home, there was a section describing the forest and noting that it is "rare to find a loblolly pine older than eighty years." Well, yes, it is rare to find one older than that, not because they all succumb to a natural death before then, but because we cut them before they reach old age. The Congaree pines show us what can be—pines two to three hundred years old and still the tallest trees in the forest. Congaree has a pine 15 feet in circumference and 167 feet tall, the largest loblolly pine in the United States (today at least). Some of Congaree's trees are as tall as a seventeen-story building.

When I tilted my umbrella back and looked up toward the top of the giant trees, I saw drops falling, as if in slow motion, toward my face. One very large drop landed directly in my eye, but even that brought me pleasure and a laugh. I felt like the whole forest was celebrating with me. Rain at last!

This is a floodplain forest, a place shaped by water, a place that welcomes water. The boardwalk trail was designed to raise visitors above the mud, but, despite the day's droplets, the ground was dry. The "buttressed" (wide-based) bald cypress trunks and the strange aerial roots called "knees," which evolved to rise above the water and the muck, were rising instead from solid ground. Yes indeed, it had been a long, dry summer.

Surrounded by the beauty, the rain, and the shared strength of so many outstanding specimens, I practically bounced down the trail. Although it was the last weekend in October, the only fall colors were the few crimson leaves sprinkled through the black gum canopy, and the small pawpaw trees in which about a third of the leaves had turned a pure yellow. As I walked through the grove-like patches of pawpaw, the light got brighter—the result of the yellow all around, even under my feet. The sunshine captured in the leaves seemed to be liberated again on this dark, gray day.

A few miles down the trail, the rain fell harder. The drops hitting millions of leaves created the sound of polite applause, and I walked along under the lofty canopy to the sound of the forest appreciating the rain and, in my imagination, perhaps even my presence. Mile after mile the applause did not die down; in fact it built to a standing ovation, the drops were hitting so hard and so fast.

It was so wet now that my fingertips began to wrinkle. The moss and lichens were fresh and plump, and after a few hours I began to feel as if I could grow some moss myself. But I was still warm under my protective clothing, and still warm and happy deep in my heart. I walked through the thunderous applause with a big smile on my face. No human audience could show such enthusiasm for so long.

SIGNS OF WOODPECKERS were everywhere—there are seven species of woodpecker here—but because of the rain I never saw a single one. When there was a report of ivory-billed woodpeckers being rediscovered in Arkansas in 2005, a team was formed to search for them in Congaree as well. So far they haven't found any, but if they were anywhere in South Carolina they would be here. Passenger pigeons and Carolina parakeets used to be here, too. No doubt the species of woodpeckers that have survived were keeping dry on a bed of wood chips in a space they had hollowed inside the giant, old trunks. Perhaps they saw me, crazy human, grinning wildly in the pouring rain. This forest is said to be taller than any other deciduous forest on Earth, and the lofty canopy had brightened my day despite the dark clouds.

I HAD BEEN hiking for four hours, but I had seen only a small portion of the eleven thousand acres of old growth in the park. Although that seems large, this forest is only a small remnant of the bottomland ecosystem that used to cover fifty-two *million* acres. When I crossed Cedar Creek, which was lined by elegant, old cypress trees with buttressed bases, I noted how similar it looked to the creek in Delaware where I searched for the largest bald cypress in that state. Indeed, that forest and this one are of the same type and serve the same ecological function. In a way, they were once connected, part of the same web of water that flows from the land toward the Atlantic Ocean, part of the same ecological cloth. Here in the Congaree, I understood what Delaware used to be, but I was in the Deep South now and a few of the species here, like Spanish moss, dwarf palmettos, and, reportedly, alligators, I would never see in Delaware.

SOMETHING THE FORESTS do have in common are the plans loggers made for them. The cutters and carvers had their eyes on this South Carolina bottomland. In fact, the cutting had already begun; the first wave of logging lasted from 1895 until 1915. In those days, the huge, old bald cypress were first girdled by cutting a strip all the way around the base, and they weren't cut down until after they died and dried out. After being dried and cut, the logs were pushed into the creeks and rivers and floated downstream. But in the Congaree, more of the cypress sank than floated—perhaps they had not dried out enough—and the unprofitable logging operation was halted.

The owners then leased the forest out to sportsmen. One of those men, Harry Hampton, wrote an outdoor column in the local paper. "The reason I ceased letting well enough alone," wrote Hampton, "was that people after people kept saying 'This place ought to be preserved.'" His idea was to hold a central five thousand acres as a sanctuary. He invited a group of influential men to tour the property, "feeling a little like Judas Iscariot, for my fellow hunters lacked all hell of wanting to give up the place."

In the 1950s, hundreds of locals were in support of protecting the forest, as were the Nature Conservancy and the National Park Service, but there was confusion about deciding who should make the offer to the owners, and at what price. So the forest stayed in private hands, unprotected, and in the 1970s logging began again. Finally, in 1976, Congress established the Congaree Swamp National Monument, and in 2003 it became one of our newest National Parks.

After hours of thunderous rain, I witnessed the depressions and seeps, which were dry that morning, filling up with water. This floodplain was doing its job.

I hope to return to Congaree someday when the sky is a clear blue, but I would not trade that rainy day for any other.

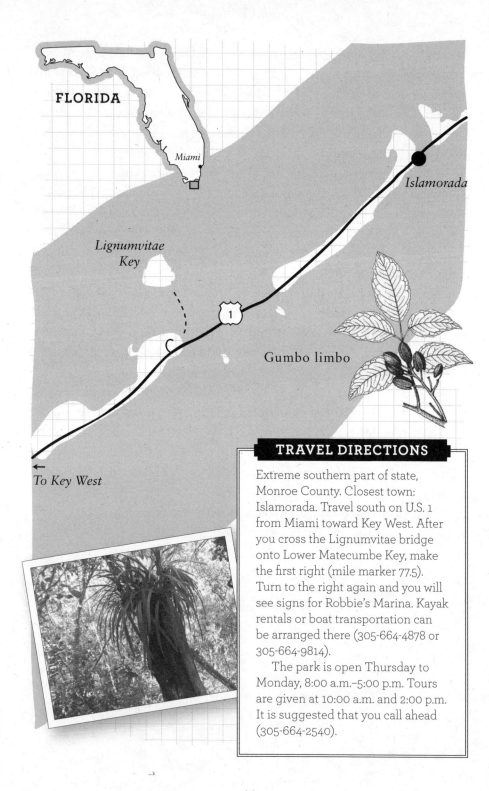

FLORIDA

Miami

Islamorada

Lignumvitae
Key

1

Gumbo limbo

To Key West

TRAVEL DIRECTIONS

Extreme southern part of state,
Monroe County. Closest town:
Islamorada. Travel south on U.S. 1
from Miami toward Key West. After
you cross the Lignumvitae bridge
onto Lower Matecumbe Key, make
the first right (mile marker 77.5).
Turn to the right again and you will
see signs for Robbie's Marina. Kayak
rentals or boat transportation can
be arranged there (305-664-4878 or
305-664-9814).

The park is open Thursday to
Monday, 8:00 a.m.–5:00 p.m. Tours
are given at 10:00 a.m. and 2:00 p.m.
It is suggested that you call ahead
(305-664-2540).

Florida

LIGNUMVITAE KEY BOTANICAL STATE PARK

A rare type...Poisonwood...Wood of life...Butterflies and crabwood...Paul Ehrlich

E ARLIER THIS YEAR, I attended a wedding where I found myself sitting next to someone's uncle. The conversation turned to forests, as it often does, and "uncle" admitted that he liked the woods, but to him they just looked green—he couldn't tell one tree from another. I knew exactly how he felt when I walked into that forest on Lignumvitae Key. Nothing looked familiar. I had been to old-growth forests in twenty-three eastern states during the past few years, and I started thinking I knew some things about eastern old growth, but this Florida island changed all that. I was humbled. Although there were sixty different tree species on the island, the only one I recognized was the introduced coconut palm. With the exception of the palm trees, it seemed that all the leaves were shiny, green ovals. How was I going to tell one tree species from another? I just stood in the diminutive forest and stared.

A FEW DAYS before I left on my trip, a colleague, who had been to the Key before, cautioned me to beware the poisonwood trees. He had developed a very bad rash from the trees after his visit. I had never heard of poisonwood before, except in the title of the novel by Barbara Kingsolver, and I had no idea what the thing I should beware of looked like.

At the marina, where I arranged for my kayak rental, they warned that I shouldn't go over to the island if it was raining. "Why not?" I asked. "I have rain gear."

"Because the poison trees will drip their toxic sap on you."

"Oh."

On the morning of my departure I was happy to see a clear blue sky. Floating on the shallow sea, in my little red kayak, I felt sandwiched between the abundant life above and below. Overhead a frigate bird circled and looked down on me, while a few inches beneath the boat a ray foraged in the eelgrass. I paddled along the island's edge until I saw the small kayak landing for the park.

Two rangers were on duty, but I was the only visitor on the island. Ranger Ben volunteered to show me around. Ben was from Indiana, and when I admitted my ignorance he responded by confessing that when he arrived on Lignumvitae Key he didn't know any of the plants either. I suppose that's not so unusual; after all, this West Indian plant community is found nowhere else in the United States except southern Florida and the Keys. It is such a rare forest type that it is not even included on the Forest Service map, and because of clearing, grazing, and development, this forest type has been eliminated from most of the Keys and most of the Caribbean islands where it was formerly found.

It was the rarity of this habitat that caused Harvard researchers E.O. Wilson, Dan Simberloff, and Bob Silbergleid to work for its protection. In the 1960s, Wilson and Simberloff were doing research in the Keys and the Everglades to confirm Wilson's island biogeography theory. Their research involved fumigating entire islands to kill every living thing except the plants, then monitoring the return of species to the island. Not exactly conservation-guided research. But when they visited Lignumvitae Key and saw the rare forest, and heard the island was soon to be covered by vacation homes, they committed themselves to its conservation. Speaking engagements, publications, donor contributions, and negotiations with the Nature Conservancy and Florida's park system led to its eventual protection as a botanical park.

*　*　*

THE FIRST TREE Ben showed me was the poisonwood tree. Think poison ivy the size of a pear tree. It is in the same botanical family as poison ivy, and if you react to the oils in poison ivy, you will also react to contact with this tree. Ben was sensitive to it, and he described the rash as being even worse than poison ivy. The native people, he said, had used it to torture their victims; the rash can sometimes get so bad it causes the skin to turn black. I asked about the rumors of toxic sap dripping off in the rain, and he showed me a scar on his face from a day it started raining while he was in the forest.

Ben bravely posed for me next to the largest poisonwood tree in the nation. The mottled bark had dark, wet patches from which the oils literally oozed. This is one tree you do not want to hug. Oddly, humans are the only species affected by the poisonwood oils. For birds, such as the rare white-crowned pigeon, poisonwood berries are an important and abundant source of food.

The next tree Ben pointed out was the island's namesake: the lignumvitae, "wood of life." Although it is small, it can live to be very old. The spreading, sinuous shape of the tree reminded me of a carefully tended bonsai in a Japanese garden. In April, blue flowers open, and the pollinated flowers eventually produce yellow, papery fruits that open to reveal bright-red berries. Ben obviously had a soft spot in his heart for these colorful trees. He would point out every one we passed: "There's one... there's another one... this one's a beauty... I'm worried about this one... this is one of my favorites." When we came to a lignumvitae tree that was dropping its ripe berries on the trail, he collected the berries and cast them into places where any seeds that sprouted wouldn't be trampled.

In their wisdom, the Florida State Parks have made a management decision to maintain all vegetation in as natural a condition as possible. So I'll never tell them there's a ranger out there who lovingly moves seeds out of harm's way, pulls aggressive species away from rare ones, and tucks fallen orchids back up into the trees.

We walked along through the sparse shade from the small trees, dry leaves crunching under our feet, as Ben pointed out some of the other tree species. The largest and easiest to identify were the gumbo limbos. In an article from 1896, Frank Cushing called them "the most fantastic of trees— the trees *par excellence*...bare, skinny, livid, monstrous, and crooked of

limb, and, compared with surrounding growth, gigantic." In contemporary times people have started calling them "tourist trees" because they are as red as a tourists' sunburned skin, and the thin bark peels off like dead skin. Beneath the peeling red layer, fresh green bark is visible. The leaves looked much like the poisonwood to me, but at least I could tell their barks apart. Ethnobotanists say the natives used gumbo limbo bark and leaves as a remedy for the poisonwood rash. Ben said he hadn't tried that yet; so far he had only used calamine lotion.

If Ben hadn't identified it for me, I wouldn't have known that the smallish, dull, gray-brown butterfly that flew across the path was the rare Florida purple wing. When it stopped on the bark of a crabwood tree, I got a closer look and could see the dusting of iridescent purple-blue on its open wings. As the wings opened and closed, six white dots flashed in the sunlight. Silbergleid, one of the scientist-saviors of Lignumvitae Key, studied ultraviolet reflectance in butterflies. Butterflies can see a part of the spectrum that is not visible to the human eye. Perhaps the wing movements of the butterfly I was watching were communicating a message to another butterfly in a language I couldn't understand and in a wavelength I couldn't see.

It's not surprising that we saw it on a crabwood tree; the flowers and rotting fruits of the crabwood provide sugars the butterflies feed on. The female butterfly then lays her eggs on the leaves of the crabwood, and the leaves become food for the larvae that hatch from the eggs. This single tree species provides for all of the needs of the Florida purple wing butterfly.

To me the leaves looked like all the rest—shiny, green ovals—but Ben showed me a rough little notch at the base of the leaf that feels like the tip of a crab's claw—hence the name crabwood. Over the next few hours, I learned how to identify many more, including torch wood, so called because it burns easily even when green; milk wood, with bark that looks like it has been splashed with milk; and mastic, once used as an ingredient in chewing gum. During our hike Ben even found a species no one realized grew on Lignumvitae Key. It was not on any of the species lists kept by the park. On the trunk of the tree I noticed the smallest ants I had ever seen, barely visible to the naked eye. Perhaps even E.O. Wilson himself, famous studier of ants, did not know this ant species was here.

Forty years after the Lignumvitae Key University Council was formed to protect this rare three-hundred acre remnant, much has changed in the other Keys. As a result of continuing development and deforestation, habitat for species is disappearing. Forty years ago, the Florida purple wing butterfly could be found from the Everglades down to Lignumvitae Key. By 2005, it was found only on this tiny island. If this forest had not been preserved, it is possible that the Florida purple wing would be gone altogether.

WATCHING THE BUTTERFLY reminded me of conservation biologist Paul Ehrlich, who, on his first sabbatical leave from Stanford University, wanted to see more of the planet. He had been hard at work catching, categorizing, and counting the butterflies of the western United States, but he wanted to put this work in perspective. His sabbatical request was approved, and he and his wife spent the next year traveling the world. Ehrlich took note of the butterflies he saw everywhere, but, more importantly, the trip opened his eyes to how one species, humans, affected not just butterflies but all other species as well. When Ehrlich returned to Stanford he never stopped studying butterflies, but his perspective had broadened beyond butterflies to the total environment, including human population and resource use. He began writing his book, *The Population Bomb*, which eventually became a best-seller. Since then he has written or edited more than twenty books and has won many awards, including a MacArthur Prize and the United Nations Environment Prize. I imagine how different his life would have been, and what an important voice we would have missed out on, if Ehrlich hadn't taken that journey, but instead stayed in his laboratory isolating butterfly DNA.

I am on leave from my university position too, and, like Erhlich, I am casting a very large net, using my time away from teaching and home to experience the Eastern forest. I want to understand what we have done to it, not just through percentages and maps, but viscerally. That sort of comprehension requires more than just hikes through the clear-cuts, it also requires its opposite—hikes through the old-growth forests. By the time I paddled up to this Florida Key, I understood not only how thoroughly we had changed the forest, but also that the forest was changing me.

AS THE MOSQUITOES hummed—in December!—I looked around and realized I was beginning to understand the pieces of this tropical forest.

When Ben pointed to a tree and quizzed me, I was right some of the time. I recognized the basic structure of an unlogged forest: numerous species, canopy of varying height, trees twisted with age, dead trees both standing and fallen, big branches fallen to the ground. Even though it seemed so strange and different to me at first, here too there was a code that could be deciphered with practice and patience.

But no one knows all the secrets a forest holds. As in all forests, many mysteries remain here. I could live on this small island the rest of my life and still have no understanding of the language of the butterflies, or even have a complete list of all the species that shared the island with me. The slow and patient work of scientists has brought us a long way, but we still have far to go. Preservation is the first and most important part of the formula.

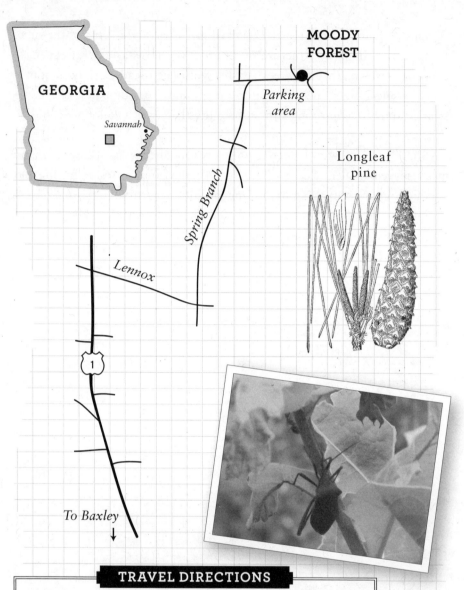

GEORGIA

Savannah

MOODY
FOREST

Parking
area

Spring Branch

Lennox

1

Longleaf
pine

To Baxley

TRAVEL DIRECTIONS

Eastern part of state, Appling County. Closest town: Baxley. From U.S. 1, seven miles north of Baxley, turn right onto Lennox Road (at the gas station). Turn left onto Spring Branch Road. Continue until you come to a T intersection with East River Road. Turn right and continue on this road approximately one mile. The parking area is on the left just before the intersection with Jake Moody Road. There is a sign, and trail maps are available.

Georgia

MOODY FOREST NATURAL AREA

The song of the pines...The Moody legacy...Wildflowers and beetles...Fire

I WAS ALONE IN the forest, far off the path, listening closely. Could I hear it? Could I hear the song of the pines described by the early naturalist-explorers? As I shifted my attention beyond the silence, beyond the chirps and whistles of birds, I did hear it. It sounded like a distant waterfall, or a train, but it was neither: it was the wind blowing through pine needles, the millions of needles that are the harp strings of this forest.

I sat to observe one of the oldest pines, said to be more than two hundred years old. Although young pines shoot arrow-straight toward the sky, the ancient ones gradually decide that *out* is better than *up*. The life energy of the tree moves to the horizontal boughs, and they grow thick and twisted. When I studied the sinuous curves of these branches, I understood that the pines not only make music from the wind but also give it form. Centuries of wind had been solidified into the shape of this tree.

THERE ARE MANY different forest types in the eastern U.S., ranging from broadleaf tropical forests in the extreme South to broadleaf deciduous forests in the central region, to evergreen boreal forests in the North. Of all these forest types, the longleaf pine ecosystem was once the most extensive.

Longleaf pines dominated the flatter, sandier coastal areas of the southeastern states. A map illustrating the historic range of longleaf pine shows that
it once covered literally half of North Carolina, South Carolina, Georgia,
and Florida, and lesser portions of Virginia, Alabama, Mississippi, Louisi-
ana, and Texas. Historic accounts tell of travelers passing through mile after mile of the flat "piney woods." Old photographs show what looks like a
monoculture of sturdy pine trunks rising from an open, grassy forest floor.
In each photo a single human, posed among the trunks for scale, occupies
less than one-sixth of the vertical height of the photo, but not one horizontal branch is seen; the wind-blown limbs are still far overhead, out of the
frame. The pines were a timber seller's dream: no steep slopes, no shrubby
undergrowth, a gentle climate. It was almost too easy. Ninety-eight percent
of the longleaf pine forests were harvested.

The forests in those photographs are gone. The only way to see even a
poor imitation of those remarkable forests is to be a quail hunter invited to
one of the few privately owned plantations where some old-growth longleaf
still exists, or to be a researcher with access to one of the military bases or
research stations where the longleaf pine groves are on life support. There
is nowhere the general public can go to see anything like the forests in the
photographs. The pines I was sitting among this day were old, but they occupy just a small area within a larger landscape that includes mostly floodplain deciduous forest.

The story of this forest, and how it still exists for us to experience,
echoes the story of so many other old-growth forests. The stories almost
always start with the native people being driven out and white settlers moving in. In this case, the Creek Indians were driven out and a lottery system
was established to distribute their land to the settlers. The Moody family
ended up with more than three thousand acres along the Altamaha River,
and from then on it was just a matter of trying to hold on to what they had.
The Moodys lived simply, in hand-built wooden cabins with no plumbing
and only wood stoves for heat. They did whatever they had to do to make
a living off their land: raised a few cows, planted a few fields, made some
moonshine, hunted squirrels, tapped a few trees for turpentine. But cutting
any timber was a last resort. Three generations kept the same promise to
protect the forest as best they could, but they were not always successful.
Some timber had to be cut, mostly to pay estate taxes owed on the now

valuable riverfront property when someone died. When the last member of the third generation died in 1999, without a will and without having made any plans for what would happen to the forest, the property passed to thirty distant heirs—mostly half-nieces and -nephews. The Moody family's legacy of forest protection ended when the heirs agreed to sell the property at auction.

It was a sealed-bid auction. Eight timber companies and the Nature Conservancy, an organization dedicated to protecting ecologically important lands, submitted bids. These bids were opened one by one on October 2, 2000, in the small local library. As the envelopes were opened, the name of each timber company and the millions of dollars it was willing to pay for the right to log the old-growth forest was read aloud. Finally, the Nature Conservancy's bid was revealed: $8.25 million—just a few hundred thousand more than the next highest bidder. Nature writer Janisse Ray, who lives near the forest, said, "The moment it was purchased for preservation I will recall as among the most blessed of my life."

The Nature Conservancy generously opened the forest to the public so we can visit it and see at least a remnant of the old longleaf pine ecosystem.

ONE WOULD NEVER guess it at first glance, but longleaf pine forests contain some of the highest levels of species diversity on Earth—not in the trees, but in the herbaceous wildflowers that carpet the ground. Normally I am able to identify most of the wildflowers I see blooming, from the east coast to the west, but I was amazed at what I saw in this small section of longleaf pines. There were many plants in flower, and some of them I had never seen before, anywhere. The best-known groundcover in the longleaf pine ecosystem is wiregrass, and I did see that all around me, but I also saw blooming candyroot, queen's delight, cat bells, finger rot, and many more. (The Latin names are in the notes.) My wildflower guides did not cover this region, so I was sketching, photographing, and memorizing. A beautiful, purple skullcap had me stumped. Of the sixteen hundred plant species found only in the Southeast, more than eight hundred of them are found only in the longleaf pine ecosystem. No wonder I was not familiar with them. These plants, called endemics by botanists, had not spread from someplace else; they had become distinct species right here. I found myself wishing for better botany books, a magnifying lens, and lots more time—but I would probably still be finding new things if I spent a decade in this forest.

The queen's delight has glossy, green leaves and a spike of flowers that give the impression of yellow. But a closer look shows that the flowers have no petals. The yellow I saw was from pollen on the anthers, and clutching every spike of flowers were a few black insects, all of the same species. Again, I investigated and photographed. I assumed that once I returned home I would be able to solve the mystery of the beetles that love queen's delight, a plant with toxic sap. But hours of research turned up no other reports of this association. Finally I sent a photograph to whatsthatbug.com, and the response came back that it was possibly some type of rove beetle. But there are more than three thousand species of rove beetles in North America—forty-seven thousand in the world—and very few people who can tell them apart. The taxonomists who can identify them are discovering new ones all the time. (If you want the opportunity to name an organism, rove beetles would be a good subject to study.) There is one, called the black lordithon, which is associated with old-growth forests. Considered globally rare, it is suspected to occur in Georgia, but no one knows for certain. I wondered if the bugs I found that day were members of this globally rare beetle species.

Later the entomologists wrote again: they had been wrong, and now thought it was a tumbling flower beetle. There are only two hundred species of that type of beetle, so the possibilities for identification were considerably narrowed, but behavior and life cycle have only been studied in a few of those. We still don't know why they are attracted to queen's delight, and what exactly it is they are doing on it. There are mysteries beyond mysteries here, too.

These mysteries do not frustrate me; I love them. Our planet is so exciting! I know that Rachel Carson, ecologist and author of *Silent Spring*, shared my way of looking at the world. In a talk she gave, she said:

> From what I have told you, you will know that a large part of my life has been concerned with some of the beauties and mysteries of the earth about us, and with the even greater mysteries of the life that inhabits it. No one can dwell long among such subjects without thinking rather deep thoughts, without asking himself searching and often unanswerable questions, and without achieving a certain philosophy.

There is one quality that characterizes all of us who deal with the sciences of the earth and its life—we are never bored. We can't be. There is always something new to be investigated. Every mystery solved brings us to the threshold of a greater one.

I think other animals, too, must be surprised by the never-ending mysteries. Sitting quietly in the open pine forest, I was able to observe the activities of many different birds. One bird plucked from the forest floor what it likely thought was a worm. It was the size, shape, and color of a worm, but was firmer and stronger. How strange. The bird flew to a branch very close to me with the "worm" dangling from its beak, and began whacking it against the branch. When the thing was subdued, the bird gulped it down, perhaps surprised by the novel taste of Florida worm lizard.

And this animal that looked like a worm, or if not that a snake, but which is really an eyeless, legless lizard? Perhaps it, too, was surprised by the mystery of a flight through the air after a life underground.

THE WORM LIZARD is a rare species, too. Fossils show that it once had eyes. The eyes evolved away on the outside, but deep inside the lizard's head are some unusual cells—a legacy from when the species could see. This reminds me of whales, whose ancestors evolved legs, but when they finally did better without them, the legs retreated. We humans are still holding on to our eyes and our legs, but we have no idea what the future will bring. We know we should expect change, for that's the way nature works.

We know that changes to species and evolution of new species occurs primarily through natural selection, meaning that some force of nature has influenced what life forms are most likely to survive and reproduce. Here in the longleaf pine forest, the primary force that determines what survives and what doesn't is fire.

Ecologists have been known to disagree about the role fire has played in shaping the landscape, but for the longleaf pine ecosystem there is no doubt: it was shaped by fire, and it remains fire dependent. It is no coincidence that this ecosystem occurs in the region of the country that has the most thunderstorms—lightning strikes start fires. Before humans created firebreaks, such as large agricultural fields or paved roads, a fire that started in one spot could burn through millions of acres. Because the fires were so frequent, they did not get very hot, and most of the fire-tolerant longleaf pines survived. The less tolerant species, such as loblolly pines and broadleaf trees, often perished. The result was more space and more light for longleaf pines, grasses, and wildflowers.

Without fire, the "piney woods" become something else. Without fire, other shrubs and trees, mostly oaks, begin growing among the pines. They block sunlight from reaching the wildflowers; the rare wildflowers disappear, the insects that eat the wildflowers disappear, and in turn the animals that eat the insects disappear. A forest will be present, but it will be a wholly different forest.

You could say these forests are *encouraging* fire: the pines produce long, resinous needles that constantly fall to the ground as tinder, and even the wiregrass holds its old, dry, brown, flammable blades above ground and stores most of its living mass below. Although these ecological tricks served the ecosystem well for many thousands of years, they were no match for the march of civilization. Given what we have left now, if we want to save any of this forest type and its many endangered species, we will have to be the ones to do the forest's bidding and light the flames.

All over the South, land managers are rising to this challenge. Countless dollars and human hours are spent caring for these forests on life support. The Moody Forest had not been burned frequently enough in the decades preceding its acquisition by the Nature Conservancy, and now the forest is the subject of intensive management. I could see where the small, invading oaks had been cut out by hand, and where a human-set fire had recently scorched the bark of the pines.

When the Nature Conservancy obtained the property, there was only one nesting pair of red-cockaded woodpeckers, another species made rare because of its vanishing habitat. Then something happened to the female bird, and for two years only a single male returned. This year a pair of captive woodpeckers were relocated to the forest. The trees here are old, and the forest has never been cleared, but the scent of humanity is everywhere.

When I approached the wind-sculpted pine I had been admiring, I saw that a numbered tag had been nailed into it. Number twelve, I touch your charred bark, I see how delicate the sinuous flakes are. And under the charred flakes I see the fresh, reddish ones; their turn for sacrifice will come next. And beneath that layer I count thirty more thin layers. And I know that deep below there is another layer forming this very moment. How much old-growth longleaf pine habitat will be left in the next century? Do we have the ability to regain any of what we have lost?

Rachel Carson says, "I believe that the more clearly we can focus our attention on the wonders and realities of the universe about us, the less taste we shall have for destruction." The song of the pines is just one of the many wonders this forest holds.

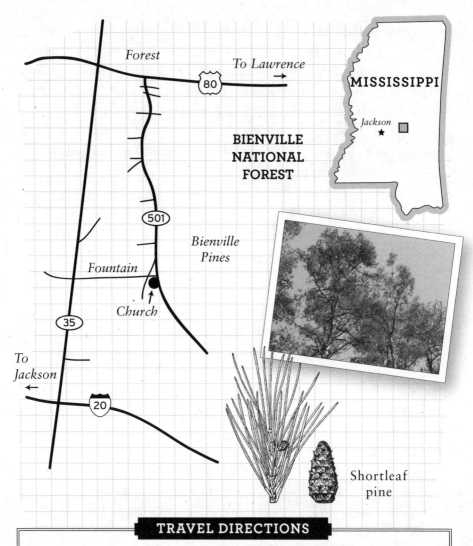

Forest

To Lawrence →

80

MISSISSIPPI

Jackson ★ ◼

BIENVILLE
NATIONAL
FOREST

501

Bienville
Pines

Fountain

35

Church ↑

To
Jackson ←

20

Shortleaf
pine

TRAVEL DIRECTIONS

Central part of state, Scott County. Closest town: Forest. From the west, take Interstate 20 to exit 88. Take Eoute 35 toward Forest, turning right on Fountain Road.

From the east, take exit 100 (U.S. 80) west toward Lawrence. Go eleven miles to the center of the town of Forest and turn left (south) onto Route 501 (Main Street). In about half a mile, you will see a sign for Bienville Work Center on the left. Do not turn there. Soon you will see Fountain Road on your right.

The entrance to the forest is directly across from this road. You can park in the lot of the brick Baptist church. From the parking lot, looking across the road toward the forest, you will see a pathway on the left-hand side. There are no signs.

46

Mississippi

BIENVILLE PINES SCENIC AREA, BIENVILLE NATIONAL FOREST

A forest gone missing...Forest management...What could have been

W**HERE ARE YOU** going in Mississippi?" asked the hiker, after I told him about my plan to visit an old-growth forest in each of the eastern states. When I answered that Mississippi was one state I was still researching, he offered to help. He said his wife's great-grandparents were in the logging business in southern Mississippi in the early 1900s and they still had contacts there.

Longleaf pine used to be the dominant forest type in the state—it covered about a third of the land area—but there are no longer any old-growth longleaf pine forests open to the public in Mississippi. My research pointed toward Bienville Pines as a good possibility for a visit, and the Internet turned up this intriguing description:

> The scenic area contains 180 acres and is the largest known block of "old-growth" pine timber in Mississippi. Towering loblolly and shortleaf pines, many over 200 years old, continue to dominate the site....The Bienville Pines Trail meanders through this area, giving hikers the opportunity to observe the plants and animals native to mature pine forests, including the red-cockaded woodpecker, an endangered species which nests only in living pines. The main trail is two miles long (shortcuts available) and is complete with interpretive stops and rest areas.

When the hiker e-mailed me, he suggested Bienville Pines also, copying this description that he had found:

> While in the forest try to visit the Bienville Pines Scenic Area. This 189-acre tract is the largest known block of old-growth timber in Mississippi. Old-growth forests are a rare and special thing in this part of America and well worth the time of a visit. A two-mile hiking trail meanders past 125 to 200 year old loblolly and shortleaf pines. Basically left to Mother Nature, this area provides visitors with a view of how nature works to maintain itself.

The 1986 management plan for the Bienville National Forest states, "The Bienville Pines is truly a unique area. It is the largest single block of old-growth southern pines known to exist in the United States." I was looking forward to my visit.

MY FIRST CLUE that something was terribly wrong was when I got to where the forest should have been and I could find no signs or trail markers. I stopped at the combination hunting goods/convenience store a few blocks away to ask about the trail. They sold boots and ammunition, fluorescent-orange wool hats, fishing lures, coffee, and candy bars; surely they would know where the trail was. But the clerk had no idea what I was talking about. He called over the other clerk, who likewise had never heard of the trail.

I called the Forest Service office, but the receptionist had no information about the trail, either. She gave me directions to the ranger station a few miles away, so I drove over there. At the station, a helpful ranger told me there "used to be" a trail, but it had been closed since before she started working there.

"Why was it closed?" I asked incredulously.

"Because someone was afraid the dying old trees would fall down and hurt someone, I think," she responded.

"But it is public land, and it's still open to the public, right?" I squeaked, trying to control myself, fearful that my long drive had been in vain.

"Yes. You can go there if you want, it's public land."

She gave me a photocopy of a map from 1964, which showed a parking area and a trail winding through a "scenic area." This looked hopeful, and

I was relieved. I imagined finding remnants of the old trail and enjoying a walk through the forest after all. She even dug out a few other documents for me from the old file. With map and directions in hand, I headed out the door and back to the forest.

But I still wasn't sure I was in the right place and had to call the office for confirmation. Finally, sure of my destination, I changed into my boots and headed across the road. The straight, unmarked path I was walking was cleared for a natural gas pipeline, but it was supposed to lead me to the old growth and the scenic area.

Soon I saw the tall, healthy pines. The loblolly pines had their characteristic rectangular-plated bark and long cones, and the shortleaf pines had thinner bark and shorter cones. But what had been done here? The pine trunks were rising out of a field of slash. Everywhere there were stumps from small trees and not-so-small trees. The forest floor looked as though it had been chewed up and spit out, and the deep ruts told me there had been some very heavy machinery in this forest very recently.

Those who judge a forest only by its oldest trees might still be tempted to call this an old-growth forest, but nothing at all felt like old growth to me, and there was certainly nothing scenic about it. I could see now why they took down the signs. The old trail was nowhere to be found, and I wandered through the pathless debris without a smile.

I can bet you it was someone with a forestry degree who ordered this done to the Bienville Pines Scenic Area. I'll bet that he or she, like a good Forest Service employee, had read the management plan, where one sentence in particular stood out: "The Bienville Pines was established for the purpose of protecting and preserving the old-growth pines, and management practices will be directed to that end."

At first glance this sounds good, but that critical sentence could be interpreted to give the nod to "management," and foresters are trained to manage. The sentence could also be interpreted to mean that the area should be left alone to age gracefully, but the evidence was painfully clear as to which way it was interpreted. The ruts and slash under my boots said it all.

Perhaps our imaginary forester has never seen an upland old-growth forest (where would he see one in Mississippi?), but he has studied his textbooks and has read the management plan. Keeping his management mission in mind—the pines!—he reads this section:

It should be noted also that, were this a "virgin stand," it would be predominantly hardwood with very few of the older pines left. The ecological climax forest in this region is an oak-hickory forest. This successional process is in effect now and if the area is left in a natural state, the area will revert to the oak-hickory type in 100 to 200 years.

Foresters are frequently taught to think of what happens in a forest as a competition. There are limited resources—primarily light, water, and nutrients—and the trees that are able to get the most resources will win. Pines need lots of light, so they do best after an area is cleared. But eventually other shade-tolerant broadleaf trees will grow under the pines, and no new pine seedlings will germinate on the shady forest floor. The broadleaf trees will compete with the pines for resources, and eventually the pines will succumb. This is a just-so story of succession, but it is an oversimplification.

The real story of the forest cannot be predicted; it is a shifting mosaic that only becomes evident once you stop believing the books and start believing your eyes. What you see as you walk through an old-growth forest is that there is often no "winner." A large variety of species can be successful all at once, and there are probably ways that they are cooperating with each other as well as competing. For instance, the leaves that drop to the forest floor help accelerate the decomposition of fallen needles and neutralize the soil so more nutrients are available to the pines. There are probably beneficial fungal and insect associations, too. We definitely have much more to learn about the relationships among tree species.

RED-COCKADED WOODPECKERS nest here. The forester thinks she is doing the right thing by manipulating the forest in a way that will benefit the woodpeckers. But, ironically, it is our management of the forests that has endangered the woodpecker in the first place. This is one of the only places left for them to nest because this is one of the only places with mature pines. But even managing for the pines does not ensure the pines will survive. A small, isolated forest of very tall trees is susceptible to windthrow. If these old pines fall in a strong wind, there will be no place for the woodpeckers to go.

Our forester was afraid the pines would lose the competition with the hardwoods, and they went to battle with the oaks, the maples, the hickories, the redbuds, the dogwoods, the hornbeams, and all the other trees growing at the base of the pines. The forest is close to town, so they didn't want to use fire to halt succession. Instead they crushed the plants on the forest floor and ground ruts into the soil in the name of "stand improvement." This decision was not made by an evil person, I'm sure, just someone who didn't see the bigger picture. And the equipment operator was just doing what he was told. If he lost this job, he'd have to go to work at the chicken-processing factory across the street—and he didn't want that.

I am convinced of the need for fire management to retain the tiny percentage of longleaf pine forests we have left, but loblolly and shortleaf pine regenerate more easily after cutting, and this particular National Forest has more than a *hundred thousand* acres of pine. Why not leave this little precious bit of old growth alone, for reasons both aesthetic and educational, halt the cutting of some of the other acreage, and allow *those* pines to age? Old loblolly and shortleaf pine forests provide important habitat, but they don't always have to stay in the same place. By the time the Bienville Pines would be replaced by the hardwoods growing underneath them—perhaps another hundred years—a new area of pines could have matured enough to meet the needs of the woodpeckers. In a landscape this large, one has the luxury of rotation—rotation for ecological rather than commercial purposes. Rotation counted in centuries, not decades.

I dream of the Bienville Pines Scenic Area the way it could have been if it had been left alone for another hundred years. I imagine some of the old pines, homes of the woodpeckers, dying. Some of the dead trees remain standing for a time, and other organisms nest in the dead snags. The woodpeckers feed on the grubs and beetles in the snags and carry them home to their nestlings. Occasionally, on a windy night, one of the snags falls to the forest floor with a crash. There it becomes home to different sorts of organisms, such as salamanders and millipedes. The rotting logs keep the soil cool and moist. Meanwhile, the oak and hickory trees are getting taller and stronger. The forest floor is densely shaded, and children love to come here on school trips. Some of the pines, those with good genes or in a fortunate location, live much longer than anyone could have imagined. Woodpeckers still nest in those trees, and sometimes the schoolchildren are lucky enough to see them, but many woodpecker families have dispersed into the adjacent acreage—land designated as an extension of the scenic area and uncut for the last hundred years.

The town's economy is doing much better thanks to the boom in eco-tourism. The mayor applied to the federal government for a brass plaque declaring the forest a National Natural Landmark. Television news programs covered the town's celebration on the day it was erected. The convenience store has started selling nature books and Patagonia clothing in addition to their usual items, and profits have doubled. Ester's little shack has become a full-scale restaurant, and tourists love to sit on the back deck watching the birds while they eat. And these words from the 1986 management plan are still true:

> Regardless of the question of its virgin state, the Bienville Pines is exceptional in its age, magnitude, and beauty. There is no other place where one can go to view an area as large and with the number of trees of the age of these. The area is also a classic example of "undisturbed" ecological succession.

If only.

I wondered about this town, named Forest, which no longer had a trail through its most famous forest. The name of the town came from a commodity that was exploited. This flatland with tall pines was the perfect place for a logging operation. So they came, and they logged. Everything. Even the biggest Bienville Pines were logged, probably between 1850 and 1860. This is not an undisturbed forest. But in the second (or third) round of logging, the pines in this one small area were left alone. It's not that they were difficult to get to—in fact, they were right next to the center of logging operations. Some have speculated that the pines were spared because the company could log there at any time, and so harvested the more remote areas first. I would speculate that the trees were left because even the loggers loved their beauty and shade, and therefore saved some for their own pleasure.

What convinced me that emotion, not economics, saved the pines was what happened in 1935, when the federal government was purchasing the Bienville Lumber Company's acreage for a national forest. The lumber company planned to donate twenty acres of the old pines to the city of Forest for a park, but, because of the Great Depression, the city had no funds for the things normally needed in a park, such as picnic tables and restrooms. The city turned down the offer, and the Bienville Pines forest was included in the land acquired by the Forest Service. According to the records, "At the time of the acquisition, a 'gentleman's agreement' was struck between the Forest Service and the lumber company to the effect that this area would be left intact and never cut." Obviously, someone cared about this forest.

The area around the big pines was designated a scenic area, and the Forest Service installed water fountains, tables, grills, and restrooms. The map from 1964 shows a winding trail, and in 1976 someone thought enough of the forest to nominate it as a National Natural Landmark. It was awarded this recognition—a fact that surprised even the ranger who found the letter in the file.

Incredulous that this abused-looking plot of trees would be considered a National Landmark, I called the National Park Service to speak with the coordinator of the National Landmarks program's southeast region. As it turned out, he had never been to Bienville Pines, so I suggested he might want to take a look. He called the Forest Service ranger and then called me back. He explained that they had done a "mechanical reduction" to reduce the risk of fire so close to a populated area, and that this was "standard forestry practice."

Yeah, whatever. This is no longer a place of recreation or non-manipulation; this is no longer a place of beauty. No wonder the people of Forest no longer know where it is.

Under different circumstances, this forest could have been the gem of the town. It could have attracted ecotourists and inspired children to study and love nature. It could have brought more customers to the convenience store and to Ester's. Forest would be called Forest for a good reason. There are 178,000 acres in this National Forest, yet they couldn't leave this little bit alone. Normally I leave a forest feeling great, but today I was feeling down.

I stopped by Ester's shack for a sweet tea on my way out of town.

"Was that you a while ago walking through the woods?" she asked.

"Yes it was. I'm interested in old forests," I answered.

"Ain't you scared?" she asked.

"No."

She just shook her head. "Ought to have a gun."

Cook Forest State Park, Pennsylvania

MID-ATLANTIC FORESTS

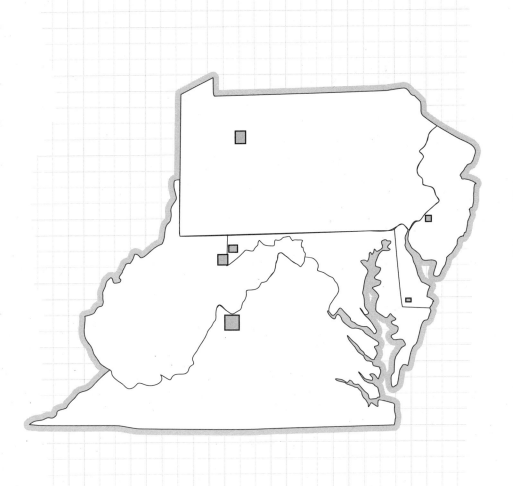

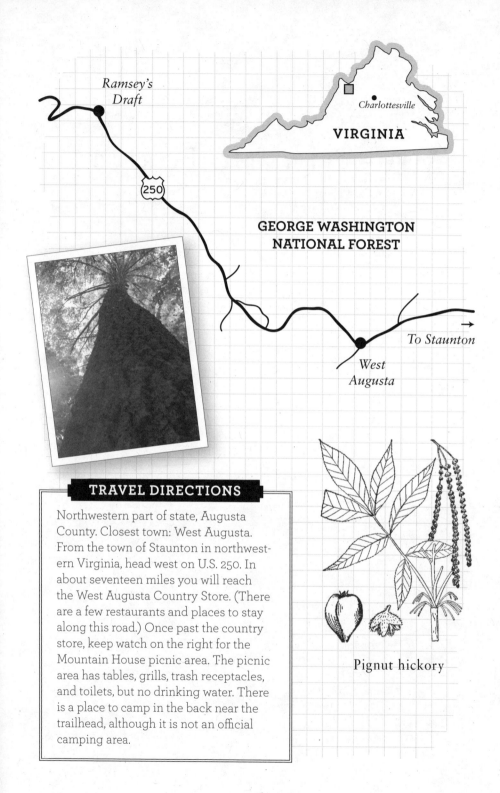

Ramsey's
Draft

Charlottesville

VIRGINIA

250

**GEORGE WASHINGTON
NATIONAL FOREST**

To Staunton

West
Augusta

TRAVEL DIRECTIONS

Northwestern part of state, Augusta
County. Closest town: West Augusta.
From the town of Staunton in northwestern Virginia, head west on U.S. 250. In
about seventeen miles you will reach
the West Augusta Country Store. (There
are a few restaurants and places to stay
along this road.) Once past the country
store, keep watch on the right for the
Mountain House picnic area. The picnic
area has tables, grills, trash receptacles,
and toilets, but no drinking water. There
is a place to camp in the back near the
trailhead, although it is not an official
camping area.

Pignut hickory

Virginia

Ramsey's Draft, George Washington National Forest

The world has changed...Nettles...Adelgid...John Seed

D RAFT IS AN old-fashioned term for what we now call a creek. This official wilderness area, in a national forest, includes the creek, the floodplain that surrounds it, and the hillsides rising up around the floodplain. If you just want to see big trees, you can see plenty on a day hike. But if you want to go further and stay longer, as I did on this journey, then you must carry a backpack that holds food and shelter.

Following a trail along the creek, I crossed the stream by stepping carefully from rock to rock. The trail continued on the other side for a distance, then crossed the creek again. Most of my day was spent like this, back and forth across the clear, rocky stream, mile after mile. In between crossings, the path was straight and level, and the giant trees cast a dense shade. I am in the old growth now. Every so often I saw a tree so remarkably large that I had to leave the trail and pay it a visit. At the base of the tree, I would tilt my head back and strain to see the shapes of the leaves so far up, silhouetted against the sky. I was most captivated by the tulip poplars, but there were also remarkable maples, hickories, and oaks. I appreciated each one, and then walked on slowly through the green wonderland.

When I looked around, I saw a carpet of low, green plants on the forest floor and trunks of varying sizes rising up around me on all sides. Away from the creek, the only sound was birdsong echoing off the hillsides. The trail was a dirt line through a rich, green, herbaceous floor, and compared with the scale of the trees, I was a very small creature moving through the forest. I felt like a hobbit, on a mission to see the world as much of it used to be...before.

But the world has changed irreversibly. Although Ramsey's Draft is now an officially designated wilderness area, and one of the places in the East least manipulated by humans, an introduced plant grows throughout the floodplain. Luckily for me, though, this plant is wineberry, and its berries happened to be perfectly ripe on this weekend. The wineberry's Latin name translates as "blackberry with purple hairs." It was purposefully introduced from China and Japan in 1890 as breeding stock, and it is delicious. As I walked, I plucked and ate. My actions may have been irresponsible, however, for the seeds from the berries can be spread by birds or by humans, and there was no port-a-potty where I was headed.

THE MOST ABUNDANT plant on the forest floor was a wood-nettle. These are edible too, but must be cooked first, so I didn't nibble on them. Cree Indians call them *masan,* which means "one who itches." In their legend, nettles once had golden shimmering leaves and a bright aura, but humans took them for granted and paid them no respect. So the plant turned green to blend in with other plants and grew stinging hairs to get the humans' attention. Now we pay more respect to *masan.*

Stinging nettles grow about knee high and cause an intense burning sensation if they hit bare skin as you brush past them on the trail. The structure of the nettle's stinging hairs has been well studied. Enlarged, they look like fine glass needles with rounded tips sitting atop pedestals. Like glass, the hairs are made of silica and are brittle. When a passing hiker brushes a hair, the rounded tip breaks off and the sharp point of the needle penetrates the skin. This alone would probably be irritating, but what happens next accounts for the nettle's bad reputation: chemical compounds stored in the hair's base are injected into the skin via the needle. These chemicals burn.

I mean no disrespect to the Cree, but as a plant ecologist, I interpret the stinging hairs as an adaptation to prevent being eaten by animals. Research on this has shown that whether or not an animal will eat nettles mostly

depends on the size of the animal. Their leaves are a favored food source for the caterpillars of a number of butterfly species. The adult butterfly lays her eggs on the nettle leaves, and the caterpillars feed on the nutritious leaves after they hatch. Because many animals avoid the leaves, these caterpillars enjoy a high survival rate. And they are small enough to avoid coming into contact with the tips of the stinging needles as they feed. Many humans, if given the opportunity, would wave a magic wand to rid the world of nettles, but without them we would be without many butterflies, too.

Snails and slugs also rely on the nettle leaves for food. The glasslike hairs have been found in snail feces, but we don't know how these mollusks react to the hairs, either on their way in or on their way out.

Bison and other very large animals can eat nettles without pause, but medium-sized grazers, such as rabbits and sheep, avoid them. Yet even their avoidance is relative. In one experiment, researchers noted that plants from different areas exhibited varying numbers of stinging hairs. They presented varying samples to hungry rabbits and sheep that had no other food source. Not surprisingly, the animals fed most on the ones with the fewest hairs. In evolutionary terms, the sheep and the rabbits were selecting which nettles would live to reproduce their genes—the ones with the greatest number of stinging hairs.

I am hard-pressed to find anything positive to say about another organism in this forest, the wooly adelgid, a tiny insect that sucks the sap out of the bases of hemlock needles and twigs; it was unintentionally introduced from Asia to the West Coast in the 1920s. In one phase of their life cycle, adelgids may drift about in the breeze and spread to formerly uninfected trees. Most commonly, however, birds carry them from tree to tree.

In the northern states, freezing winter weather has kept populations of this pest somewhat in check, but in the South many hemlocks have been killed and now stand like gray ghosts on the hillside. Trees that have survived for centuries despite fire, logging, or wind are now dying because of something almost too small to see. Here in Ramsey's Draft, most of the hemlocks were still alive, but when I inspected young branches I saw the white, cottony, telltale signs of adelgid infestation. My heart sank when I thought about what might be missing from this forest the next time I visit.

But it was difficult to stay sad for long in a forest this beautiful. As I walked, I thought of John Seed, who, as a young man, was involved in an "action" to protect a rainforest in New South Wales, Australia, from logging. He felt so good about protecting those trees that he decided to make it his life's work. He started the very influential, nonprofit Rainforest Information Centre. Formerly a systems analyst with IBM, Seed threw himself fully into trying to save rainforests across the globe. But none of us can do it alone, and soon he felt burned out. Then Seed met Joanna Macy, an American who had developed practices to help prevent burnout in activists.

Both Seed and Macy recognized the powerful and deep connections that we humans share with our planet. We evolved in the Earth's bosom, and when the Earth is damaged we instinctively feel pain and anxiety. But at the same time, we often feel powerless to stop the damage. No one enjoys the pain that comes with caring for something that is being destroyed, so we may begin to shield ourselves by shutting down, by trying not to care so much. But shutting down is not the answer. The best way to deal with the pain, Macy says, is to use it to empower you. Both Macy and Seed lead "despair and empowerment" workshops to help others through this transition.

As I moved my hobbit-self and my backpack through the large, green landscape, I thought of a talk by John Seed I had attended in Eugene, Oregon. One young woman had raised her hand at the end. "When I go away to one of these workshops, I come home feeling so energized," she said. "But then after a few days, it begins to wear off, and after a few weeks it has really worn off, and after a few months I feel lousy again. How can I keep that good feeling I came home with?"

Seed paused. "Well, yeah," he answered in his wonderful Australian accent. "It's not a magic pill is it? You don't just have one experience and—poof—you're fine for life. You must keep at it. The only advice I can give you is to spend as much time as you can in the wildest places you can find."

Bingo, that's it. That's why I was thinking of Seed. Look, here I was, doing it, and he was right, I felt better. *Spend as much time as you can in the wildest places you can find.* It's as simple as that.

Later, lying on my sleeping bag in the darkness, I heard the water splashing over the rocks in the creek and the wind moving the leaves far above me. Nearby, a night insect trilled. It was the best of all lullabies.

Gerald Manley Hopkins wrote a poem, almost a prayer, that seems perfect for the occasion:

What would the world be, once bereft
Of wet and wildness? Let them be left,
O let them be left, wildness and wet;
Long live the weeds and the wilderness yet.

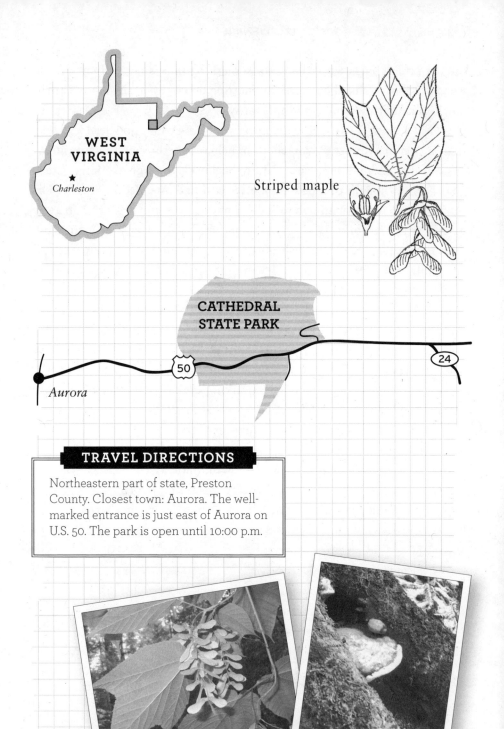

WEST
VIRGINIA

★
Charleston

Striped maple

CATHEDRAL
STATE PARK

50

24

Aurora

TRAVEL DIRECTIONS

Northeastern part of state, Preston
County. Closest town: Aurora. The well-
marked entrance is just east of Aurora on
U.S. 50. The park is open until 10:00 p.m.

West Virginia

CATHEDRAL STATE PARK

Arrivals...Partridge berries...Funnel-web spiders...Caterpillars...Drought

IN THE BOOK *Blue Highways,* William Least Heat Moon describes taking off for a long road trip after his marriage fails. Moon travels alone in his van, taking the smaller, more scenic roads shown in blue on his map. On those roads he experiences the real America that he writes about. On my map, the largest highways are shown in blue and the smaller roads in red or gray, but my impulse is the same as Moon's. I have a destination—the old growth—but along the way I want to see an authentic landscape. I feel anesthetized traveling on superhighways where the land has been made to fit the road; I want the road to rise as the hills rise and to drop back down through the valleys. I want to drive on a small road where the branches hang over and I can tell if I'm passing through oak or poplar. I want to be able to stop at the next little store and be the only stranger there.

The red road to the forest at Cathedral State Park is especially lovely. Travel to old-growth forests is different from other sorts of travel. In almost every case, I had not been to the forest before nor met anyone who had. As I checked and rechecked the directions, getting nearer with every mile, a certain tension built and grew, finally bursting into exhilaration when at last I saw the sign.

You pull in and park. You have made it to the forest! Perhaps there is another car in the parking lot, perhaps not. But certainly there will be trees, clean air, and birdsong. You get out and stretch while the truck makes little ticking noises as it cools off. It seems so quiet after the noise of the road. You are anxious to step into the forest—which is right there—but it is best to delay that gratification until you've changed your shoes and put a few things in your pack. Then, finally, finally, you take your first few steps on the trail and it all comes rushing at you—the green, the damp, the fragrance, the bird calls. The trees seem large, but they are not overwhelming. The landscape is complex but in a subtle way.

I FOUND MYSELF just wanting to walk at first. Just walk, breathe, listen, look. Just become part of the forest for a while and let it become part of me. I didn't try to take notes or pictures or identify anything; there would be time for all of that later. For now, I would just be, just feel what the living earth under my feet is supposed to feel like, and imagine when this forest stretched so far that you couldn't walk out of it in a day or even a few days. I would have liked to be in that forest, but already the Giant Hemlock Trail had ended at a farm field, and I needed to decide whether to turn onto the Partridge Berry Trail or the Cathedral Trail. These trails were measured in feet instead of miles; they were easy and well maintained.

I eventually walked both trails, and on the Partridge Berry Trail I was pleased to see the partridge berry plants in bloom. I stopped to watch a bumblebee visiting the flowers. Heavy with nectar, she didn't even bother to fly but just crawled from blossom to blossom.

My observations had slowed me, and I was ready now for a closer look. I had taken in the whole of the forest and was ready for the pieces, the minutiae, the pleasure of beholding "the other." I did not have far to look. Surrounding me were dark columns of trees. The hemlocks' short evergreen needles cast a deep shade. As I reached out to touch their bark, I noticed webs in some places. We tend to think of bark as somewhat lifeless, but of course it isn't. Numerous organisms live on bark and spend their entire lives there.

The webs I saw were a few inches across and not the type strung between branches; instead they were like webby sheets attached to ridges in the bark. As I looked closer I noticed, somewhere on each of these webs, a circular hole receding from the surface down toward the trunk like a funnel. This was the work of a funnel-web spider. The sheet of webbing isn't sticky like some other webs; it functions more like the head of a drum. When a small insect causes the web to vibrate, the spider senses it and zooms out of its funnel hole. He captures the insect, bites it, wraps it in silk, and drags it down into the hole. Some types of spiders spin a new web every evening, but the funnel-web keeps the same one all year, making repairs as necessary.

I could see a spider perched at the edge of the hole closest to me. When I raised my camera to snap his picture, he ducked back into the hole. I put the camera down and watched for a few minutes, and he soon climbed back up to the edge. Again, I raised my camera, and, again, he backed away. I spoke to that spider as one might with a recalcitrant three-year-old. *Come on, pleeaasse, just one picture.* And the unspoken threat: *don't make me collect you.* It was an idle threat, of course.

Spiders are critical components of the ecosystem, primarily because their feeding reduces other insect populations, but also because other organisms, such as wasps, birds, and lizards, feed on them. I didn't believe that collecting one spider would harm this ecosystem—I had probably stepped on at least one unknowingly—but feared more that it might harm my spirit. The Dali Lama recently was asked what sort of things should be taught to children. "Teach them to be kind to the insects," was his reply.

SPIDERS ARE LONERS. They are aggressive predators and will not hesitate to capture and eat other spiders, even ones of their own species. And other spiders would not hesitate to eat them, either. This makes mating especially tricky; a spider must make direct contact with another spider without becoming its dinner. As a result, they have evolved elaborate attractants and mating rituals.

Much of the information about spider mating comes from R. Gering, who devoted his career to studying the topic. The funnel-web mating story begins with an adolescent male spider who feels a "sensation of fullness in the testes and of emptiness in the palpal organs." (The palpal organs, or pedipalps, are feeler-like structures near the mouth that resemble short legs.) In response to this feeling, he builds a small web and rubs against it.

I will leave it to Gering to tell what happens next: "The male's action pre-sumably produces a tactile stimulation which causes the extrusion of the seminal fluid droplets. These droplets coalesce to form a single drop of sem-inal fluid which remains on the web." The spider then takes his pedipalp and dips it into the seminal fluid, which is drawn by capillary action into a narrow duct in the "palm" of the pedipalp.

In male spiders the pedipalps, located on either side of the head, bear genitalia that will deliver sperm to the female. The female's genitalia are un-usually positioned, too, in a cavity beneath a hardened plate on the under-side of her abdomen, up near her thorax. The male must insert the complex structures on the end of his pedipalp into this cavity. These structures are so tiny but so complex that illustrations of them remind me of diagrams of the inner ear, with their miniature interlocking bones and curled cochlea.

The sexually mature, virgin female funnel-web spider produces a chemi-cal pheromone that attracts males to her web, and, once there, the male performs a well-studied routine. First he sways his abdomen back and forth rhythmically. Next he flexes the web by raising and lowering his abdomen (think spider push-ups). These motions produce vibrations that the female can detect. The male that sways the fastest is the most likely to get lucky, but the female is not easy to persuade. He may have to continue this dance for up to an hour and a half. Occasionally he will stop and rest, but the male that takes the shortest breaks has the highest probability of being ac-cepted by the female.

When he has finally proven he has the right stuff, he walks toward her and she doesn't retreat. They face each other for a few minutes, motionless. As he reaches out to touch her, she faints, overcome by a chemical he has released. The now passive female is no longer a threat, and he strokes her, takes one pair of her legs in his mouthparts, and turns her on her side. She must be positioned just right for him to insert the complex structure on his pedipalp. At this point, the male begins cleaning his pedipalps in his mouth, causing his spines to become erect and pulsate. It is believed that "the clean-ing process serves to lubricate the genital bulb and its component parts."

Now the most challenging part of the copulation begins. Like a blind man feeling the features of someone's face, the male spider taps his pedipalp across the female, searching for the lock that will fit his key. At last the two engage and the key is literally turned, the male organ a hardened coil

that spirals into the female. Scientists tell us that, when rotation has been completed, a "particularly strong paroxysm is observed." After the male ejaculates the seminal fluid, the coiled organ deflates and is withdrawn. The "female may make feeble attempts to right herself," but generally she remains immobile. After withdrawal, the male cleans his pedipalps and repeats the entire sequence. In the eighty-five spider matings Gering observed, there were between three and eighteen repetitions per mating event.

Must I be concerned that these scientifically documented facts will narrow my audience, and that this chapter will never be assigned to an eighth-grade class? As Ralph Waldo Emerson reminds us: "Eyes, ears, taste, smell, motion, resistance, appetite, and organs of reproduction that take hold on eternity,—all find room to consist in the small creature. So do we put our life into every act. The true doctrine of omnipresence is that God reappears with all his parts in every moss and cobweb."

THE FEMALE LAYS her fertile eggs in a silk cocoon she has produced. She attaches the cocoon to the underside of a loose piece of bark and positions herself next to it to guard it. When the cold weather arrives, she will die in place next to her egg-mass cocoon. But the eggs will survive and, come spring, the tiny newborn spiders will instinctively head off by themselves. They will climb until they find a place where they might produce a web and capture enough food to keep themselves alive until it is their turn to conceive the next generation.

I saw many of these funnel-webs on the bark of the hemlock trees. They seemed to prefer hemlock over other species, perhaps because the deep fissures in the bark offered good protection. I noticed that the placement of the webs was not random: Most of the spiders chose to build directly under a knob where a branch had broken off long ago. I hypothesized that this meager roof protected their one and only web from pelting rain or blazing sun.

Nature is full of patterns like this. Some are well documented, and you can recognize them from someone else's description, but it's most rewarding to discover patterns yourself. Pattern recognition is a skill that can be developed. Once you have identified a pattern, you can then take the next step and hypothesize *why* this pattern exists in nature. Normally it will have something to do with survival of the organism, or at least survival of its genes. Scientific testing and close observation are the best tools we have for determining whether a hypothesis is correct. I could have easily spent the next two years collecting data to support or refute my hypothesis about the webs, but I had other plans.

I searched for more patterns and noticed that many nettle plants had a daddy longlegs perched on them, top and center. What was happening here? There is so much we don't understand. There is no forest on Earth for which we have finished cataloging all its living species, and our understanding of all the patterns and relationships is even less complete. Discoveries await many generations of scientists to come. But the Earth holds the most beautiful and complex jigsaw puzzle there is, and we must keep all the pieces if we ever hope to understand the final picture.

In his book *The Hidden Forest,* Jon Luoma asks, "Can there be anything more extraordinary or bizarre or perverse than a culture that pours its resources into the study of the mystery of other worlds, even as it fails to take far more modest steps to uncover the interwoven wonders of life on its own?"

WHEN I ENTER an old-growth forest, however large or small, I stay on the paths at first. The part closest to the parking lot always gets the most use—and abuse—so there, especially, I stick to the trail. But to really feel part of these wild forests it is helpful to occasionally stray. After I have walked off my initial excitement and gathered my first impressions, I will usually look for a quiet spot off the trail where I can't be seen. There I will sit and experience being an animal surrounded by an intact ecosystem. We are always animals supported by the ecosystem, of course, but it is easy to forget that riding in a vehicle or shopping at the mall. Here, in the forest, I am reminded of my wild, ancient lineage.

Sitting quietly, I see more and hear more. The small things I would otherwise walk right by begin to attract my attention. This fern here by my knee: why is it curled up like a ball on the top? Not the usual fiddlehead pattern that emerges in the spring, but a globe, as if something has stitched the *pinnae* of the fronds together into a ball. And something has: a green caterpillar. The caterpillar climbs to the top of the frond, binds the top leaflets together, and connects them to the stalk—called the *rachis* in ferns—with a strong silk thread. This causes the top of the fern to curl downward. The caterpillar then fastens the side leaflets with more silk and pulls the resulting ball down further along the rachis "in a manner analogous to rolling up a carpet," according to scientists who studied this procedure. At a certain distance from the tip, the rachis gets too stiff to roll well, so the caterpillar bites a notch in the rachis, enabling the rachis to curl. The notch is cut so skillfully that the moisture- and nutrient-conducting vessels are not damaged. Wow.

All this rolling goes on between 10:00 p.m. and 6:00 a.m. It allows the caterpillar to feed on the fern tips day or night without being exposed to harsh weather, hungry birds, or parasitic wasps. But, although there is plenty to eat and the temperature is comfortable, the problem with being in such an enclosed room is that your wastes stay in there with you. If you were to open up one of these fern balls, you might or might not find the caterpillar, but you would always find a dark crumbly material, *frass*—a polite biological term for caterpillar poop.

Some caterpillar species that build shelters forcefully fling their frass great distances away from their shelters at great speed. But in this particular globe-making species, the caterpillar will eventually get so large and the frass so abundant that a new globe shelter must be made. A typical caterpillar will make five of these globes before it pupates. The pupa forms inside the fern globe and a medium-sized tan and white moth later emerges. Another life cycle successfully completed.

ON MY WAY here, the news on my truck radio was all about the drought, the worst this part of West Virginia had seen in a long, long time. The creeks had dried up, forcing some farmers to cut down trees to feed to their cows—because of the moisture and nutrition in the leaves—and others to sell their herds. This was happening all around the state, yet here in the ancient forest the streams were still running.

Many people are still unaware of the relationship between logging and hydrology, although naturalist George Perkins Marsh was trying to educate people about it as early as 1864. In his book *Man and Nature*, he wrote, "In many parts of those states which have been cleared for above a generation or two the hill pastures now suffer severely from drought, and in dry seasons no longer afford either water or herbage for cattle."

Forest soils and even dead logs on the forest floor act like thick sponges shaded by an overhead canopy, soaking up the rains and then releasing them ever so slowly, thus buffering both floods and droughts. This capacity to hold water is just one of the valuable ecological services our mature forests provide. I wonder if the same farmers that were having problems with their cows had sold timber off their land, and now had money in their bank accounts but no water in their streams? That was the case with one family I visited in West Virginia.

THE HISTORY OF logging the virgin forests of West Virginia is well documented, and it will break your heart. Roy B. Clarkson, in his book *Tumult on the Mountain,* tells the story of how technological advances, such as steam trains, accelerated the forests' doom. The speed with which the forests were destroyed is difficult to imagine. In 1870 the majority of West Virginia was covered in old-growth forest, an estimated ten million acres; by 1910 old growth covered only 15 percent of that; and by 1920 only a few small pockets remained.

Cathedral State Park covers 133 acres, and the park's brochure touts it as "one of the last living commemorations of the vast virgin hemlock forest that once flourished in the Appalachian highlands."

The history of forests further to the south is documented in another heartbreaking book, *Old Trees: The Illustrated History of Logging the Virgin Timber in the Southeastern United States.* The two stories are very similar, and the lesson of both is that "improvements" in technology made the destruction of our forests faster and more complete.

I remind myself that, although I cannot forget what happened to our land, my visits to the old growth are designed to be a small-scale antidote to all of that. Others have had the difficult task of documenting the destruction. The task I have chosen for myself is to focus on what remains. I want to find what is left and celebrate the amazing life forms that have survived. Today I celebrated the partridge berry, the bumblebee, the funnel-web spider, and a fern-curling caterpillar.

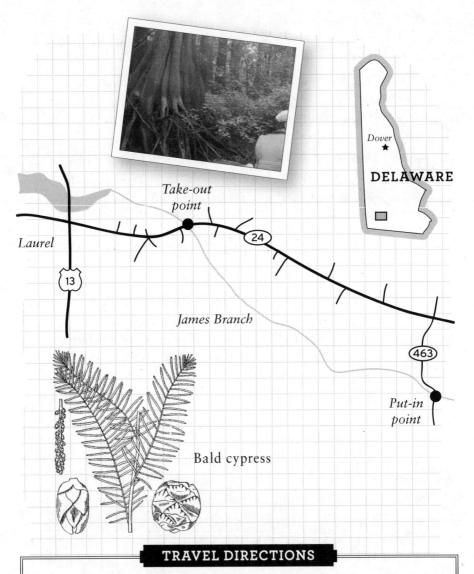

Take-out point

Laurel

13

24

James Branch

Dover ★

DELAWARE

463

Put-in point

Bald cypress

TRAVEL DIRECTIONS

Southern part of state, Sussex County. Closest town: Laurel. From U.S. 13 in Laurel, turn east onto Route 24. In about one mile you will cross a small bridge. This is your take-out point, so you may want to leave a vehicle in the parking lot just beyond the bridge. Continue east on Route 24 another two miles to Hitch Pond Road (Route 463). Make a right, and in less than a mile you will again come to a bridge over James Branch. This is your put-in point.

I would suggest making the trek in early spring when the water is high, but, whenever you go, expect to come out muddy and tired. Nearby Trap Pond State Park has camping areas and rents cabins (www.destateparks.com; 302-875-5153).

Delaware

JAMES BRANCH, TRAP POND STATE PARK

Tucker La Prade...Canoeing...The Patriarch...Dragonflies

T HERE IS NOT MUCH to choose from when selecting an old-growth site open to the public in Delaware. I read about one forest in the extreme northern part of the state that was said to be old growth, but it was not open to the public on a daily basis. I was considering my options when out of the blue of my computer screen came this e-mail:

Dear Professor Maloof,

Hello, my name is Tucker La Prade. I am a college sophomore at Hillsdale College and during the summer I serve as an Americorps Environmental Educator at Trap Pond State Park. Recently, we ordered your book *Teaching the Trees* for our nature center. I wanted to let you know how much I love the book. Thank you so much for writing it. I, too, am passionate about trees, so it was a joy to find someone who understands, for example, the simple bliss of beholding a tulip poplar. Your writings about trees have stirred my imagination and spurred me to pursue my passions all the more.

I was very excited when I looked at the back flap of the book and discovered that you taught at Salisbury University. I lived in Salisbury for ten years before moving to Seaford, Delaware. I would love it if you could come to visit at Trap Pond sometime. Reading your book was such a revelation, I know a

real walk in the woods with you would be even more of one. You have probably visited Trap Pond before, but if not, I know you would love it. Most
people come for the stately bald cypress trees in the middle of the pond, but I
love it for its hauntingly beautiful foot paths and canoe trails.

Among my other projects this summer, I am designing a trail guide for
our Island Trail, which features beautiful variation between beeches, cypress,
oaks, maples, holly, gum, and a few stalwart chestnut trees. I would love your
insight on that trail. If you came, perhaps we could canoe down the James
Branch trail to see "The Patriarch," supposedly the park's oldest cypress tree,
said to be about 600 years old. If you teach a summer class, perhaps you
could take them to Trap Pond to do some field study.

Well, these are just some of a few ideas to get you to the park. I'd love to
meet you and talk to you further about trees and nature. Thank you again for
your moving book.

Sincerely,

Tucker La Prade

I answered back. Of course, I wanted to meet Tucker and see the Patriarch
Tree. By all accounts, the Patriarch was in a stretch of cypress that had
never been logged. This would be my Delaware old growth.

Dear Dr. Maloof,

Thank you for your enthusiastic response, I am very excited about your
visit to the park. I've been thinking a lot about what to do when you come,
and I think it would be the most fun to visit the Patriarch. Have you ever
visited it before? According to an article by our former Naturalist, Ed Lewandowski, the Patriarch is 550 years old, making it Delaware's oldest tree.
According to the same article, the tree is 127 feet high with a trunk circumference of 25 feet and a crown spread of almost 63 feet. In the meantime before
your visit, I will explore the trail to discover the best way to get to this tree. If
the trail is too overgrown or the water level is too low (unfortunately this is a
bad time of year to follow the James Branch Canoe trail), we have many other
forests and old trees I would love to show you.

Again, I am thrilled about your visit; I am saving up all my tree questions.

Sincerely,

Tucker La Prade

Dear Dr. Maloof,

Good news about the Patriarch! In an effort to locate the tree, I called former Trap Pond naturalist Ed Lewandowski and State Senator Bob Venables and received a good description of the general area. Yesterday I canoed to that area and saw the landmarks of where the tree should be, but didn't have the time to wander off the path to find it. In a way I am more excited, because I've reserved the pleasure of discovery for your visit.

I think the morning will be the best time for our trip, and judging from my canoeing yesterday, it should take about 5 or 6 hours. How about meeting at the Nature Center at Trap Pond at 9:00 AM? Since we probably won't be off trail 'til 2:00, I suggest bringing a lunch; there's a good spot to stop for lunch midway down the trail. As for transportation, we can definitely provide canoes and paddles, but if you'd like to bring your own kayak, that's fine too. Honestly, for this trip, I suggest canoes, because fallen trees abound and one has to get out of one's boat often to drag it over these spots.

I should warn you, the trail is pretty rough. It's often more wading through the stream than canoeing. There is also a good deal of spiders, stinging bugs, poison ivy, etc. I think it's well worth the effort, though. Besides the giant bald cypress trees, the trail is teeming with wildlife, from mammals to birds. I saw fresh deer, raccoon, and beaver tracks, as well as prothonotary warblers and red-headed woodpeckers perched on trees directly in front of me. I heard many more bird songs than I could recognize. By all accounts, this trail is one of the more wild in Delaware.

Let me know if you're good for the 7th at 9:00, and we'll go from there.

In great anticipation,

Tucker

I was good for the 7th at nine.

THE RAIN STOPPED just as I pulled into the nature center, where I was greeted by a band of six children of both sexes and various skin colors. Tucker turned out to be a young man with a smile that turned sharply upward at the corners. In truth, I don't think any of them were younger than seventeen, but even the oldest was less than half my age and I kept wondering if there shouldn't be an adult in charge. *I* certainly wasn't in charge. I had no clue where we should put in or take out or where this giant tree was supposed to be. The young ones scurried about readying the canoe trailer and gathering the paddles, life jackets, radios, maps, sunscreen, and all the other items necessary for an adventure such as this. I felt as if I were Wendy, deep in the forest of Neverland with the Lost Boys. I just tried to relax and enjoy my status as the honorary mother-naturalist.

We unloaded the canoes at a bridge over a very small and smelly black creek. I shared a boat with Tucker. The water level was low, and a submerged log soon prevented our passage. I had worn my trusty black rubber knee boots for exactly this sort of situation. But with my first step out of the canoe, the muddy water came rushing through a hole in my right boot. The boot that had served me reliably for thirteen years picked this very day to begin leaking. Now it kept water in instead of out. Oh well, wet feet didn't really matter on a day this hot. Once across the log, we climbed back into the canoe and paddled for at least two minutes before we came to another log that blocked our way. Out again, drag the canoe over, then back in. Soon there was another limb blocking the only deep section of the creek. Out again. Only this time, as we looked ahead we could see that soon we would be out again, so we didn't bother getting back in. We just waded through the shallows, pulling the canoe along. I would have been happy to walk the entire length of the creek, but that wasn't possible either. My left foot sank into a hole so deep that water rushed over the top of my only dry boot, and soon I was in water up to my thighs. I hauled my wet and muddy self back into the canoe before I had to start swimming.

Occasionally, we were lucky, and the log crossing the creek was high enough that we could bend backward in the canoe and slide under it. During those passages, our noses practically scraped bark. But the next log would be too low to pass under, and the water beneath it too deep to wade through, forcing us to climb out by balancing on one foot in the boat while stretching the other onto the log. (This journey is not for those who lack good balance!) Once both feet were on the log, it was a back-aching task to hoist the canoe up and over it. In most canoeing situations, one would step ashore and carry the canoe around rather than over a log like that, but we were in the midst of a trackless way, a swamp, and stepping "ashore" would have meant sinking deep into the mud. The other three canoes were ahead of us, and I was marveling at how well the youngsters were doing when the quiet was pierced by screams for help. Tucker and I paddled as fast as we could, imagining all sorts of horrible things. As we approached, we saw a girl in mud up to her hips and still sinking. She had tried to go ashore to relieve herself, but started sinking so quickly and deeply that she feared for her life.

Ed Lewandowski, the naturalist Tucker mentioned in his e-mail, wrote, "As far as canoeable streams in Delaware are concerned, they do not come any smaller or wilder." It may have been passable eight years previously, in the early spring when Ed took his trip, but I was now beginning to wonder whether this stream really was "canoeable."

ON TRIPS SUCH as this, the first moments are a time for giving thanks that you have managed to make the great escape from furniture and cars and all things civilized. This escape takes effort, and you feel inclined to congratulate yourself. You have managed to do it again! The resulting adrenaline creates a sort of ecstatic glee. The length of this phase varies from person to person and place to place, but after Phase One comes Phase Two. Now the initial rush is gone, your brain is quieter, and the rest of nature becomes more audible. You finally hear the water dripping from the rocks, the woodpeckers tapping, the birds scuffling for seeds under the shrubs, and the wind rustling the treetops. During this phase, you also begin to feel the rub of your boots or the blisters forming under the paddle in your hand. But it feels good to be using your body this way, in nature, and you think you could go on forever. This second phase lasts much longer than the first, but its duration depends on your age and physical condition.

At the very end of the novel *Peter Pan and Wendy*, Wendy says, "I am old, Peter. I am ever so much more than twenty. I grew up long ago." I knew exactly how she felt. I generally am not a complainer, but after two hours of climbing in and out again I felt ready to grumble. Amazingly, the Lost Boys (and Girls) stayed positive and cheerful. Even the girl who had sunk into the mud was soon laughing about her experience. I was reaching my personal Phase Three, looking forward to the end of the adventure, but maturity brings a few rewards, and one thing it has taught me is that asking "how much further?" is generally a mistake. The distance is what it is, and the answer won't make it any shorter. It just shows the others that you're through with Phases One and Two. It's like showing your cards to everyone in a poker game; it spoils everyone's fun and your reputation.

I HAVEN'T SAID a word about the trees yet. Survival comes first and botany second, even for this tree lover. In the beginning, the trees were unremarkable—mostly red maple, ash, and loblolly pine, none too large. Then, suddenly, a good-sized bald cypress appeared, and soon many more, until we were in a forest dominated by these lovely wetland trees. We were in a cypress swamp—always a special place to be. There used to be fifty thousand acres of cypress swamp in this area, but now it is down to five thousand, and almost all of what remains has been burned or logged in the recent past. Many of the giant old trees were used to make shingles for houses and roofs; the rest became charcoal for the iron forges. Only a precious handful of the ancient cypress trees remain.

As we paddled and pulled among hundreds of trees, we were searching for just one: the granddaddy, the Patriarch. I tried to stay in the moment and enjoy each tree as it slipped past, or as we dragged our canoe over its roots. At one narrow bend in the creek, I remarked at a real beauty, "Look at that one!"

Dutifully, Tucker looked and said, "Wait a minute. This place looks exactly like the place they described to me. Do you think this could be our tree?" I had no idea what had been described to him or how he could tell one place from another in this black swamp, but it was a lovely tree, and suddenly there was an air of certainty and celebration. It just felt right. We had found the Patriarch! Tucker called the others back, and we climbed out of our canoes and stood on its buttressed roots, stroking the stringy bark. For this momentous occasion, I dug my camera out of my wet pack and was relieved to see it dry in its baggie.

But wait a minute—look at *that* tree. It is even bigger. *That* must be the Patriarch. Yes, of course, now we have found the *real* Patriarch. The *real* Patriarch must be touched now. Oh...my...God. Look at *that* one! It's much bigger than either of these two. Yes, we all agree, that must be the *really real* Patriarch. We repeated our adulations for that one, too. If this were a group of grown-ups, they would have been making wisecracks and cynical remarks, but the only one there that day kept her mouth shut.

* * *

WE ATE LUNCH in our canoes under the shade of the really real Patriarch, and then cast off to complete our journey. The second section of the creek was even more beautiful than the first. Here the cypress dominated the forest almost entirely, and their August foliage cast a dark shade onto the even darker water. The trees growing by the waterline flared out so abruptly at their bases they looked like southern belles attending a ball in their hoop skirts. Many of the flared roots had become hollow, and it wasn't difficult to imagine a snake, frog, spider, or even bat tucked up in the end of the narrow chambers. Even though I was wet, muddy, and tired, I appreciated this dark and complex beauty, so rare in flat, agricultural southern Delaware. What would those in the world of furniture and cars think of this Neverland? Some would envy me, I guessed, and others pity.

OCCASIONALLY, WE WOULD paddle past a giant dragonfly dipping her tail repeatedly into the water. My young companions didn't know it was a female laying her eggs. The eggs would hatch into larvae that looked and lived nothing like dragonflies. The larvae live underwater for a year or two, eating snails, tadpoles, and fish eggs, and sometimes even snatching insects, such as water striders, off the surface. After a year or two of this wet diet, the ugly larvae crawl onto land, shed their skins, and emerge as creatures of the air—lovely dragonflies. Imagine having spent all your life crawling underwater, and then suddenly becoming a creature with wings to fly through the air! And not just any wings; dragonflies have been described as "the best fliers this planet has produced." Now your food is also winged, and instead of eating tadpoles and snails you must capture bees and flies. You must also accomplish the tasks that will ensure a future generation: mating and laying eggs. But your predators have changed as well. Instead of hiding beneath rocks to avoid hungry fish, you must now dive to avoid hungry birds, even as you migrate among them.

The dragonflies we saw were of the largest type, commonly called "darners." But a number of different darner species live in Delaware, and I was not practiced enough to identify them by sight. I would have to capture one and bring it back to the land of books and microscopes to know for certain which this was. After that it would either be dead, or wishing it were. Some darner species in Delaware are listed as very rare, and perhaps this was one of the rarest. After all, the rarest species are usually found in the rarest habitats, and an old-growth cypress swamp in Delaware is just such a place. Surrounding this gem of a spot were hundreds of thousands of acres of corn and soybeans, lawns, and roads. Many scientists would argue that the possibility that this dragonfly was a rare one gave me good reason to capture and identify it and record its location. The death of this organism is just an unfortunate side effect of the process, they would say. But to my way of thinking, its potential rarity is exactly why I would *not* want to capture it. We had passed only three of these intriguing creatures—what if those three were all this habitat held? Some believe in capturing until the end in order to record for future generations what we have lost. I am not one of them.

WHEN IVORY-BILLED WOODPECKERS and Carolina parakeets became rare, ornithologists collected more instead of fewer. Today, I can see hundreds of these birds in museum drawers across the world, but not a single one in the wild. They became extinct before anyone had even studied their behavior.

John James Audubon left us a lovely painting of Carolina parakeets in the wild, but when I read his account of producing the painting, it no longer seemed so lovely to me:

> The living birds, as if conscious of the death of their companions, sweep over their bodies screaming as loud as ever, but still return to the stack to be shot at, until so few remain alive, that the farmer does not consider it worth his while to spend more of his ammunition. I have seen several hundreds destroyed in this manner in the course of a few hours, and have procured a basketful of these birds at a few shots, in order to make a choice of good specimens for drawing the figures by which this species is represented in the plate now under your consideration.

When the early American nature writer John Burroughs had trouble identifying a bird he, too, would shoot it. "It is for such emergencies that I have brought my gun," he wrote. "A bird in the hand is worth half a dozen in the bush, even for ornithological purposes; and no sure and rapid progress can be made in the study without taking a life, without procuring specimens." When I read his account of shooting a screech owl, I was almost pleased to note that Burroughs's "sure and rapid progress" ended with him six feet underground.

ALTHOUGH JAMES BRANCH was beautiful, it did seem to go on forever; I even lost interest in watching for darners. Finally one of the Lost Boys reached Phase Three. "How much further?" he called back to Tucker. *Bless you my son*, I thought. Tucker said we had about an hour to go.

He was right. We got to the bridge after another hour of paddling, swimming, wading, tugging. My feet felt like giant prunes floating in rubber sacks of water. For the first time in my life, I didn't load my own canoe onto the carrier; I stood by gratefully while the Lost Boys did it for me.

One of the best things about adventure is the relief in having survived it without harm. I'll call that Phase Four. The hero's journey: she goes out, she returns.

TWO WEEKS LATER, I got another e-mail from Tucker. Note that he has stopped calling me Professor Maloof.

Dear Joan,

Yes, I made it back safely. I just came from my first two classes and in an hour will be happily going to my first Plant Taxonomy class. I am so grateful you came to our park. You don't know how much our excursion meant to me. I would say it was the pinnacle of my summer, but things have been going up ever since then. I thank you for that, as well as the Patriarch. As the seven of us canoed that day, I felt as though I was learning something about myself, nature, and the art of living well. Thank you for imparting your wisdom, not only about trees, but also about living. I especially took to heart your advice that a career isn't set in stone, and that, no matter what I do, I can continue to change.

Thanks again, have a great school year!

Tucker

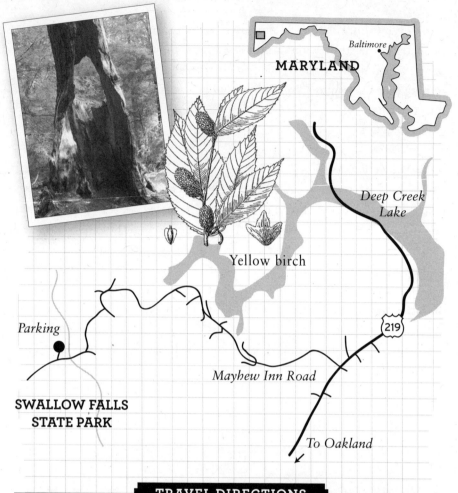

MARYLAND

Baltimore

Deep Creek Lake

Yellow birch

Parking

219

Mayhew Inn Road

SWALLOW FALLS
STATE PARK

To Oakland

TRAVEL DIRECTIONS

Western part of state, Garrett County. Closest town: Oakland. From U.S. 219 between Deep Creek Lake and the town of Oakland, turn west onto Mayhew Inn Road. Follow this road to the end (4.3 miles) and turn left at the stop sign. In less than a mile, turn right onto Swallow Falls Road. After two miles, you will see a sign on the right for Swallow Falls State Park. Immediately after you go through the gate, there will be a parking lot on the right.

The trail is an easy walk, well marked, from the parking lot. There is a short wheelchair-accessible trail as well. You won't really need a map, but they are available at the camper check-in office located next to the parking lot, or online at www.dnr.state.md.us/publiclands/western/swallowfalls.asp. There are bathhouses and camping spaces available in the park, and cabins for rent at the nearby Herrington Manor State Park. It is advisable to reserve ahead for campsites or cabins as they fill up quickly (301-387-6938).

Maryland

SWALLOW FALLS STATE PARK

Henry Ford...White wood-sorrel...The uses of forest...Fred Besley

S WALLOW FALLS IS a small bit of old growth that can be seen in an hour or two, but what a delightful hour or two it is! Hemlock, white pine, yellow birch—my old friends. I was reminded again of what watery, rocky places many of the ancient forests are. The drought was definitely over. It was hard to believe that this was *my* Maryland when I saw the rushing freshwater and the clouds of mist pouring over rock ledges.

In the eastern part of the state, where I live, one has to search to find even the smallest rock. But here at the western end, there were huge slabs so delicately balanced that it was almost frightening to walk by them for fear that they would choose that moment to let go.

The thought of letting go reminded me of my forest friend Bob DeGroot, who had recently let go of this life. The last time I had been in this forest, Bob was with me. He had been making a video to educate others about how important uninterrupted tracts of old forest are for wildlife, and I had agreed to an on-camera appearance in return for a ride to this area and information about the locations of lesser known old-growth remnants.

As you enter the trail at Swallow Falls, a sign notes, "The towering hemlock and white pine here are the oldest in Maryland.... Some of the trees have never been touched and others are over three hundred years old." The same ancient trees that drew me here attracted other, more famous visitors during the summers of 1918 to 1924. Henry Ford designed a dozen of his early automobiles specifically for nature expeditions, giving birth to the era of car camping. On the banks of the creek where I was standing, Ford camped with Thomas Edison; Harvey Firestone, the maker of the first automobile tires; and John Burroughs, a well-known nature writer. They stayed up late into the night, sitting by the fire discussing science, their latest inventions, and their views on religion. Other movers and shakers would sometimes join them, including Presidents Warren Harding and Calvin Coolidge.

As I try to imagine those leaders of industry and government gathered under the old growth, sleeping among the sounds of splashing water and calling insects, I find myself wishing for the same today. I would like to see Bill Gates, Steve Jobs, and writer Wendell Berry talking for days with President Barack Obama under the deep shade by the creek's edge. How would our tools and our policies change if our leaders were truly *grounded*?

THE SHADE HERE was deep, as only coniferous shade can be. Evergreens cast year-round shade. Only a few special plant species can photosynthesize in this sort of gloom, and I saw one of these all around me—at the edges of rocks, on rotting logs, on the brown-needle-covered forest floor. It is *Oxalis montana*, the white wood-sorrel. This plant loves old growth and lives in many old-growth forests in the East. A different species of wood-sorrel thrives under the old-growth redwoods in California.

How appropriate, I thought, that this old-growth-loving plant has leaflets shaped like little, green hearts. Three such leaflets join together at their bases to form a cloverlike leaf, the shamrock, considered sacred by the Druids of Ireland. (Folklore says St. Patrick used the shamrock to teach the Druids about Christianity and the Holy Trinity.) I walked along through the deep shade of Swallow Falls fantasizing about the goddess Gaia sprinkling her best forest creations with little hearts—the way girls in my seventh-grade class would dot their i's.

The little hearts captivated me, so I was lying down on the ground trying to photograph them when two young men, just a bit older than my students, stopped to express interest. Ever the teacher, I suppose, I showed them that this plant has two types of flowers: one that opens for insect pollinators, to share its genes with other flowers; and another that never opens and has sex only with itself. A handful of other plant species have permanently closed flowers, too, but only the wood-sorrel produces more closed flowers when living in a place where it grows best.

The handsomer of the pair smiled broadly. "I just love learning new things like that," he said with a sparkle in his eye. And he really meant it too, I thought. Feeling a bit like Eve, I told him the leaves were edible and asked him if he'd like to taste one. I went first, placing a green heart on my tongue, and declared it a bit lemony as I chewed. I handed him his own heart, and he followed suit. "Hmm, yes."

IN 1916, MARYLAND'S first state forester, Fred Besley, wrote, "The most important use of the forest, here, as elsewhere, is for *Lumber*." I would disagree with him, of course. If asked, I would probably start with Air Quality, reminding him that forests are both the largest producers of oxygen (a gas we cannot live without, by the way) and the largest sink for carbon on the land. I might also mention pollutants such as nitrogen oxides and sulfur oxides that damage human lungs but are removed from the atmosphere by forests. I might mention Water Quality, and how forests prevent floods by slowing runoff from the land and prevent water pollution by purifying the runoff that does occur. I might add that each tree transpires and returns to the atmosphere hundreds of gallons of clean water a day, and that forests can alter precipitation patterns in a whole area. I might mention Soil, our truest wealth. Intact forests create deep, fertile, healthy soils, and logging them by the usual methods often results in this wealth being literally washed away. I would stop there if I could, but if I were wound up by then, which is likely, I would have to mention Beauty. "At some point the world's beauty becomes enough," wrote Toni Morrison, and I agree, perhaps because beauty encompasses all the things mentioned previously. What we consider beautiful in the natural world may be a complex, though unconscious, awareness of what is healthy, of what is intact and functioning; perhaps we can sense all the energy captured and recycled in the myriad relationships and movements of molecules. Lastly, I would remind him, and myself, that this Earth is home not only to humans; it is also home to Other Living Things. There are some places where the skin of the Earth should just be allowed to be the skin of the Earth. There. I would probably stop there.

Besley, who thought lumber was the most important use of the forest, became state forester in 1906, after Robert and John Garrett donated nineteen hundred acres to the State of Maryland. The original, ancient white pines on their acreage had been logged out in the 1880s and again in 1906, just before they donated the land to the state. Remember, these were dark days for the eastern forests, when tree cover reached its lowest level. When explorer John Smith sailed up the Chesapeake Bay in 1608, more than 98 percent of Maryland was covered in forests, but by 1920 that had fallen to only 17 percent. I try to imagine what nineteen hundred acres of old-growth white pine and hemlock forest would be like in Maryland today—a dream for sure—but it is unlikely a forest like that would have remained untouched through more than eighty years of state management.

The acreage in state forests continued to increase as other lands were donated or purchased. The federal government was also interested in purchasing Maryland forest land, to add to the growing National Forest system, but Besley opposed federal ownership of Maryland land. In 1927 he convinced the state legislature to reverse a law that had previously granted the federal government "power to purchase lands in the state for the purpose of establishing a national forest." Although Besley has been dead for almost fifty years, his misguided legacy lives on: Maryland is one of only seven states with no national forest.

Besley also opposed creating state parks, and by 1927, twenty-one years into his reign as state forester, Maryland was one of only thirteen states without a single one. Besley was furious when he learned someone was trying to form a state parks commission. He also deflected every attempt by the federal government to create national parks in the state, fearing that parks would result in forest preservation rather than timber production.

But Besley *was* good at acquiring land. Under his leadership, state forest holdings increased from two thousand to fifty thousand, and finally to one hundred thousand acres. Some of those state forests happened to contain old growth, such as this small area of hemlock and pine near Swallow Falls and, just a few miles away, a three-hundred acre tract of "virgin" oaks donated to the state in 1917.

A newspaper article from 1940 tells the story of what happened to that grove. "Hundreds of mighty oaks are crashing to the ground this summer as lumbermen move through what is believed to be the last big stand of virgin timber in Maryland's mountains," the article begins. It is difficult to continue reading. This was not a private forest, remember, but public land donated by a forest-loving citizen. Are we to be reassured that the state foresters "held out for a premium price on the timber," or that "they thought their great white oaks, which made up 80 percent of the timber on the tract, were better for something else than railroad ties or ordinary lumber"? And what did they deem the highest and best use for those trees? Whiskey barrels. Are we to feel compassion for the logger who told the reporter, "A man ought to put on a white shirt to cut trees like these"?

Fred Besley retired fourteen years before I was born, but his decisions still shape the landscape around me. If someone else had held that post, there's a good chance Maryland would have national forests and many more parks. There's a chance those oaks would still be standing and I'd be walking beneath their limbs today. We tend to forget that our short lives can have such long-term effects on the landscape. The past president of my university once mentioned to me that he'd like the sprawling Deodar cedars removed from the front of one of the university-owned houses. "Blocking the view of the building," he said. I considered those two cedars the most beautiful trees on the street. "I'm afraid I'll have to chain myself to them if you try to remove them," I told him, only half joking. Not long after that conversation, he was diagnosed with lung cancer. He died before ordering the trees cut and has been dead now for twelve years. I really liked the man, but I pass those trees frequently on my way to and from work and a part of me is pleased they outlasted him.

The trees I witnessed at Swallow Falls are the same ones that were standing there less than two years earlier when Bob DeGroot made his video. Continuity is another forest value I might mention to Besley. Imagine an organism that can live three times longer than the longest-lived human. We need to recognize that in trees, and honor it.

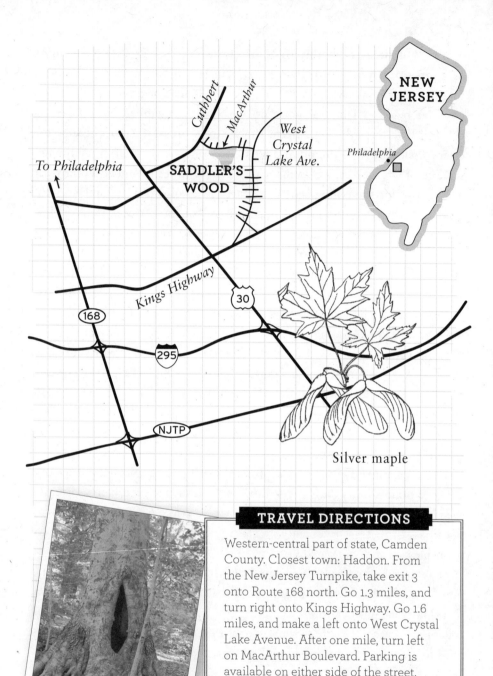

NEW JERSEY

To Philadelphia

Cuthbert

MacArthur

West Crystal Lake Ave.

SADDLER'S WOOD

Philadelphia

Kings Highway

30

168

295

NJTP

Silver maple

TRAVEL DIRECTIONS

Western-central part of state, Camden County. Closest town: Haddon. From the New Jersey Turnpike, take exit 3 onto Route 168 north. Go 1.3 miles, and turn right onto Kings Highway. Go 1.6 miles, and make a left onto West Crystal Lake Avenue. After one mile, turn left on MacArthur Boulevard. Parking is available on either side of the street.

More information, including directions for using public transit, is available from www.saddlerswoods.org or 856-869-7372. Open daily from sunrise to sunset.

New Jersey

SADDLER'S WOODS

An urban tract...A freed slave...Land trusts...Near miracles

W HEN I READ that this forest was "one of the oldest and best preserved ancient forests in New Jersey," I put it on my list for a visit. But what I found was an urban tract, very different from other forests I had been to. I had to park at a high-rise apartment building and run across a busy street to get to it. No vegetated buffers surrounded the small parcel, so it was open to all sorts of influences from the city around it: invasive species, city sounds, and air pollution. Young people need a place to hang out, and urban forests can provide nature experiences for everyone, but the users here had left broken glass and other trash.

The giant beech trees, tulip poplars, and impressive silver maples cast welcome shade, and there was a delicate stream running through the center, but I hesitated to call this an old-growth experience. The only wildlife I saw was a single chipmunk and some robins.

Some birds, such as the wood thrush and many of the warblers, need a large block of unfragmented forest to be successful, and when forest acreages drop below 250 acres, fewer species will be found. Robins, unlike those other birds, do very well in places inhabited by humans.

Robins are never found far from a source of water, because they need mud to construct their nests. They carry it from the water's edge in their beaks, and make the nest by layering mud and grass. But I wondered about the cleanliness of the water in the stream—its source was at least partly the storm water that ran off the surrounding parking lots and roads.

ALTHOUGH THIS FOREST was not what I expected, it is a good example of how very different humans, living in very different times, were able to rescue a forest. Saddler's Woods was saved, in turns, by a former slave and a high school student. That alone is worth celebrating, I suppose. Each of these forests has its own unique history, but as I consider the eastern old-growth forests as a group, it seems to me that very few were preserved by governments, whether local, state, or federal. Rather, most were preserved by individuals, and then by other individuals after those passed on.

Most of those who preserved eastern forests from the rampant logging of the 1800s and 1900s were white-skinned. This didn't have anything to do with attitudes toward nature among people with different skin colors, but with who owned the land. "Ownership," of course, meant something very different to the native people than it did to European immigrants. As the New World was explored, it was claimed in the name of various European kings and queens, who could then grant land to whomever they liked, or to whomever they owed a favor. These land grants involved massive numbers of acres that today would cover entire counties. The grantees, of course, were other Europeans, who then had exclusive control of the land and could log, sell, or protect it as they saw fit. When grant holders died, their family members could inherit the property and, again, do with it as they wished. The land was frequently divided up among the heirs; these early land grants are the original source of wealth for many white families in America today.

The African blacks brought here as slaves were not granted any land, and the inequity of those two different settlement histories persists today. The wealth disparity between whites and blacks in America stems from ancestral land ownership, and it is perpetuated through inheritance. If we really want equality we will have to do away with inheritance, but I don't foresee that as long as those who benefit from the system as it stands are the ones in power. Many politicians argue that we shouldn't even tax inheritance.

The man who protected Saddler's Woods didn't get his property through land grants or inheritance. His name was Joshua Saddler, and he was a

black slave on a Maryland plantation. In the early 1800s, he escaped to New Jersey with his wife and two daughters. Fearing recapture, he began working for Cy Evans, a Quaker farmer. When Saddler learned that Evans opposed slavery, he confessed that he was an escaped slave. Evans eventually bought Saddler's freedom from his former owner and helped him purchase a plot of wooded land on which to build a house.

Saddler must have loved his forest; a clear stream ran through it and many different species of trees, animals, and birds lived there. He had freedom *and* property! And he could leave his land to his descendents. But the thought they might log his beautiful forest must have troubled him, because his will, dated 1868, stipulates that none of his heirs "shall cut the timber thereon." Thus began the chain of events that led to this forest being in existence today, surrounded by roads, shopping centers, schools, and high-rise apartments.

I wish more of us would make the simple effort to preserve nature that Saddler, the freed slave, did in writing his will. I would just make one suggestion: instead of writing these instructions into your will, preserve your forest now by changing the deed to your property. Simply add a deed restriction stating what can and cannot be done to the forest. The property will still belong to you, and it can still be sold or passed on to your heirs, but any new owners will not be able to log it easily. You can do this with the help of a real estate lawyer or a land trust organization. Protecting your land through a land trust may result in substantial tax advantages and will also help educate future owners about what can and cannot be done on the property.

Be cautious, however, if you really want to protect old growth (or future old growth). Some land trusts support forest management and may try to convince you not to "tie the hands" of future generations by prohibiting logging. They repeat what they are told by foresters about the necessity of management to maintain a "healthy forest." But management almost always means logging, and that is not the best path to an old-growth forest. Old-growth forests contain many dying and "unhealthy" trees. They should. Some species of fungi and insects can survive only through the death of trees, and some birds and frogs can survive only through the survival of insects. Soil organisms depend on the deaths of members of all these species, and only through their work can a healthy soil exist. Healthy trees need healthy soil, so the death of some is balanced by the abundant health of others. This is sometimes difficult for those who think of dead trees as a waste to accept. No one has been paid for the fiber they contain, nor have paper, pencils, or furniture been made from them. No cardboard boxes or toilet paper will enter the market as a result of their death. They will just lie there, slowly providing the materials for new life.

Some see a log lying on the ground as rotting money. When I attended a forest management meeting and argued that some areas ought to be off limits to logging, or at least that more time elapse between cuts, an earnest young logger remarked, "Some trees will just die."

"Exactly," I replied, "and that is not a bad thing. A healthy forest needs dead wood."

I HAVE NOTHING against land trusts; they are doing good, important work. I am simply warning that preserving your land from development through a trust does not mean you have protected it from logging. Where I live, most forests with conservation easements held by land trusts can be logged. If you want to leave the legacy of an old-growth forest, you must be firm and clear, even when dealing with the good guys.

* * *

So, for a long time the freed slave's forest didn't get logged, but by 1970, Saddler's heirs and his instructions to them were long forgotten. The property, now in the middle of a crowded and bustling area, was owned by a man who wanted to construct high-rise apartment buildings on it. And if it weren't for one local high school boy, he probably would have done so. Doug Hefty loved that forest and didn't want it destroyed. He wrote a report about the ecology of Saddler's Woods and presented it to the owner. In another of the continuing string of near miracles that preserved this forest, Hefty's report persuaded the owner to build his high-rise apartments across the street instead.

In 1987, the forest was threatened again, this time by a new owner planning to build townhouses. The town's planning and zoning board favored the tax revenue that development would bring, but many citizens of the area felt differently; more than three hundred of them attended a meeting to protest the development. Also, although the trees—like trees in most places—had little protection, the stream on the property was protected by federal wetlands regulations. By 1988, the proposed development had become so unpopular and problematic that the mayor and commissioners began to question the plan, citing the "need to further study impacts to traffic, sewage treatment capacities, and water supply." In 1990, Haddon Township applied for state funds to buy the woods and, in 1999, purchased fifteen acres on which to develop athletic fields. You can't play soccer in a forest, of course, so the trees would have to go.

Once again, many individuals and organizations worked together to save the forest. In 2002, a trio of old-growth experts was invited to visit the forest and decided that, as some of the trees were more than 150 years old, it was officially "old growth." In a heated election year battle, eighteen hundred citizens signed a petition to protect the forest, and eventually the mayor and the commissioners agreed to place a conservation easement on the property. In 2004, they formally named it Saddler's Woods in honor of the slave who made the first move to protect it.

I wonder what he would think if he walked this grove with me today.

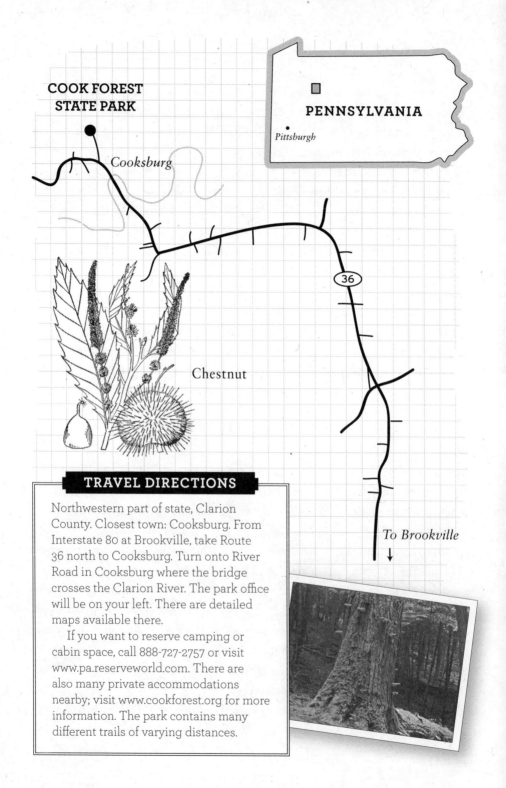

COOK FOREST STATE PARK

Cooksburg

PENNSYLVANIA

Pittsburgh

36

Chestnut

To Brookville

TRAVEL DIRECTIONS

Northwestern part of state, Clarion County. Closest town: Cooksburg. From Interstate 80 at Brookville, take Route 36 north to Cooksburg. Turn onto River Road in Cooksburg where the bridge crosses the Clarion River. The park office will be on your left. There are detailed maps available there.

If you want to reserve camping or cabin space, call 888-727-2757 or visit www.pa.reserveworld.com. There are also many private accommodations nearby; visit www.cookforest.org for more information. The park contains many different trails of varying distances.

Pennsylvania

Cook Forest State Park

Abundance...Chestnut blight...The family Cook...Bacteria

*I*F BIG MOTOR HOMES are the McMansions of the road, my compact truck is like a one-room cabin—without electricity or indoor plumbing. It keeps me warm and dry in a storm but is rustic enough to require a sense of adventure. Last night, I slept in the back of my truck under a canopy of hemlock trees. In the morning, I crawled out and made myself breakfast in the clear, cool, evergreen air. The trail to the old growth began right next to my campsite. Life is sweet.

What does it feel like to walk through Cook Forest? Well, if I were a cartoon character on my way to see the seven dwarves, I would have been skipping and singing. The rest I didn't have to imagine—the chipmunks were scampering along beside me, the birds were chirping and hopping on the trail in front of me, and patches of moss were glowing green from the slender beams of light that made their way through the canopy far overhead.

I felt almost as if I had been drugged. I was so filled with joy I had a cheek-splitting grin on my face. (Fortunately, I was the only one on the trail.) In every direction, the forest floor was an art installation composed of moss and rocks, mushrooms, and twisted roots. Looking more closely, I saw miniature compositions of berries and acorn caps, tiny spore-bearing parasols, and leaves in abstract shapes. Each composition was more beautiful than the last.

Trees of all sizes and types loomed overhead. Around every bend the species composition changed slightly. How could one pick a favorite forest type? But finally, I decided my favorite must be the hemlock groves with their dark shade and a soil so spongy it seemed to spring back as I lifted my foot. Overhead were dark, feathery boughs; underfoot was a soil created by hundreds of years' worth of tiny, fallen needles and the organisms that feed on them.

Conservation biologist Aldo Leopold's most often quoted lines read, "A thing is right when it tends to preserve the integrity, stability, and beauty of the biotic community. It is wrong when it tends otherwise." As an ecologist, I have been trained to focus on the *integrity* and *stability* of ecosystems, but here in the old growth of Cook Forest I was thinking more about the *beauty*. We tend to discount beauty because it is so difficult to define and measure, but beauty is a physiological reality: The experience of beauty changes the levels of neurotransmitters in the brain. We may need the beautiful more than we know.

The abundant variety of tree species here can be intimidating for anyone trying to identify them, even a tree lover like myself. But even more important than the tree species is the rich treasure of genotypes that has been preserved here. During one hike, I identified a red maple with a bark texture I was familiar with, but next to it a maple of the same size and leaf shape had very different bark. I puzzled over this for a while before deciding that I was probably looking at one species, but two genotypes. Trees have genetically based individual differences, just as humans do.

Environment does have some effect, and both well-nourished trees and well-fed people grow taller than others not so well-nourished, but genetics cannot be totally overridden. If you are born into a family of short people, you are likely to be short also. Here in Cook Forest, the trees must have good genes and good nutrition. For many years, it was thought that a tree in this forest—a white pine named Longfellow—was the tallest tree east of the Mississippi River. But a few years ago someone found a taller white pine in the Smoky Mountains, so Longfellow became the second tallest tree in the East, at least for now. Searching for champion trees is a sport for tree huggers, and, like in any sport, champions come and go. One tree might grow quickly and regain the title, or perhaps its challenger will fall to insects or a

storm. But there are enough record holders in this forest—tallest hemlock, pignut hickory, American chestnut, and black cherry—to award the forest as a whole the title of tallest canopy in the Northeast.

Even here, though, everything has not been perfect. One species that used to be an important part of this forest is all but gone. In 1904, an American chestnut tree in New York City was infected by a fungus from Asia, and the dreaded Chestnut blight had begun. Chestnuts, like all other tree species, were already being cut heavily across the northeast, and the spreading blight only amplified the destruction. Some landowners were cutting their chestnuts quickly to get an economic benefit from their trees while they could; others were advised by foresters to cut them to help slow the spread of the pathogen. But the cutting didn't help. In hindsight, it might have been better not to cut any of the chestnuts once the blight started. Perhaps, somewhere in all those chestnut groves, there were some trees with genes that made them resistant to the blight fungus. We'll never know.

Because Cook Forest was not logged, it was one of the few places chestnut trees were allowed to take their chances against the blight. Most of them lost the battle. Although they are long dead, gravity hasn't yet won, and many of the snags still stand. Today these ghosts have a unique, ethereal beauty. The bark has all been shed so the pattern and texture of the wood shows, but the pattern is not that of a tree reaching straight for the sky. It spirals like a unicorn's horn.

This spiral pattern is not uncommon in trees, although we still do not completely understand it. Many trees, especially conifers growing in harsh environments, show spiraling. Most of them spiral left to right, although there are exceptions, and in some individual trees the spiral eventually reverses direction. Hardwoods tend to be more straight-grained than the conifers, although when they do spiral it is more often toward the right. We still don't know if the spiraling is genetic, environmental, or a combination of the two. Perhaps some minuscule early unevenness becomes exaggerated with age. I recognize this in myself and other aging humans—why not trees?

One book about spiral grain says, "If extreme spiral grain presents conceptual difficulties to the scientific mind, the trees themselves clearly have little difficulty adapting to it." The chestnut ghosts I saw here mostly spiraled to the right. I put my hand to the grain and appreciated an organism that was no longer living but was still influencing the forest ecosystem, slowly releasing the resources it had gathered and benefiting other organisms. The smaller, still living chestnuts give me hope for the future. Extinction is forever, but the American chestnut is not extinct.

The air was absolutely calm, but suddenly there was a loud crack, followed by a ground-shuddering boom. One of the ghosts had gone from standing to supine. If I hadn't paused to appreciate this particular ghost, might I have been made a ghost myself?

THERE CAN BE no doubt that the male of our species has cut or ordered cut most of our forests. One may question whether this is because they had the power to do so, and whether women with the same power would have made the same choices. Or one might speculate that men are simply more prone to conquest, either over other men or over the natural world. Whatever the reason, it should be noted that men have played a dominant role in forest preservation, too. Some men logged without any notion of preservation; some preserved forests without doing any logging; and some played dual roles as both loggers and preservationists. It is rare for me to meet a man these days who does both. Most men I know see themselves as either one or the other—timber beast or tree hugger. The Cooks of Pennsylvania were unusual in that they embraced both roles.

In 1836, John Cook was hired by the government to survey waterways in western Pennsylvania. In one area, he noted a beautiful forest with many white pine trees and a nearby river suitable for getting the logs to market. He returned to the area later that year and purchased hundreds of acres. Fulfilling his dream, he began logging the pines and floating them down the river, but he wasn't greedy. He intentionally left certain sections of the forest untouched—not because they were difficult to get to, but because he wanted to preserve them. Demonstrating remarkable restraint, he even preserved the ancient forest on the hill behind the sawmill.

John Cook fathered seventeen children, ten with his first wife and seven with his second. His son Anthony inherited his father's business skills and his love for the forest. The younger Cook acquired many more acres of forest, built his home in the middle of the ancient forest, and refused to allow any logging there. After he died in 1891, his son, Anthony Wayne

Cook, also a forester, was determined to preserve the vast forest around the family home, but other members of the family were more interested in financial gain.

In 1910, the thought arose that the area should become a park. But it took seventeen years to convince the state legislature. Anthony Wayne Cook's son, Anthony E. Cook, who still lives on the property, documented the history of this political battle in his book *The Cook Forest*. The arguments for and against the park were economic: Some people encouraged the Cook family to cut the remaining old-growth forest to provide jobs; others promoted the park as a way to develop the local economy through tourism.

When I see the many visitors who have come here just to enjoy the forest, I know those who argued for development through tourism were right. Miles and miles of driving on my way to and from this forest took me through town after town where the original forest was completely logged out. Today those towns are economically depressed. No one wants to rent a cabin or invest in real estate there, but the towns surrounding the Cook Forest are thriving. Many people work in real estate, restaurant, and entertainment businesses that cater to ecotourists. The chairman of the University of Montana's Economics Department insists that wild lands' greatest economic value lies in maintaining its wildness. These lands will only grow in value as the years go by.

DEEP INSIDE THE large Cook Forest, it is possible to feel that you are indeed in a *wild* place. I lay on my back on the forest floor and looked up at the canopy far above. I heard only the sounds of nature—birds, insects, wind in the leaves—and imagined the network of fungal strands and plant roots underneath me, tunneling through the damp soil. I know enough biology to imagine water entering the tiny root hairs, then moving into vessels in the larger roots, and finally into vessels in the stem. Water molecule linked to water molecule for the entire height of the tree's trunk, drawn upward toward the leaves far above me where the sun shines and sugars are made. Water is needed to make the sugar, but most of it escapes through the leaves into the atmosphere. Imagine a molecule's journey, from the dark depths up to the bright air! With a certain type of attention, I could feel the liquid moving beneath me in the soil, around me in the stems, and above me in the leaves, the vapor finally circling back to enter my own dark bronchial passageways.

I had yet another view of the forest, and felt biologically connected to it, when I considered the bacteria essential to both the forest ecosystem and my bodily system. The soil beneath my back teemed with these microbes, and these trees wouldn't be here if not for the important work being done by them—decomposing the dead and converting nutrients into forms they can use. Likewise, my dark gut was filled with bacteria working to help digest my breakfast. Bacterial cells are small, but there are ten times as many bacterial cells in my body as human cells. My skin, too, is covered with a thin layer of microbes. The species and counts vary from person to person, but forty-eight different kinds live on the average person, just on the surface. The trees, too, host a layer of bacteria on their bark and leaves. When I touch these trees, I leave some of my bacteria and acquire some of theirs. I may ingest some while eating my lunch. We are just beginning to understand this invisible ecosystem that is all around us and within us.

This forest is rich with lessons from history, art, and science. Philosophers call this kind of aesthetic appreciation, combined with scientific understanding, "serious beauty."

Cook Forest is seriously beautiful.

JOHNSON WOODS, OHIO

CENTRAL FORESTS

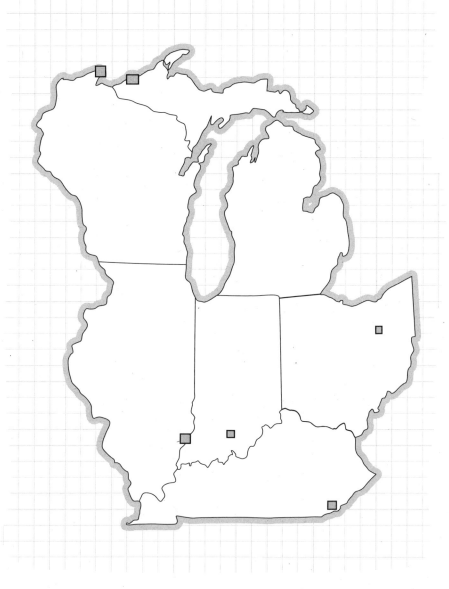

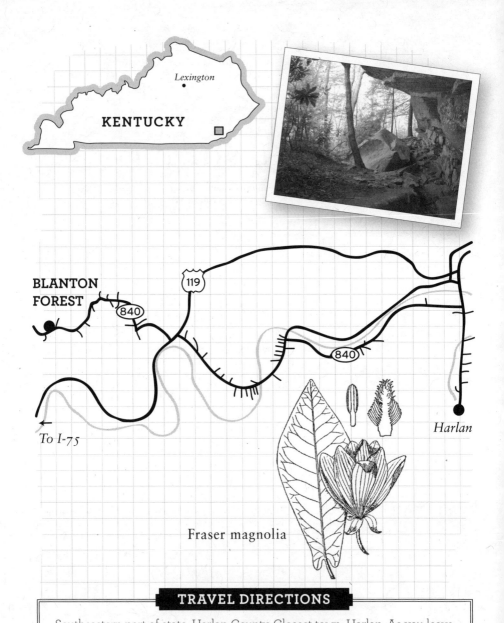

KENTUCKY

Lexington

BLANTON FOREST

119

840

840

To I-75

Harlan

Fraser magnolia

Southeastern part of state, Harlan County. Closest town: Harlan. As you leave the town of Harlan heading north, you will see a left turn onto Route 840. Follow 840 for a few miles until it runs into U.S. 119. At this intersection, make a left and then an immediate right at the sign for Camp Blanton. If you are coming from Interstate 75, take exit 29 onto Highway 25 east to Pineville. Make a left on U.S. 119 north and continue for 23.5 miles. Turn left at the sign for Camp Blanton. Follow this very windy road for one mile, and you will see clearly marked signs to the parking area on the right.

Kentucky

BLANTON FOREST STATE NATURE PRESERVE

Dog...Fraser magnolia...The maze vs. Serra...Smooth rocktripe

A S SOON AS I had parked at the trail, gotten out for a stretch, and reached for my daypack, a smallish white dog approached me wagging his tail. At the sign-in station, he waited patiently. He knew exactly what I was there for and seemed eager to accompany me. My furry new friend then escorted me through an eerily empty Boy Scout camp and led me to the trailhead.

The densely shaded trail was lovely right from the start. The spring wildflowers had passed, but many varied and beautiful mushrooms entertained me as I walked. Here were my old friends the hemlocks, and under them evergreen-leaved rhododendron shrubs, and there, a new tree, the Fraser magnolia. If I had been here in the springtime, I would have seen their white blossoms, up to a foot wide, but in this season I had to be satisfied with their red cones littering the forest floor. One type of tiny white mushroom grows only on magnolia cones, but I saw none of those.

By evolutionary standards, the family of plants called *Magnoliaceae* is ancient. They originated in Asia, where they were among the earliest seed-producing plants, and some of the first to be insect-pollinated. When the Earth's climate warmed considerably, about fifty million years ago, the magnolias spread across the high latitudes of the Northern Hemisphere and eventually into the land mass we now call America. Ten million years later, the climate cooled drastically again, and the warmth-loving magnolias across much of North America died off. The survivors, cut off from the larger gene pool, evolved into new species over time. So the Fraser magnolia has Asian ancestry, but is 100 percent American now. It occurs naturally nowhere in the world but the hilly parts of these Appalachian states. I never would have seen this tree in the wild if I had stayed home.

ECOLOGIST LUCY BRAUN called this area of Kentucky the "mixed-mesophytic forest," which means the climate is neither very wet nor very dry and the forest is composed of both evergreen and deciduous tree species. In fact, it is the most tree species–rich of all the eastern deciduous forest types and was her favorite place to be. Trees with restricted ranges, such as the Fraser magnolia, grow here alongside more widespread species. This diversity is a result of many factors—varied terrain, a favorable rainfall pattern, mild temperatures—but past climate changes were the primary driver. When the Ice Age arrived and the glaciers advanced, much of the South came to be covered in conifers, but some of the older, warm-climate vegetation survived in scattered refuges. When conditions turned more favorable, the various species could begin their outward migration from these refuges. Some species, such as oaks, migrated very quickly to occupy land left behind after the glaciers or seas retreated, but other species, such as this small magnolia, remained very restricted in range.

We tend to think of tree migration as something that happened in the past, that species are now "set" in their distribution range, but this viewpoint is completely wrong. For as long as trees have existed, they have been moving across the landscape. They migrate slowly, to be sure, dependent on animals or chance events for seed dispersal, but trees have always moved and continue to move. The wild sweetbay magnolia that grows near my Maryland home is probably migrating very slowly northward at this moment, helped along by global warming.

Like me, Lucy Braun used to seek out old-growth forests. She would drive for days, and then walk for days, to reach a special location. In 1936, she visited an old-growth, mixed-mesophytic forest in southeastern Kentucky. She described what it was like:

We are entering a veritable cathedral, its roof upheld by towering columns—the tall and stately tulip trees. Where before they had been scattered, rising here and there between the other trees, now they outnumber all others, sheltering in their shade large beech and sugar maple. The herbaceous growth is even more luxuriant than before; masses of narrow-leaved spleenwort and silvery spleenwort, waist-high are all about. Hidden more or less by this luxuriance, and inconspicuous because past blooming, are yellow lady's slippers and showy orchids.

The leaves of trillium, bellwort, phlox, spotted mandarin, buttercups, foam-flower and a host of other spring flowering plants stirred our imagination and painted the hillsides in spring bloom. But dominating all is the primeval grandeur of a forest....And then, ahead, rises the majestic column of the "big poplar"—straight, sound and perfect, towering eighty feet to the first branch, lifting its crown far aloft. In reverence and awe we stood and gazed upon this tree, the largest living individual of its kind in North America. Such monarchs of the forest are not grown in decades, nor yet in centuries.

In the last part of the article, she pleads for the preservation of this particular forest, but it was logged just a few years after the article appeared, and the new trees that grew on the site were logged again fifty years later. Now it is a young forest dominated by spindly tulip poplars. I wish I could have seen the forest as she described it, but I have no desire to see it now.

Loggers and foresters defending what they do will tell you that trees grow back where they have been logged, and indeed they do. But how long will it take? Will that Kentucky forest ever again look the way it did in 1936? *Not...in decades, nor yet in centuries.*

That story is terribly sad, but on this summer day I was walking through a shady old-growth forest with little room in my soul for sadness. "Dog" walked down the trail a few paces ahead of me, and when he stopped to look into the forest so did I. His hearing and sense of smell were much better than mine. Besides having larger ears, he could control them in ways I never could: The eighteen muscles in a dog's ears can precisely raise, rotate, and tilt them. Dogs can hear higher frequencies than we can and can even hear animals underground. But their hearing is feeble compared to their sense of smell.

Humans tend to rely on vision, but dogs interpret the world through smell. A canine's long snout is lined with ridges covered in scent-detecting

cells. Dogs have twenty-five times more smell receptors than we do, enabling them to detect odors in minuscule concentrations. These enriched senses of hearing and smell are especially advantageous in dense forests where vision is of limited use. So, when Dog stopped for something of interest, I believed there really was something interesting there, even though I could not detect it. Experiencing the forest through him made it richer for me.

Hiking alone together, I also noted how quiet he was. We hiked along silently, both hoping to sneak up on the wildlife. Occasionally I would step on a twig and snap it, accidentally alerting other animals to our presence. Dog would look back, as if to say, *Oh well, I guess you can't help it; you're just a human after all.*

When we got to a knobby rock overlook, Dog led me directly to the spot with the best view and, while I sat to enjoy it, ambled off to rest in the shade. Noon was approaching, heat advisories were in effect, and that morning the radio announcer had reported five people already dead from the heat wave. Dog looked at me questioningly when I continued hiking uphill after our rest, but he continued his faithful service.

TWO POINTS OF interest were noted on the trail map, the "maze" and the "sand cave." There was no sign at the maze, but I didn't need one to tell me I was there. Gigantic boulders and slabs of granite tumbled and leaned in every direction. The play of light on the boulders was an artist's dream. Photographers travel to Zion or Canyon de Chelly for this light; I never would have imagined seeing such images in Kentucky. A human on foot would have to go across, around, over, and under the boulders to navigate the maze, and I felt dwarfed by their massive size. For someone as directionally challenged as I, it was especially helpful to have Dog lead me through its wondrous passages.

Logging, like war, is not an act of nature. It doesn't just happen, like an earthquake or a tornado; someone must choose to log. But in this forest that choice was never made, and instinct tells me it was because of these special rock formations. I imagine it was more than just the difficulty of logging; I want to think it also had something to do with aesthetics.

A few weeks ago, I visited the Museum of Modern Art in New York City. Thousands of people were paying twenty dollars each to get in the doors. The featured exhibition, by Richard Serra, one of the preeminent sculptors of our era, consisted mostly of massive steel plates curved to enclose the viewer. The museum describes his work as "emphasiz[ing] materiality and the engagement between the viewer, the site, and the work." At the exhibit, people *oohed* and *ahhed*, took pictures, and touched (even when they weren't supposed to). But here in the hills of Kentucky, where there was no charge and no other people, I was moved in a much deeper way. This was grand sculpture, indeed. Is it still art if not made by human hands?

* * *

THE STATE OF Kentucky began protecting this area in 1995 by purchasing slightly more than a thousand acres and has added to the preserve almost every year since then. The state is serious about protecting this tract, the largest old-growth forest in Kentucky. In addition to saving the old growth, the government and the land trusts aim to protect the entire ridgeline where Blanton Forest is located. Many agencies, from federal to private, have joined efforts to keep the entire mountain range a natural, intact, functioning ecosystem. Although the Blanton Forest Preserve now includes more than three thousand acres, even that is not large enough to be considered a truly intact and functional ecosystem with enough shelter and food sources for top predators, such as bears and mountain lions.

CLINGING TO THE steep, shady sides of some of the smooth granite rocks, where it seemed nothing at all should be able to grow, were what looked like thin strips of mocha-brown leather. At first, it was difficult to believe these were living, growing organisms, but they were, in fact, lichens called smooth rocktripe. The name comes from the French Canadian *tripe de roche*, which translates literally as "rock guts." For thousands of years, Native Americans have used species of this lichen as emergency food, usually boiled in a broth. It was even eaten by George Washington's troops at Valley Forge, who were probably taught about this lichen by Indians.

Dog and I paused while I photographed the rocktripe and then, after a moment's hesitation, I broke off a little piece and put it in my mouth. Not bad, but not good either; it was somewhat tasteless in this dry condition. I wouldn't have opposed eating this lichen to survive, but it grows so slowly that I would only consider eating more if I really had to. One study, in which individuals were measured annually, discovered that rocktripe grows only a few millimeters—about the width of a caper—every year. Knowing that the lichen I was looking at had been growing on that rock, undisturbed, for at least ten years, and probably more, made me want to leave it there a while longer.

ON THE SHADY backside of the massive summit rock, Dog and I stopped for a drink of water and a snack. I ate half a banana nut muffin and gave him the other half. He didn't seem to mind drinking from the creek, so I kept the bottled water for myself. Farther down the trail, someone had erected a ladder to facilitate climbing over a particularly tricky spot. Even though Dog couldn't climb the ladder, he led me to the bottom of it before running around on a longer, more dog-friendly route. That was when I changed his name to Angel Dog.

Back at my truck, I thanked him for his service. I considered inviting him onto the passenger seat and making him my trail companion forever. But his collar and demeanor told me that he was already well loved and his disappearance would cause someone sorrow. Sometimes, even the best relationships are meant to be brief.

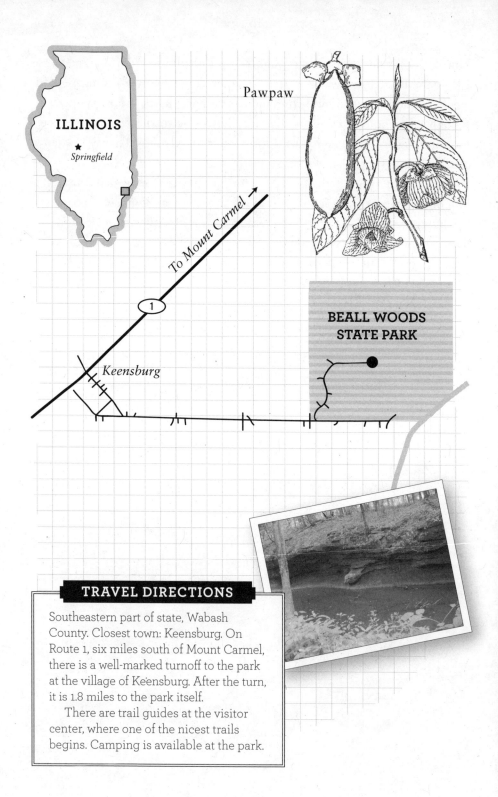

ILLINOIS

★
Springfield

Pawpaw

To Mount Carmel →

1

Keensburg

BEALL WOODS
STATE PARK

TRAVEL DIRECTIONS

Southeastern part of state, Wabash
County. Closest town: Keensburg. On
Route 1, six miles south of Mount Carmel,
there is a well-marked turnoff to the park
at the village of Keensburg. After the turn,
it is 1.8 miles to the park itself.

There are trail guides at the visitor
center, where one of the nicest trails
begins. Camping is available at the park.

Illinois

BEALL WOODS STATE PARK

The Bealls...University of Trees...Pawpaw...Butterflies...
Patent leather beetles

I N THE 1800S, Edward Beall purchased one square mile of land along the Wabash River in southern Illinois; half was covered by forest that had never been logged. By the time Beall moved there, he was a widower and accompanied only by his daughter, Laura. Unlike most men of his era, he chose not to allow any logging on his property other than what the sharecroppers needed for firewood or repairs to fences and cabins. I imagine Beall and his daughter shared a love for the forest, because when he died and left it to her, she didn't allow it to be logged, either.

Laura Beall never married. She lived to be a very old woman, and when she died, in 1961, she left no will and no heirs. The property was sold at auction in 1962, and the purchaser planned to log the large, valuable trees. By then the forest was already recognized as one of the last remnants of old growth in Illinois, and the public outcry at its imminent destruction caused state authorities to step in and halt the cutting—just a week before it was to begin. The new owner was not happy with the state's interference, and a lengthy legal battle began. Eventually, the state prevailed, paying a few thousand dollars more than the purchase price to take over the land. In 1965, Illinois dedicated Beall Woods as a National Natural Landmark and opened it for all to enjoy.

Stories like this gladden me, of course, but I wonder how many forests we cannot visit because no one was able to save them. I think of the forest in Kentucky that Lucy Braun pleaded for and the Primeval Forest in North Carolina, both gone.

NOW, THOUGH, I was in an old-growth forest that got saved. I was alone in the forest on this green-gold afternoon. This place is sometimes called the "University of Trees," and I could see why. My head was spinning from trying to identify all the different tree species. I can name more than most people, but I still shrugged my shoulders at a few. I thought of my students and how they feel when I take them to the forest.

I am always amazed by how many young people cannot recognize any tree species at all. The forest must be just a green blur for most of them. To many college freshmen, all evergreens are "Christmas trees" or, at best, "pine trees." Out of hundreds of students, I've only had a few each year who enter college able to tell the difference between oak, hickory, maple, and gum. Maybe one or two students in fifteen years have been able to identify different *kinds* of maple—or oak or hickory or pine. In this University of Trees, I was a student again; there are *five* kinds of maple, *six* kinds of hickory, and *thirteen* kinds of oak! And there are forty other tree species in this forest of fewer than three hundred acres.

Those not familiar with tree identification tend to think the answers are all in the shape of the leaf. Most guidebooks would lead you to the same conclusion as you turn the pages and see one leaf illustration after another. Leaf shape might help with some types of maple, oak, or nut; but what if someone brings you an elongated oval leaf with a pointed tip and asks what kind of tree it is from? If the edges are serrated, it could be birch, cherry, hornbeam, beech, or elm. If the edges are smooth, it could be magnolia, black gum, sourwood, or persimmon. In a diverse old forest, the leaves don't really help much anyway, as they're usually very far away. Who can tell from a hundred feet below whether the leaves are serrated or the veins are forked? Sometimes you get lucky and a branch has fallen from the canopy, but proper identification usually requires a number of other clues. The texture of the bark helps, but it can vary from tree to tree of the same species. Fallen flowers or fruits are even more helpful, if you're lucky enough to find them.

Even autumn hues can be a clue. Black gum, for instance, is always the first to change color in the autumn, and it always turns deep red, never yellow, while tulip poplars turn yellow, never red.

I could even use my sense of smell. Here there was a small tree with oval, alternate, smooth-edged leaves in the understory. There were no flowers or fruits on the trees, and the bark was unremarkable, a smooth gray. I could reach the leaves, so I tore a small piece and inhaled. To me it smelled like creosote tar, so I knew for sure it was pawpaw.

The closest botanical relatives of the pawpaw all grow in the tropics. Native Americans cultivated them for fiber and fruit. Those facts make me wonder if the pawpaw spread across this country naturally, or if prehistoric humans helped it along. Some say pawpaw fruits kept Lewis and Clark from starving on their exploratory expedition, after the natives taught them how the fruits could be eaten.

A beautiful butterfly called the zebra swallowtail, white with dark stripes and long tails, has larvae that feed only on pawpaw leaves. A doctor claims that pawpaw twigs can cure cancer. This is just a bit of the lore collected by pawpaw aficionados, but the most frequently referenced book about trees, the *Silvics Manual*, doesn't even mention them. Why? Because they have no commercial value. When a forest with a pawpaw understory gets logged, the loggers just crush or push the small trees to one side. If the forest is to be converted to pine, they spray the pawpaws with weed killer. Never mind the zebra swallowtails.

I saw another plant here in the understory—more a shrub than a tree—with oval, smooth-edged leaves that alternated position along the twig. Again I tore a leaf in two and sniffed. Mmm, good, kind of spicy—a spicebush. The females of this plant have bright red berries, making them easy to identify in late summer, but for the plain, green males the sniff test works best. This plant is another important host for butterfly larvae. The spicebush swallowtail butterfly lays her tiny eggs one by one on spicebush leaves. After the caterpillars hatch, they hide in folded leaves during the day and emerge at night to feed. The young caterpillars are brown and white, and some claim they resemble bird droppings. Perhaps that is their means of camouflage. The full-grown caterpillars are an almost comical sight, painted with big clown eyes. A large, velvety, black butterfly emerges from the chrysalis it creates. The bottom half of its wings appear to be dusted with pale blue powder, and at the margin of its bottom wings are blue-green half moons. This gorgeous creature then silently wafts through openings in the forest searching for another of its kind.

I WAS WALKING and listening and sniffing, watching butterflies and ID'ing trees with no idea what diversion I would encounter next. Up ahead a huge tree had fallen across the path, and a trail maintenance crew had sliced it into sections and rolled them off the trail. The sections looked weathered, so I guessed this had happened quite a few years ago. Depending on the species and the weather patterns, trunk decomposition can be very slow. It may take as long for a tree to decompose as it took to grow. Many organisms depend on the coarse woody debris, as it's called, for both food and habitat. As the organisms decompose the wood, the trees release nutrients back into the soil over decades or even centuries—the ultimate slow-release fertilizer. We don't often see these decomposers, because they are either very tiny or hidden from view. I approached a large section that came almost up to my hip (wondering if I should take the time to count the growth rings) and idly peeled off a small section of bark. I was excited to find two big, black, shiny beetles underneath.

When asked to name an insect that eats wood, most people immediately mention termites, but these large, black beetles eat it, too. If they only knew how many different names humans had given them—horned Passalus, bessbugs, Betsy beetles, patent leather beetles. The last is my favorite, because they do have the texture and color of the Mary Jane shoes I wore in first grade—a shiny, deep black. But deep, longitudinal grooves on their back ends give the beetles a ridged look. This species even has many Latin names, having first been called *Passalus cornutus*, then *Popilius disjunctus*, and currently *Odontotaenius disjunctus*. Who knows when the name will change again? But no matter what you call them, these impressive beetles become more fascinating the more you learn about them.

Most insects, and most spiders, spend their lives alone except when mating. Other insects, such as termites and honeybees, lead very social lives in a colony. Patent leather beetles fall somewhere in the middle, sharing their lives only with a partner and their offspring. In this species, it is impossible to tell males from females by examining their exterior. The only way you can tell is by squeezing the abdomen; if the beetle is male, his genitalia will be forced out. Unfortunately, this usually kills them, so I chose to assume that the two I found were a male and a female. This is almost certainly correct, as the male and female live and work together.

They literally eat themselves a home—eating tunnels through rotting wood, and later raising their young in these tunnels. And, if that's not cool enough, they feed their babies on the poop they excrete after ingesting all that wood. If another male enters the tunnel, they respond by gnashing their mandibles and making a squeaking noise by rubbing their inside wings against their abdomens. Apparently, unlike most other insects, the sounds they produce have nothing to do with mating; even the larvae can make noise.

Noisemaking is the only purpose so far discovered for the wings of the adults, who cannot fly at all. One researcher commented, "No way has been found to make them use their wings. Tossing in the air and dropping from tall buildings...have brought negative results."

If the beetles are lucky enough to avoid discovery by eager scientists, they spend their lives crawling and chewing. Adults eat an amount equal to one-third of their body weight per day, which would be like me eating two whole, average-sized turkeys and a ten-pound bag of potatoes.

In the spring, the fertilized female prepares a nest in a tunnel lined with finely chewed wood. She lays two bright red eggs at a time over the next few weeks, until she has laid between twenty and sixty eggs. These eventually turn dark green, and the larvae hatch in about sixteen days and begin feeding on the predigested pulp (poop) right away. One experiment determined that larvae excrete twice their own weight in a twenty-four hour period. The adults, meanwhile, keep busy enlarging the living space and predigesting pulp for the larvae. After seven weeks, a larva is ready to pupate and will begin hollowing out a depression by rolling over and over, signalling the adults to build a cocoon of mud or wood pulp around the fat grub. After another ten to twelve days as a pupa, the beetle emerges, but, with a red head and white wing covers, it looks very different from its solidly black parents. The young beetles turn completely black after a few weeks or months. An adult beetle will live at least three years, probably more.

These beetles cannot live and feed on living wood. Their preferred habitat is a large, decomposing oak or hickory log on the floor of a shady forest. They like the old growth, too. The rotting logs retain moisture, so, even in a summer this dry, the beetles were in a moist environment. In the cooler months, the decomposing wood releases some heat, keeping the beetles warm. And, if you know how nature works, it should be no surprise that the beetle itself is the preferred habitat of another organism—a tiny worm-like nematode. Rarely is an adult beetle found without these in their gut. The *average* number of nematodes found per beetle in one study was 471. As another researcher put it: "This seems like a heavy infestation, but one has only to open a beetle or two to be convinced. It is very startling indeed to open a fresh adult and observe the wriggling mass of nematodes in the body cavity." Then, there are the mites, found under the wing covers of these beetles, and the microbes, found only in the gut of the mites, and so on. Habitat creates more habitat.

I replaced the chunk of bark I had peeled off and continued my walk through the University of Trees...and butterflies...and beetles. In the late afternoon, the dusk-singing cicadas started calling again—my cue to leave this splendid university from which no one will ever graduate.

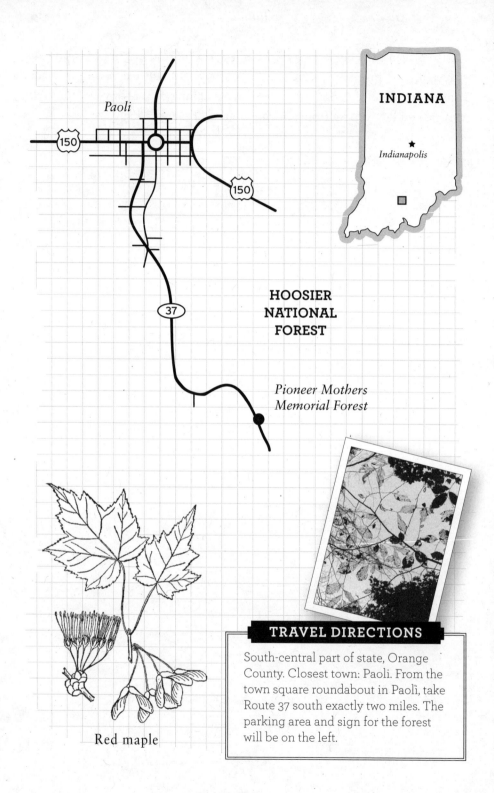

Paoli

150

150

INDIANA

★
Indianapolis

HOOSIER
NATIONAL
FOREST

37

*Pioneer Mothers
Memorial Forest*

Red maple

TRAVEL DIRECTIONS

South-central part of state, Orange
County. Closest town: Paoli. From the
town square roundabout in Paoli, take
Route 37 south exactly two miles. The
parking area and sign for the forest
will be on the left.

Indiana

PIONEER MOTHERS MEMORIAL FOREST

Sleeping...Song of the forest...Characteristics of old growth...Individuals

I'LL ADMIT I was pushing it; I had been driving for thirteen hours. All I needed was a dark little corner off the road where I could sleep in my truck. My friends are always warning me about traveling alone and *all the crazy people out there*, and usually I just laugh them off, but tonight nothing felt right. I felt inexplicably fearful. Finally I circled back to a small, darkened parking lot across from a church. It would have to do.

I pulled in and it was perfect, surrounded by trees and a chorus of night-singing katydids. It felt good and safe. And then I saw a small sign: *Hikers Welcome*. Like a moth to a flame, I had been drawn to the back entrance of the Pioneer Mothers Memorial Forest. I climbed out of my warm driver's seat and breathed deeply of the old-growth air. I lifted up the truck cap's back window, lowered the tailgate, and stretched out on the mattress to listen to the songs of the forest. Lines from a Wendell Berry poem came to mind, "...It is as though I descend / slowly earthward out of the air. I rest in peace / in you, when I arrive at last." I soon fell asleep.

THE LOVING CONCERN of my friends and family has caused me to examine my actions. Why, indeed, do I prefer camping in my truck to sleeping in a motel? I have generated a long list of reasons, but few would guess one of the most important: I love the sounds of an old forest, especially at night when the owls hoot and the coyotes howl. And then there are those strange sounds so difficult to tell apart. Frog? Insect? Bird?

We are all familiar with the summer chorus of insects, but perhaps less so with the individual "voices." This year I had a newfound appreciation for the "songs of insects," having just read a book by that title before leaving home. The book came with a CD, and I had been listening to it on the drive. I already knew the songs came from crickets, cicadas, and katydids, but was astonished by how many species of each there are. Thirteen species of katydids and twenty-one species of crickets populate the eastern U.S.— and each species plays a different song! Oh yes, and these are only the *common* species. These are the sounds of the healthy earth, and you hear none of them in a motel.

I WAKE EARLIER when I sleep outside, which for me is a good thing. My body senses the shift from black to pearly gray, and the gentle stirrings of the dawn-singing insects and birds. I was up and walking in the forest before the sun rose above the horizon. Alone, I moved very quietly through the cool, predawn forest. The symphony had been changing hour by hour. Last night as I drifted to sleep, I was listening to various species of katydids and tree crickets. When I woke, the katydids had fallen silent but the tree crickets were still making their music—like tiny fairies shaking glass maracas. Now the early birds were beginning to call to each other. As I started down the trail, a high, whistled *peowee* call alternated between two birds across the top of the forest canopy. Past sunrise, most of the tree crickets stopped singing, and the squeaky, chattery birds started up. By the time I left the forest, the sun was high and the cicadas had begun their electric buzzing.

THE SONG OF the forest changes not only by the hour, but also by the season. In winter, this forest would be nearly silent; in spring, frogs, toads, and birds would be singing. Only in summer and early autumn would I be able to hear the full insect chorus. Most singing insects start the year as eggs. In spring, they hatch into tiny nymphs, and they must eat, grow, and shed before becoming sexually mature. Only then do they sing.

In ancient Asian cultures, city dwellers took vacations to remote areas of the country in autumn to appreciate particular insect songs or choruses renowned for their beauty. Although ecotourism is catching on in the States, I have yet to see any place advertise its insect concerts. As in many things, the Asians were ahead of us in recognizing aesthetic beauty. We know that trees clean the air and water, but the forest's songs may be a service we have forgotten.

Unfortunately, this forest is quite small, so natural sounds must compete with the din of human industry. In the middle distance, I could hear a factory roar: big conveyor belts, perhaps, large ventilation fans, and the beep-beep-beep of a backup warning. Cars. And the sounds of the animals that humans keep: a rooster crowing, dogs barking. This forest is a good thing to have saved, and it is convenient for those who live nearby, but it will never have the auditory quality of a forest large enough or remote enough to be beyond the sounds of manufactured things.

Walking on this hillside path so close to town, I wondered if the average visitor would even recognize it as an old-growth forest. Knowledge about old forests seems to have been left out of most easterners' education. People who have heard of old-growth forests but have never been in one—knowingly—imagine they are going to see nothing but redwood-sized giants and heavenly light streaming in from the tall canopy. They may even imagine their hearts opening in an epiphany of love and instantly *knowing* they are in a special place.

The danger with this way of thinking is that any forest that causes a lesser reaction is at risk—considered "ordinary" and therefore fair game for clearing or whatever else one wants to do to it. In reality, eastern old growth often appears very ordinary at first glance.

Once, while I was giving a talk at another university, and going on at length about old growth, a student raised his hand and asked candidly, "What *is* old-growth forest?"

I took a deep breath. This student didn't care about the semantics of a bunch of bean-counting scientists still arguing about the definition of old growth. He wanted to know what old-growth forests *looked* like, what made them different from the forests he passed every day, what it *felt* like to walk through one.

"That is a wonderful question, thank you for asking it," I began. "Some people imagine that eastern old-growth forests are filled with very, very large trees, but in reality large trees are the exception. Yes, there are *some* very large, old trees, but there are also many young trees. The trees are likely to be of many different species. There are also many dead trees, some still standing, and others fallen over on the forest floor. Some of the fallen trees will be quite large. The forest floor is likely to be undulating with pits and mounds from where trees have fallen over long ago. The ground layer will usually be quite open because of the dense shade cast by the large trees. In other words there will not be much brush; you will feel like you could walk in any direction without much trouble. You will usually notice the birdsong, and there may be many different species of fungi growing out of the trees or the ground." I paused.

He was completely engaged in my description, and at the end said earnestly, "I think we have some forest like that on our farm. It is a section in the back. I don't know if it has ever been logged, but it looks just the way you describe it."

I urged him to find a way to protect it. Maybe together we had found, and will save, an old-growth forest.

TRUE TO MY description, there were trees of all sizes in this forest. The largest were not just of one, or two, or even three species; there were big trees of many kinds, including maples, oaks, hickories, and beeches. I was starting to recognize (as I was starting to appreciate the insect songs) that the oldest trees were not the most remarkable just because of their size, but also because they were so interesting *as individuals*. With ancient trees, the unique character of each is revealed, even in two of the same species growing side by side. Young trees differ from each other, too, but the disparities are much easier to see in old trees. Many have a ridge of callus bark in a line down the trunk—a scar from a long-ago lightning strike. Many ancients also have large bumps, like tumors, bulging from their trunks. Although we might be repelled at the sight of a tumor bulging from the skin of an elderly person, on these old trees I was beginning to see them as interesting or unusual, not ugly. The trees were teaching me to view a human tumor the same way, without judgment. Most of the elderly trees will live for many more years with their bumps, bulges, and scars. Although they are considered *overmature* by forestry standards, they will probably grow new leaves next year and the year after that and the year after that. In fact, many will outlive not only me, but also most of the young trees growing beneath them. And the energy they continue to harvest from the sun will nourish the cicada nymphs sucking on their roots and the katydids and tree crickets feeding on their leaves.

The old trees were teaching me that victory does not go to the swiftest, but to those with the most endurance. They were teaching me that we will not look perfect when we get to old growth, but will be most perfectly ourselves. Most women in the Pioneer Mothers group who raised money to save this forest have grown old, developed tumors of their own, and passed on. But many of the trees they loved still stand, and the chorus they preserved sings on.

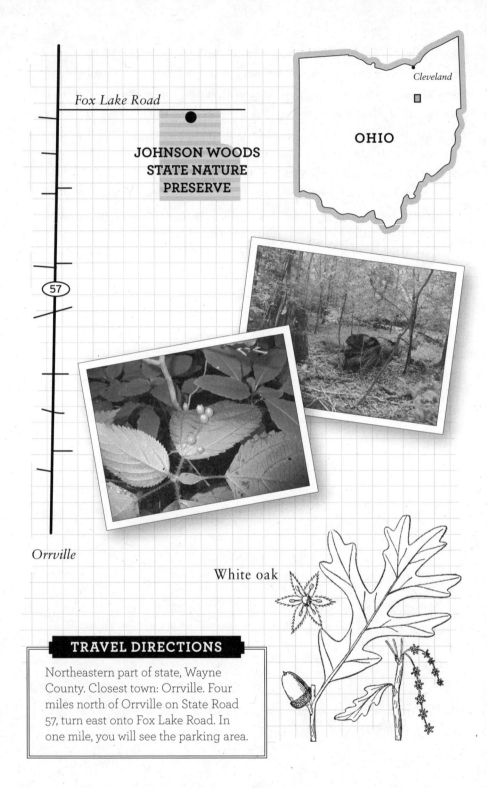

Fox Lake Road

JOHNSON WOODS
STATE NATURE
PRESERVE

57

Orrville

Cleveland

OHIO

White oak

TRAVEL DIRECTIONS

Northeastern part of state, Wayne County. Closest town: Orrville. Four miles north of Orrville on State Road 57, turn east onto Fox Lake Road. In one mile, you will see the parking area.

Ohio

JOHNSON WOODS STATE NATURE PRESERVE

Death...Whitetail deer...Mayapples and rust fungus...Lucy Braun

I WAS ON THE back roads again, this time driving through the wide-open agricultural countryside of Ohio, only a few miles from my destination. When I made the next turn, the speed limit dropped and I entered a town. Passing the library, the school, the video store, and a handful of fast food franchises, it was hard to imagine an old-growth forest nearby. It was even harder to imagine that 95 percent of this state was once covered in forest. After passing through the small town, I found myself in cornfields again, until my truck was suddenly enveloped in shade from the forest on both sides of the road. This was it; I had arrived at an old-growth oasis in the landscape. A few other cars sat in the small parking area.

The only trail was a nicely designed boardwalk. Just to be different, I decided to go the "wrong" way around the loop to see who else was in the forest with me. At first I saw only a few power walkers and a couple who apparently wanted to get their overactive children out of the house. They would have been amazed had they known I drove 650 miles to reach this forest, but other than a quick hello, I kept to myself.

Finally, near the end of the loop, I passed an elderly man moving slowly through the forest. He seemed ill, and I could see a clear plastic tube poking out from between his shirt buttons. I imagined him at home on his bed thinking of one last walk in the forest—perhaps the last he would ever take. I imagined him making the extreme effort to be among these trees. Perhaps he would die in this very place on this very day. It's not such a bad place to die, I thought.

Dying in nature does not seem to be a goal for many Americans, but philosopher Arne Naess noted that a dignified death in nature is important to many Norwegians. A poet who calls himself "Antler" wrote a poem that begins, "I want to lie down in dappled leaf-shade, / In quivering shadows of quivering leaves," and ends, "after all is said, / after all is done, / This is the way / I would die."

A GREAT DEAL of death was happening here anyway, as in any old-growth forest. Johnson Woods has impressively large specimens of oak, hickory, beech, and maple, but many of the big, old white oaks were reaching the end of their life spans, and dead trees—standing and fallen—were everywhere. These are indicators of an old-growth forest. Standing dead trees and large fallen limbs and trunks mean that the forest has been left alone long enough for the natural processes of life and death to occur. The largest, most ancient trees must have witnessed many deaths.

My grandmother lived to be a hundred years old, which seems enviable until you realize that by the time she died she had witnessed the deaths of most of her friends and family members. I suppose that as we get to old growth, we will experience the deaths of others at accelerating rates, too. When death becomes more commonplace, does it become easier to accept? Or more difficult?

SOME OF THE dead trees here were still standing, and I was pleased to see that the parks department had not made the mistake of cutting them out of fear for visitors' safety. Standing dead trees—called "snags"—play an important ecological role in the forest, providing safe nesting and resting places for many creatures. In a standing dead tree, there are many cavities and hollows up away from the forest floor, away from the rain and from predators. Once a snag has been cut and rests on the soil, it no longer provides the same type of protection. On the forest floor, the cavities are exposed to flooding from rainwater, to all sorts of crawling insects, and to ground-dwelling animals that would eagerly feast on eggs or young. Deadwood on the ground has its own, equally important role in the forest ecosystem, but it is very different from the role that standing deadwood plays. If you cut the standing deadwood in a forest, you are removing critical habitat; the living trees may still be "old growth," but the forest won't function as a healthy old-growth forest.

In this forest, there are very few younger oaks to replace those that are dying, so the forest is gradually shifting into a beech-maple forest. This pattern of forest succession has been well studied in a similar Ohio forest, Dysart Woods. The authors of that study seemed puzzled by the changing forest composition and speculated about causal factors such as fungus, pollution, drought, or understory cover. They noted that "browsing by deer is possible, but unlikely." But data released by the U.S. Forest Service shows whitetail deer populations rising quickly in Ohio. And during my visit to this Ohio forest, I was entertained by a number of deer snorting and running past.

Whitetail deer prefer the taste of oak saplings to beech or maple. In Pennsylvania's Cook Forest, a small area was fenced off to exclude deer and thereby study their effects. The results were visually striking. Inside the fence, the ground was covered with oak seedlings while outside there were none. I think the reason for the change in this Ohio forest is quite clearly the increasing deer population, but what to do about that is a completely different question. Humans deserve much of the blame for the deer population increase. As we opened up habitat by cutting dense forests and creating farm fields, the deer population multiplied; as we hunted the larger predators for skins, sport, or safety, the deer population expanded even more.

Some ecologists would like to see almost every whitetail gone, but I don't count myself among them. The forest is changing because of an animal; the animal is influenced by human actions. Who is to blame? What should be done? I found a quiet spot off the path and sat in the forest as it was—while the oaks still towered above me. According to a sign here, some of these ancient trees were producing acorns when the Mayflower landed at Plymouth Rock in 1620. So much has changed since then.

* * *

IN MY SHADY spot off the trail, I was surrounded by the low, parasol-like leaves of mayapples. This plant always grows in colonies. In early spring, clusters of green umbrellas, with deeply undulating edges, open on the woodland floor. Many of the plants are just a single leaf with a central stalk. These single-leaved shoots will not produce any flowers or fruit, but stalks with two leaves will form a large, white flower in the crotch between the two leaves. The flower cannot pollinate itself; it depends on an insect to bring pollen from a different mayapple. That may seem simple when you see a colony of hundreds of shoots, many of them flowering, but most of those are genetically identical and thus self-incompatible, meaning they cannot pollinate one another.

If the flower is pollinated, it forms a greenish-yellow, egg-shaped fruit. The fruit is more noticeable than the flower, because by the time it ripens, the leaves have begun to wither. The pulp of the ripe fruit can be eaten raw or used to make jelly, but eating the roots, leaves, seeds, or green fruit would all cause a vicious case of the runs. There have also been reports of the roots causing birth defects and miscarriages. Personally, I have never tasted the fruit, because I never wanted to risk the possible side effects. I put it under the heading of "not worth it."

The mayapples here today are past flowering and have beautiful, angular, yellow spots on the leaves. They are infected with a rust fungus. The Latin name of this fungus species, *podophylli*, is very similar to the genus name of the plant, *Podophyllum*, because this fungus can only live and reproduce on a mayapple. No mayapples, no mayapple rust. The life cycle of the rust fungus is very complex—much more complex than that of its host.

In the middle of winter, if you were to sift through the debris on the forest floor with the tiniest of tweezers and a powerful microscope, you might eventually find a dark, spiky, club-shaped thing smaller than a grain of sand. In very early spring, just exactly when the tiny, green mayapple shoots start pushing through the soil, the dark object germinates and produces even tinier spores. These spores might be carried by wind or water onto a mayapple shoot. If a fortunate spore lands on a mayapple, it will produce a microscopic, threadlike filament called a hypha. The hypha can tunnel between the mayapple cells and draw out enough nutrition to live, but its other mission—searching for another hypha thread, produced by another spore—is even more important. If these two threads find each other, their

cells will merge and form a different type of hypha, with two nuclei in every cell instead of just one.

Only a few days have passed since the plants broke dormancy, and the mayapple shoots are only a few inches tall, their leaves not even opened, but the hyphae that have found each other begin their next phase of reproduction. They produce more of the dark, club-shaped spores, inside of which the nuclei from the two hyphae have merged. If this were a plant or an animal, we'd call the event fertilization, but biologists who study fungi use different terms.

It is still early spring, the mayapple leaves have just unfurled, and already the second generation of dark, club-shaped spores has germinated, producing a second generation of tiny spores. Many of these will eventually be carried, again by wind or water, onto the stems and leaves of mayapples—perhaps the same plant their ancestors started from. Once again the spores germinate on their one and only host, and the hyphae set out in search of nutrition and each other. At this point, Mother Nature adds a twist. What happens next depends on which part of the plant the spore lands upon. If the hyphae cells fuse on the stem or a vein, where nutrition is abundant, they will once again form the club-shaped structures that will live on dead leaves over the winter, but if the hyphae fuse on the leaf blades, they will form pockets filled with rust-colored spores. This type of spore cannot live through the long winter, but it can reinfect the plant, germinate, and eventually form the dark overwintering clubs. The yellow spots I see on the leaves result from the fungus using up the sugars and nutrients in the leaf cells. Viewed one way, these leaves are *infected*, a term with negative associations, but viewed another way, the leaves with rust are the most beautiful and interesting: Mother Nature's yellow and green abstract artwork.

These things I write about—the fungi, the small plants, the insects, the birds, the soil, and the water—may seem like digressions, but they are the forest, too, and deserve our attention. They are equal in importance to the tallest of trees. And in ways we do not yet fully understand, these small things may determine the lives and deaths of the trees.

ONE CANNOT BE in Ohio, interested in trees, and not think of Lucy Braun. In her book *The Woody Plants of Ohio,* she quotes P. B. Sears: "The State of Ohio, containing 40,000 square miles, was once a magnificent hardwood forest.... But somehow it never occurred to anyone to set aside a square mile, much less a township six miles square, of primeval vegetation for future generations to see and enjoy."

Braun made it her life's work to describe the woody species and forest types of Ohio, piecing together hints from what was left before all traces of the original forest were gone. She never married and lived her entire life with her unwed sister, Annette Braun, the first woman to earn a Ph.D. from the University of Cincinnati. Annette's degree, received in 1911, was in zoology. In 1914, Lucy earned her Ph.D. in botany from the same university. Together the sisters created a laboratory in their home and traveled widely studying the natural world and collecting specimens. Lucy Braun died in 1971 at age 81, after devoting her life to teaching and writing about plant ecology.

In Ohio, I feel Braun's presence, and I think she would approve of my journeys. She wrote: "As a result of man's continuing destruction of his natural environment by the plow, lumbering, urban sprawl, and ever enlarging highways, few natural habitats will remain shortly in Ohio." Unfortunately, those words are even truer today than when she wrote them, but in Johnson Woods I had a chance to see a bit of what Ohio used to be, and to think of death and its counterbalance, life, and to hope that perhaps our society's attitude toward the natural environment has a cycle of its own that will swing back around in time.

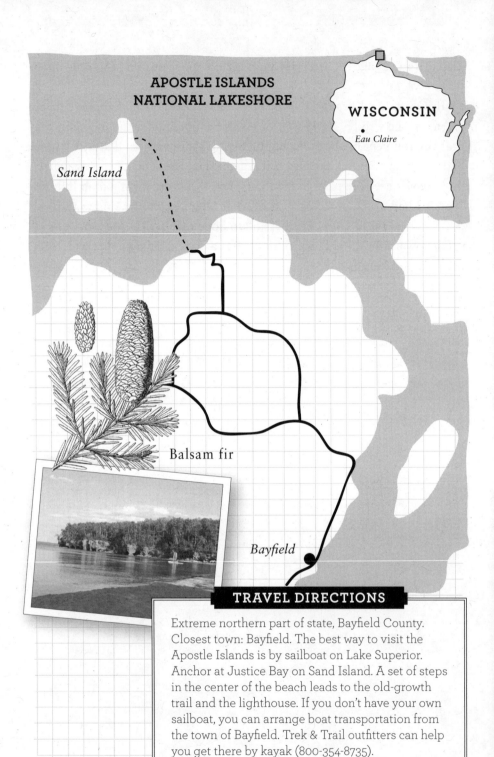

APOSTLE ISLANDS NATIONAL LAKESHORE

WISCONSIN

Eau Claire

Sand Island

Balsam fir

Bayfield

TRAVEL DIRECTIONS

Extreme northern part of state, Bayfield County. Closest town: Bayfield. The best way to visit the Apostle Islands is by sailboat on Lake Superior. Anchor at Justice Bay on Sand Island. A set of steps in the center of the beach leads to the old-growth trail and the lighthouse. If you don't have your own sailboat, you can arrange boat transportation from the town of Bayfield. Trek & Trail outfitters can help you get there by kayak (800-354-8735).

Wisconsin

SAND ISLAND, APOSTLE ISLANDS NATIONAL LAKESHORE

Balsam fir...Arranging the excursion...Safety training...
Where's the old growth?

*I*WAS IN THE North Woods. I knew this because, although it was mid-July, it was sixty degrees and the cool air smelled like Christmas morning. I was surrounded by Christmas trees—the popular balsam fir. Although pockets of this species can exist further south, it lives mostly in Canada and within a few hours drive of Canada. Besides the delicious, clean fragrance and the medium-length green needles with double white stripes underneath, you know you're in the presence of balsam fir when you see that bumpy, gray bark. The bumps are filled with resinous sap that emits the same delicious scent as the leaves. Press your thumbnail into one of those bumps and inhale as the fragrant sap oozes out. The only problem is that now you're sticky. Balsam fir sap is so adhesive it has been used as glue for mounting microscope specimens. "Balsam" is related to the word "balm," meaning a healing ointment. Native Americans used the sap as a remedy for a long list of maladies, from gonorrhea to sore throat. Although I love the smell, I can't imagine swallowing the stuff.

Perhaps deer enjoy the fragrance, too. Although they don't eat these trees, deer frequently visit fir groves, presumably using them for shelter. And there, right ahead of me on the trail, stood a young buck, his antlers still covered in velvet. He was unafraid of me and I was unafraid of him, but if one of us was to continue on this trail the other had to give way. I waited politely, not wanting to exploit my human arrogance, and eventually he deferred and stepped gracefully into the forest. I watched as he grazed on a young sugar maple, tearing the leaves off and chewing them one by one. I know whitetails do not favor red maples, so I wondered if the sugar maples tasted sweeter. As I walked by, I tore a leaf from the same small tree and took a bite. The deer watched, and I wondered what he was thinking. The leaf wasn't sweet to my tongue, but neither did it have the harsh green taste I imagined it might.

There is another "balsam" here, another denizen of the North Woods, but this one is a broadleaf, not a conifer. In fact, the balsam *poplar* is the northernmost American hardwood. Its range is mostly in Canada and Alaska, but this tree, which resembles the cottonwood or aspen, also grows in this part of Wisconsin. Native people used its fragrant buds to relieve coughs and congestion; when European settlers saw this, they called the tree "Balm-of-Gilead."

The true Balm-of-Gilead was a fragrant, medicinal ointment made in Greco-Roman times from a completely different plant species that grew near the Jordan River. Because it was mentioned in the Bible, it remained well known throughout the centuries.

Humans are not alone in collecting resin from the balsam poplar; bees collect it too, to encase hive invaders such as honey-stealing mice they have stung to death. Because a dead mouse is too heavy for them to carry, and a mouse carcass left to decay would infect the hive, the bees entomb it like a mummy in fragrant plant resin.

Although the two balsams were delightful, they were very obviously not old growth and not what I had come all this way to see. I was here to see grand, old white pines that had never been logged. I had read all about them in the park brochure: "Some of the best examples of old-growth forests in the region." And on the park's website: "When lighthouses were established on the islands, land was acquired as a reserve around the station so that the keepers had access to wood for fuel. No one was allowed to cut trees on the reserve except the lighthouse keepers. Unintentionally, the keepers protected these virgin stands.... Larger islands like Outer and Sand had 200 to 300 acre areas reserved adjacent to the lighthouses. If you hike a trail near these lighthouses today, you will see some big trees." When I read that, I decided I must see the island forest in Wisconsin.

*   *   *

BUT HOW COULD I get there? Most of the old-growth forests on this continent are accessible by car and then foot, but for this one I would need a boat. Ferries visit some of the Apostle Islands, either to islands with no old growth left or stopping only for a brief lighthouse tour—not the sort of trip I was looking for. I could have hired a private water taxi to Outer Island for a steep $480. Sand Island was only a few miles off the shore of Lake Superior—within kayaking distance—but Wisconsin was a long way from my home and I planned to fly. I couldn't easily bring my kayak on the plane. By now I was working the phone and the Internet simultaneously. I found an outfitter who would rent me a kayak, but I'd have to take a three-hour safety course first, pay for the shuttle, rent my own camping space, and, of course, bring all my own gear. When I added it all up, the kayak rental would have cost well over a hundred dollars. Or, the woman on the phone told me, I could go with a guide and a small group and all the details—camping permits, tents, meals, etc.—would be taken care of. They happened to have space on an overnight excursion to the very island I wanted to visit on the very weekend I wanted to go.

I could almost feel the plastic sliding out of my wallet. We were to meet very early in the morning, so I would need lodging nearby the night before; they just happened to have a cabin available. There were no frequent flyer tickets available, so I had to buy a full-fare ticket. I also needed to rent a car. The grand total of $1,125 was more money than I ever imagined spending on an overnight kayak trip, but it seemed like the best of all possible alternatives.

Soon I was standing by myself on the shore of Lake Superior gazing across at Sand Island. I would have only one day on the island and wanted to make sure I knew exactly where the old growth was, so I stopped at the visitor center. The volunteer at the desk called for the ranger in the back. "You will land here," he said, pointing at the map. "The trail starts right by the camping area. It is two miles long. Just follow it toward the lighthouse and you will pass through the heart of the old growth."

Early the next morning, I met the rest of the group at the outfitters: two women my age who were avid kayakers and a father and son team from Chicago. We shivered around the picnic table while introductions were made. Then the guide informed us we had to go through safety training before we could paddle to the island.

Safety training, we were not happy to learn, involved intentionally flipping one's kayak upside down in the freezing cold lake, removing the skirt (which normally keeps water out of the boat) while upside down in the water, wiggling out of the narrow boat, swimming to the surface for a breath, blowing up a float that slips over the paddle, climbing up the paddle and back into the kayak, pumping out all the water, controlling your shivering enough to get the skirt back on, and then flashing everyone a smile as if to say, "No problem." (OK, I added this last part myself.)

We did it because we had to. We did it because otherwise we couldn't get to Sand Island. When it was over, we paddled to shore, changed into dry clothes, and loaded the kayaks with what seemed like a mountain of gear. At last we set off for the island.

Once on the water, I quickly realized this was not a few miles down a slow-moving Maryland creek, but a few miles in the choppy open water of Lake Superior. Phase Two. My arm muscles started burning about halfway across, but I don't think the others could tell. I wasn't sure, but I imagined their arm muscles were burning, too. At last we landed on Sand Island. The others wanted to paddle around to the sea caves (maybe their arms didn't ache after all?), and so left me on shore alone to hike to the old growth.

It was only a two-mile trail, and at first I was entertained by the fragrant northern tree species, but soon I grew worried. The first mile went by and I hadn't seen any old growth. The beautiful beach at Justice Bay was some consolation, but I was almost incredulous when another half a mile up the trail I *still* hadn't seen any unlogged forest. I passed the lighthouse volunteers heading back to camp after a day of leading guided tours, so I asked them.

"Don't worry," they said, "You can't miss it. Just keep going." Finally, in the last quarter mile, I came across a giant old-growth white pine. Hurray! And then another and another, and then…the trail ended. I was at the lighthouse. *That's it?!* That's the old-growth forest I came all this way to see?

On my way back down the trail, I paid closer attention, counting every ancient white pine I could see from the trail. Nine. There were nine of them. Nine beautiful, big, old pine trees.

I don't usually add up what these journeys cost me, but I found myself doing just that on the way back. *Let's see, there was the drive to the airport, the plane ticket, the cabin, etc., etc. Oh yes, don't forget that table for one in Bayfield, and parking at the airport.* It came to $124.90 *per tree.* Part of me wanted to cry, not only because of the money, but because this is what it has come to. These lovely, giant trees, once everywhere in the north, are now only found in tiny, isolated preserves.

I turned back to the last big white pine. This rough-barked tree—so wide, so tall, so ancient—my outstretched arms couldn't reach even halfway around it. Its crown swayed in the wind that was blowing across the large lake. Its roots had been anchored in this same soil for centuries. I spent some time just being with the tree. It felt like times I have spent with an extremely elderly person. There was no need to talk or *do* anything; just the presence of one another was enough. *Presence* contains its own energy—a healing energy, a balm.

Could I turn my anger at the forest destroyers into love and appreciation for this tree they left behind? Which attitude would make me a more effective champion for the old-growth forests that remain?

I wondered what my philosopher friends would say, how they would feel. I tried to imagine the centuries of storms and floods, droughts, and fires this tree had survived, and I honored its stamina. Besides surviving natural threats, this tree also had the remarkable luck to survive the human's axe. It is difficult to describe my feelings toward this tree; I was not worshipping the tree so much as witnessing with it. I felt, as the philosopher Martin Buber put it, "bound up in relation to it."

Here is his full, rich passage on trees:

I consider a tree.

I can look on it as a picture: stiff column in a shock of light, or splash of green shot with the delicate blue and silver of the background.

I can perceive it as movement: flowing veins on clinging, pressing pith, suck of the roots, breathing of the leaves, ceaseless commerce with earth and air—and the obscure growth itself.

I can classify it in a species and study it as an expression of law—of the laws in accordance with which a constant opposition of forces is continually adjusted, or of those in accordance with which the component substances mingle and separate.

I can dissipate it and perpetuate it in number, in pure numerical relation.

In all this the tree remains my object, occupies space and time, and has nature and constitution.

It can, however, also come about if I have both will and grace, that in considering the tree I become bound up in relation to it. The tree is now no longer It. I have been seized by the power of exclusiveness.

Buber is saying that we can consider the tree from many different viewpoints. We can consider how it looks, what it does physiologically, its named identity, and as one from a population of its kind. But just as you or I would not want to be thought of exclusively in these terms, neither should we consider a tree only in this way. This tree is not just *any* tree—it is a *particular* tree. If regarded with discernment, it becomes an individual just as you and I are individuals. We have the same life force within us, and it is within us *uniquely,* in a way that cannot be replicated. Our ability to see the uniqueness in other beings makes our lives richer.

IT WAS BEGINNING to get dark, so I parted from the white pine and turned back toward camp. I walked quickly, alone in the woods, and started humming to myself. What came out, in cadence with my footsteps, was Joni Mitchell's song about putting the trees in a tree museum.

At a dollar and a half to see them, the people in the song got a bargain, I thought. But a tree museum is better than no trees at all, at least until we wake up. This small museum could be one more model, one more bit of living truth, one more glimpse of the planet's true face, until then.

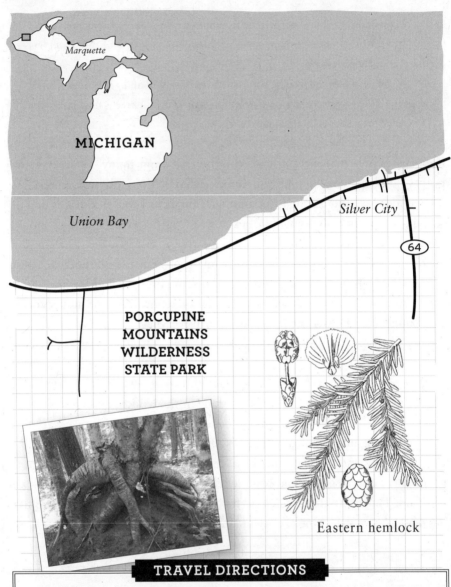

MICHIGAN

Marquette

Union Bay

Silver City

64

PORCUPINE
MOUNTAINS
WILDERNESS
STATE PARK

Eastern hemlock

TRAVEL DIRECTIONS

Extreme northwestern part of state, Ontonagon County. Closest town: Silver City. Once you get to Silver City, on the southern shore of Lake Superior, you will see signs directing you to the park.

The visitor center is a good place to get a map and see if there are any cabins or yurts for rent. There is also a display map showing where the old growth is (almost the entire interior of the park). If you want to reserve ahead call 800-447-2757 or check www.mi.gov/porkies. There are also hotel rooms nearby in Silver City.

Michigan

PORCUPINE MOUNTAINS WILDERNESS STATE PARK

*Bluebead lily...The yurt...Hummingbirds, warblers, and thrushes...
Phoebe nest...White pine*

I WAS TOLD THE hike to the yurt was about a mile. My pack was strapped to my back, and the green and brown arms of the forest surrounded me. The sun was already setting. Although I had never been to this particular place, I had been spending so much time in forests recently that I immediately felt at home. The species I had come to know so well were all around me: there was sugar maple, there yellow birch, and look, hemlock again. The ground-level plants seemed to vary more from forest to forest than the trees did. There were no mayapples here; instead, the glossy, green leaves and blue berries of the bluebead lily were everywhere.

This is a plant you almost never see in a garden, because it grows only in dense shade and doesn't begin flowering until it reaches age twelve. If I had been here earlier in the spring, the pale yellow, lily-like flowers that grow in clusters on its stalk would have been everywhere; but by now the flowers were pollinated, probably by bumblebees, and where each flower had been there was now a blue berry. Bluebead lilies, like mayapples, depend on insects for cross-pollination, so the abundant blue berries indicated that pollinators were plentiful in these woods. Earlier in the summer, the oblong leaves with parallel veins that grow close to the forest floor, usually in clusters of three, would have been shiny, green, and looking good enough to eat—which they are—but by now the leaves looked a little dull and some had begun to yellow.

I was alone now in the darkening woods, and all I could hear was the whine of mosquitoes. They were starting to take more blood than I was comfortable giving. Where was that yurt, anyway?

At last I saw a sign for a side trail leading to the yurt. I didn't know what to expect, but high on the hillside I reached a newish-looking circular structure with an attached deck. This forest, like many others, has cabins for rent, but more and more frequently the managers are erecting yurts instead of new cabins.

Mongolian nomads get credit for designing the yurt, a circular building not fixed in place, but rather constructed to be collapsed and moved if necessary. The original yurts were covered in animal skins, with rugs spread over the ground for flooring, but this one was instead covered in thick plastic and built on a wooden deck that served as its floor. Clear plastic windows with screens were manufactured into the walls. Like the Mongolian yurts, this one had a woodstove inside for heating, connected to a stovepipe that carried the smoke outside. Two sets of bunk beds and a small table with four chairs completed the furnishings. The sign on the door warned, "No cooking in the yurt"; a compact kitchen built into a cabinet was out on the deck.

I stashed my pack on a bed and opened the windows. Was this plain old fatigue or blood loss from all the mosquitoes? Whatever it was, I collapsed on a bunk and fell asleep without supper. Had I been with someone else, I would have carried on. Had I been with someone else sympathetic, perhaps he or she would have taken over while I rested. But there was no one here except me—tired, dirty, hungry.

I woke early, took a sponge bath, made a good breakfast, and started down the trail to see what this wonderful, shiny new day had in store for me. Just a half-mile from the yurt I came upon a diminutive moss-covered waterfall, the kind of shady, ferny, moist place that people stuck in the city daydream about. Across the stream was a dry, level place perfect for lounging the day away, but I had barely started my hike, so I continued on. A little farther along, however, I found myself in the midst of hemlock heaven—a place so lovely I had to stop. It was visually beautiful, of course, with towering hemlock trees lining both sides of the path and nothing but deep woods in all directions, but I think there is something even beyond physical beauty in these old-growth places unchanged by humans. Four billion years of evolution and planetary change, and *this* is what had come to be on this very spot. There is another type of beauty contained in that history of life.

Humans have dominated much of the planet and altered it profoundly, but here, just off the trail, was the "actual world," as Henry David Thoreau called it. Judging by how frequently this phrase is quoted, it clearly resonates with many. While hiking up Mount Katahdin in Maine, Thoreau was struck by the deep, mysterious relationship we have with the Earth. I think it was no coincidence he was hiking through a forest when this epiphany happened. These places feel more real—they *are* more real—than the landscapes through which we generally pass.

When you are back in contact with the skin of the actual earth, you know why you worked so hard to get there. Going to bed hungry was worth it. And now I was slowing into the forest again. I sat to listen to the birdsong and look up into the tall hemlock canopy. The vibrations of a hummingbird in flight rewarded my stillness. I watched it pluck something, perhaps an insect, from the hemlock needles.

Researchers in the Great Smoky Mountains discovered a small, green spider found only among hemlock needles. I wondered if this hummingbird might be eating those spiders. I couldn't tell from where I sat, way down below on the forest floor.

One way to find out would be to capture the bird in a mist net and dissect it to identify its stomach contents. For one study on avian diets, researchers did just that, capturing 826 birds in a forty-acre forest during the summers of 1949 and 1950. They dissected all the birds and examined their stomach contents. The list of birds almost made me lose *my* stomach contents. Forty-five different species were captured, none spared. They even killed woodpeckers, thrush, and a dozen different types of warbler. I'm sure they killed some birds I have never even seen. Biologists usually excuse their methods as necessary and disparage those who criticize them, but I doubt any biologist would conduct such a study today. That tells me there is room to be wrong and room to improve in the biological sciences. Robert T. Mitchell, author of that bird study, I wonder where you are today. I wonder if you are still alive, and if you have reconsidered what you did.

* * *

A GOOD THING about being alone is that it is easy to get very quiet. While watching the hummingbird, I noticed other little birds beginning to move in close to me. I am not an expert at identifying birds: this one was small, black and white with some yellow on the head and neck and white under the tail—perhaps a Blackburnian warbler? One study comparing old-growth forests and younger forests found forty-five times more Blackburnian warblers in the old growth.

A naturalist friend of mine used this information to get a tax break to protect future old-growth forest on his property. In order for it to qualify as agricultural property, which carries a lower tax rate, the state required a forest management plan done by a registered forester. During this part of the process, landowners are often encouraged to manage for forest products, primarily timber. The foresters often assume owners want to manage their land for profit. Some do, of course, but some don't, and the options aren't always fully explained. Many owners don't realize they are in control and can manage for anything they want. My well-educated friend cleverly declared that he wanted to manage for Blackburnian warblers, and because these birds prefer old, unmanaged forest, my friend's management plan prescribed simply leaving the forest alone to be a beautiful and ecologically complex place filled with birdsong.

No one understands exactly why Blackburnian warblers are more common in old-growth forests. A famous warbler ecology study published by Robert MacArthur in 1958 observed that, out of five species of warblers studied, the Blackburnians were most frequently found at the top of the canopy. They seem to prefer feeding and nesting in the loftiest spots, hopping along the highest branches looking for beetles and other insects to eat.

WHILE THE LITTLE warblers and I were checking each other out, I heard in the distance a musical melody from another bird. I had no idea what species it was, so I tried memorizing the tune. I decided it sounded like a waterfall played on a flute, with the water falling up instead of down. When I got home, I played through bird recordings and recognized it at once as the song of a Swainson's thrush, possibly the loveliest birdsong there is. The same study I mentioned earlier found that Swainson's thrush were twenty times more abundant in old-growth forests than in younger forests. So,

in addition to looking more beautiful and smelling more wonderful, old-growth forests also sound better.

I TRY TO travel light, but perhaps I should start carrying a bird identification guide. I had to look up yet another bird when I got home. For a few days, I spent more time and had a closer relationship with this bird than with any human. She behaved somewhat like the swallows I was used to seeing at home, but her tail was not forked and her colors were duller—brownish on top and tan on her belly. She had built a nest out of mud, like the swallows do, attached to the wall of the outdoor kitchen where a little overhang from the roof protected it. The nest's edge was trimmed in moss, still alive and green. I thought this was a nice touch, as the baby birds could rest their chins against moss instead of mud. Inside the perfect cup of the nest were three perfect baby birds.

When mom was away from the nest, the babies kept silent, their eyes closed and their heads down, but when she flew near they lifted their heads, opened their mouths, and noisily begged for food. She would stuff worms or insects into their gaping mouths and then, before flying away, pluck what looked like a fecal pellet from the nest. This I assumed she would drop in the forest somewhere before foraging for more insects. I watched this avian family for hours, but finally I could put my hunger off no longer and disturbed them by opening the kitchen cabinet and lighting the stove. "Sorry," I told her, "my turn to eat."

Mother bird must have chosen this nesting spot in early spring, when there were few hikers in the forest. While I cooked only a few feet from the nest, she didn't dare come near enough to feed the chicks. She sat on a near-by branch watching over me and cheeping her dissatisfaction. She'd flick her tail, flutter to another branch, and "cheep, cheep, cheep" some more. As I cooked, I could hear her nervous activity and rushed through my tasks so the feeding could continue. "Almost done," I'd say, and finally take my bowl of backcountry food to the corner bench to sit quietly and watch the joyous reunion. I became so attuned to their patterns and sounds that even from inside the yurt I could tell what was happening at the nest. I knew my darling bird well, and would say she knew me and my patterns, but until I got home I didn't know she was an eastern phoebe. Thumbing through my bird guide, there was no question; I recognized her the way you'd recognize an old friend in the school yearbook.

I became protective of the phoebe and her family. Once, in the middle of the night, I heard wings flapping around and around the yurt. *The bird*, I thought as I woke from a deep sleep. *Something is raiding the nest, perhaps a snake, and the mother is upset.* This was a reasonable thought—70 percent of all nest losses are due to predators such as chipmunks and snakes. Should I go out and see, I wondered? Perhaps even rescue the babies? But as I lay in bed deciding what to do, I felt a rush of wind on my face, as if from a wing. Wait a minute! How could I feel air from the wing of a bird that was *outside*? As I pondered that thought, a wing brushed my face. This was no dream, this was real, and it occurred to me that it was probably not a bird. Just then the creature whizzed by so closely I experienced the primal fear that it would get caught in my hair. I've told countless people that the bat-in-the-hair thing doesn't happen—their sonar is too sophisticated—but at that moment intellect gave way to instinct. I have very long hair and it was all sleep-messy, and the thought of wrestling a winged mammal out of my hair while alone in the dark didn't appeal to me. Laughing at myself, I covered my head with a towel, reached for my flashlight, and confirmed my suspicion: *There was a bat in my yurt.*

Many people enjoy hearing about the nesting bird, but when I tell them about the bat they are frightened for me. I simply crept to the door (with my head still covered), opened it, and hoped the bat would fly out. It only took a few more darting turns around the yurt before finding the exit.

All was quiet once more, and I went back to sleep. Bats are more abundant in old-growth forests, too.

I REALLY LIKED these Porcupine Mountains, or "Porkies," as the locals call them. They were named by the native people who lived here, because the hills reminded them of porcupines hunched side by side: up, down, up, down. This rough terrain of hills and valleys saved the old growth in these mountains.

In the early 1600s, the British began harvesting American white pines, and the British and Americans continued to do so for more than three hundred years, until almost all the white pines had been cut down. The British used these trees to make masts for their ships because they were tall and straight, strong and light. They played a role in the American Revolution, because the King of England declared that all white pines more than twenty-four inches in diameter belonged to him, and property owners who cut one down would lose their land. This angered the American colonists and was one of the disputes that led them to revolt. A white pine decorated one of the first Revolutionary War flags, to remind the soldiers of what they were fighting for. In those days, people thought these forests, two hundred feet tall and stretching for miles, would last forever. They didn't.

The logging that ravaged the Atlantic states in the 1800s swept through this region, too. White pine logs were wonderful for loggers, because they floated, which made transportation easy. The felled logs could be rolled or dragged to the water and floated to the mill. Here on the shores of the Great Lakes, many of the ancient pines were milled into boards or cut to supply fuel for steamships.

Once the pines close to the waterways had all been cut, railroad tracks were laid so trains could transport the more remote trees. But the locomotives didn't operate well on steep terrain, so forests in hilly areas such as the Porcupine Mountains escaped the saws for a bit longer. With the development of logging trucks and roads that dug ever deeper into the interior, even forests in the mountains were at risk of being logged.

Fortunately, the Porcupine Mountains escaped this fate until the 1930s. People slowly came to recognize that the hills contained some of the last, rare remnants of original forest. This living "forest museum" was brought to the attention of the federal government, which designated it as a potential site for the next national park. But then World War II changed everything. Federal funds were diverted to the war effort and other plans were put on hold. The war also increased demand for wood products, so loggers turned with renewed interest to the giant trees in the Porcupine Mountains. There was money to be made in lucrative wartime contracts.

These days we don't think much about the relationship between war and logging, but during my research I came to realize how frequently wars have influenced our actions in the forest. In some places, war was a good excuse for cutting down trees, but in Michigan, concerned citizens refused to let that happen. The state stepped in where the federal government had not, and in 1945 the Porcupine Mountains were declared a state park. But ordinary state parks are only protected as long as the elected governor and legislature are willing to protect them, and in some years proposals for more roads, entertainment facilities, and even logging in the park had to be vigorously contested. After years of political battles, in 1972 an environmentally friendly state government passed the Wilderness and Natural Areas Act and made the Porcupine Mountains a *Wilderness* State Park, thereby protecting it from logging for all time.

AFTER PACKING UP my gear and sweeping out the yurt, I faced a bittersweet hike down the trail to my car. I had developed deep feelings for this beautiful, intact old-growth-forest ecosystem. As I walked, a Rilke poem bubbled up from somewhere deep inside my brain:

> One space spreads through all creatures equally—
> inner-world-space. Birds quietly flying go
> flying through us. Oh, I that want to grow,
> the tree I look outside at grows in me!

I assured myself I would return to the Porkies.

Mohawk Trail State Forest, Massachusetts

NORTHEAST FORESTS

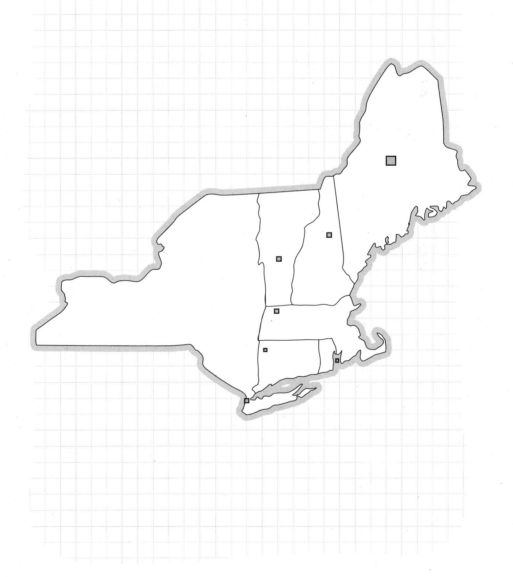

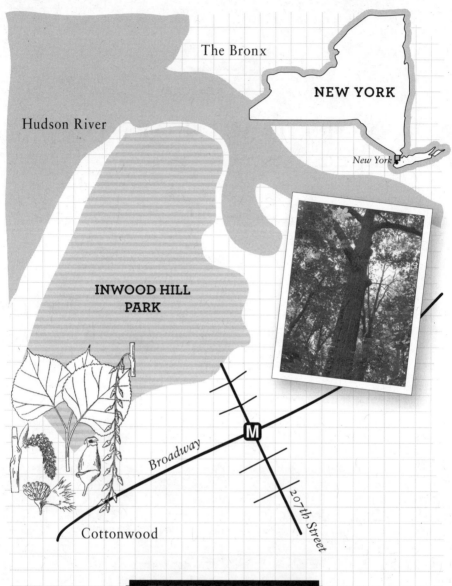

The Bronx

NEW YORK

New York

Hudson River

INWOOD HILL
PARK

Broadway

M

207th Street

Cottonwood

TRAVEL DIRECTIONS

Extreme southeastern part of state, New York City. From anywhere in Manhattan, take the 'A' subway line uptown to 207th Street. Cross Broadway and walk two blocks straight ahead.

The trails are confusing and unmarked. You can get a map online at www.nycgovparks.org/sub_about/parks_divisions/nrg/forever_wild/pdf/fw-trailmap-38.pdf, or pick up a copy at the Urban Ecology Center in the park (the center is closed Monday and Tuesday).

New York

INWOOD HILL PARK

Manhattoes...Gingko...Nesting hawks

MANHATTAN WAS ONCE covered in old-growth forest. When Henry Hudson and his comrades sailed to the island, anchored, and rowed ashore in 1609, Hudson thought it "as pleasant a land as one need trod upon; very abundant in all kinds of timber suitable for shipbuilding and making large casks."

He also encountered a friendly group of native people who called themselves the *Manhattoes*. Anthropologists estimate that ancestors of the Manhattoes (a tribe of the Lenape) had lived in the region for more than three thousand years. They carved dugout canoes from the giant tulip poplar trees; gathered acorns and beechnuts; hunted deer, raccoon and bear; caught fish; and harvested oysters. Beavers, otters, wolves, foxes, bobcats, and minks also lived there. Passenger pigeons flew through in great flocks. For the native people, the trees provided heat, light, shelter, transportation, and food.

Just seventeen years after Henry Hudson "discovered" the Manhattoes, Dutch colonists "purchased" Manhattan from them for trinkets and beads. Some say the value of the beads was twenty-four dollars, some say it was twenty-four hundred, but it doesn't really matter. The native people had no idea this treaty meant the white man would ravage the forest on which they depended. They could not have guessed that less than four hundred years later no beavers, otters, wolves, foxes, bobcats, minks, or bears would roam the island.

No one eats from this land any longer. Food is brought in by truck or train; no one dares eat oysters from the Harlem River. The passenger pigeons are long extinct, but a few trees from those days may still stand, silent witnesses to vast changes in the land. The trees, if they could talk, might tell us how white immigrants colonized the island, restricting the native people to smaller and smaller areas at the extreme northern tip of the island. One hundred and fifty years after the treaty was signed, the settlers themselves started fighting over it. During the Revolutionary War, they built a fort on the northern part of the island and shot at other white-skinned people who arrived by ship. In the years after that war, some white settlers began to feel crowded in the southern part of the island (there were hundreds of thousands of them by then) and so built country homes in the northern part. These were the richest inhabitants of the island, and many of them were uncomfortable sharing the area with wild animals. By 1890, they had killed the last of the wolves, foxes, and bobcats. Wild food had become scarce, and so within a few decades the last of the native people had left, and much of the land that wasn't used for buildings was cleared for playgrounds and athletic fields. John D. Rockefeller donated his large country estate, which eventually became Inwood Hill Park, to the city.

WHEN I WAS planning to visit the park, I pictured a tiny undisturbed corner on the heavily populated island, one small area that had stayed forested through all the paving and construction that went on around it. When I arrived, I inquired about the old growth. "Oh yes," the park naturalist told me, "almost the entire park is old growth."

I started up the trail wondering when the asphalt would stop. It didn't. Occasionally, I would come across a fire hydrant or storm water drain. There were even old streetlamps in some sections. The undergrowth was crowded with invasive, introduced plants, such as daylilies and andromeda. Many of the trees were impressive in size, but then I spotted a ginkgo tree as massive as any of the so-called old growth.

Now, ginkgos are lovely, with their fan-shaped leaves, but they are about as far from a native species as you can get. In fact, scientists are not even

sure any native ginkgos remain on the planet. The ginkgo evolved 200 million years ago, long before any of the other tree species in this New York
forest appeared on the planet. A westerner first saw a gingko tree in 1691,
growing in the garden of a Buddhist monastery in Nagasaki, Japan. Apparently, the monks had brought it to Japan from a monastery in China. It is
said the monks prayed to the trees, and one monk known for his wisdom
claimed to be guided by the tree-spirit of Japan's oldest gingko.

How strange that a tree species so tough it survived a number of mass extinction episodes, has lived millions of years longer than any of its close biological relatives, and was the tree most likely to withstand the nuclear attack on Nagasaki, is now so dependent on humans. For three hundred years, it was thought to survive only in gardens.

Recently, a few small ginkgo groves were found in the Chinese wilderness. DNA testing revealed that these trees were all very similar genetically. They may have been planted long ago in a garden, and then eventually the forest grew up around them. The same thing had obviously happened here in New York; this huge gingko tree must have been planted.

There was something else different about this place, although it took me a little while to identify it: not only didn't it look like an old-growth forest, it didn't sound like one, either. I heard no beautiful songs from forest birds such as thrush or warblers; I didn't even hear cicadas buzzing. Missing from this tract was "the divine music of the natural world," as nature-sound recorder Bernie Krause so beautifully put it. When I stopped to listen, I heard the roar of jets taking off from Newark Airport every five minutes, and sirens and train whistles in the background.

I WAS PUZZLING over my small black and white map when an official-looking trio of men stopped nearby to consult their large color map. I sensed that their mission was similar to mine. "You guys have a good map," I hinted, hoping to get a peek at it. But they had no time to help a "tourist," and we headed off on separate trails. Months later I would read about this encounter from their perspective in *The New Yorker*. They, too, were in this remote corner of Manhattan trying to understand what the island had been, and to see if any hints of that history remained.

The next day, I returned to the Ecology Center to inquire again about the old growth. Perhaps I had missed it. While waiting for the naturalist, I studied the displays. A reproduction of a painting of the Revolutionary War battle at Fort Washington hung on the wall. I recognized the landscape as the one I had walked through the day before, but the painting showed the land completely cleared of trees. Here was proof: the forest at Inwood Hill Park was not original forest. It had been logged, like most of our forests, but so long ago that the replacement forest was now hundreds of years old, ancient enough to contain very large trees. Some people would call it a secondary old-growth forest, but I resisted applying that moniker to this grove with its introduced species, human construction, and missing ecological links.

When the naturalist came out, he assured me that the trails I had taken went through the old-growth forest. "But look at this painting," I said, "It shows the whole area clear-cut." "Well," he replied, "it's as close as you can get to old growth around here."

I'm glad the people of Manhattan have a green oasis to visit, but I wouldn't want them to think they were experiencing what it feels like—and sounds like—to be in a *real* old-growth forest.

YOU MIGHT BE wondering why I didn't visit the Adirondacks or the Catskills, which contain millions of acres of forest that New York State declared "shall be forever kept as wild forest lands.... nor shall the timber thereon be sold, removed, or destroyed." The estimates of old growth remaining there range from 150,000 to 500,000 acres—plenty to choose from. All the animals gone from Manhattan still live in the vast forests of western New York, where I might find solitude and nature's music.

Instead I chose to visit Inwood Hill Park in Manhattan, perhaps from the hope that, even in the places densest with humans, we would leave space for the forest and habitat for other species. It would have made such a nice story.

The rangers in the park haven't given up hope. They pointed out a pair of red-tailed hawks nesting in one of the tall trees. The hawks have been nesting there for a decade. Every year they return to the park to mate, lay eggs, and successfully rear young.

The Adirondacks must have thousands of nesting hawks, but I bet none are more watched, or more loved, than this pair.

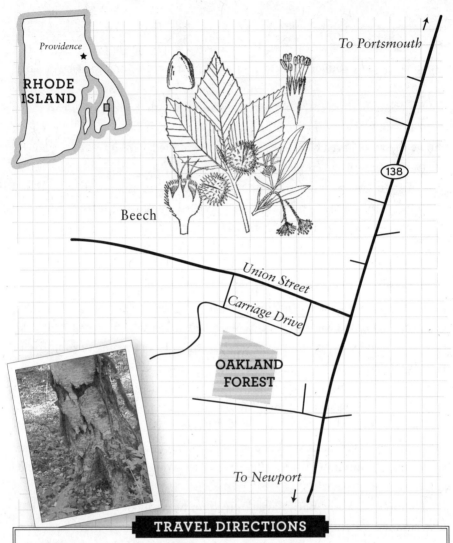

Providence

RHODE
ISLAND

Beech

To Portsmouth

138

Union Street

Carriage Drive

OAKLAND
FOREST

To Newport

TRAVEL DIRECTIONS

Eastern part of state, Newport County. Closest town: Portsmouth. From Fall River, Massachusetts, take U.S. 24 south toward Portsmouth. Exit onto Route 138, and turn right. Go 3.5 miles to Union Street (which is next to the State Police Department), and turn right.

If you're coming from the south across Newport Bridge, follow signs for 138. It is nine miles from the bridge to Union Streey in Portsmouth (the street will be on your left). From Union, make the first left onto Carriage Drive, which winds through a subdivision. There is parking across the street from 271 Carriage Drive.

No pets or overnight camping allowed. You are right in the middle of town, with many services nearby.

Rhode Island

OAKLAND FOREST

Infill…Perc test…Responsible forestry…Health

ALMOST NO ANCIENT forest is left in tiny Rhode Island. The Oakland Forest covers a mere twenty acres, right in the middle of a subdivision. I didn't expect much.

What I found was a welcome surprise. Although the forest was small, it was healthy and diverse, and the tops of the tall, centuries-old trees were waving in the wind. The trees were mostly leafy types, such as maple, beech, and tulip poplar. Down below on the level, leaf-strewn forest floor I couldn't feel any breeze at all. This forest felt hopeful, not like a monument to what was lost. It felt like what we could have—should have—if only enough of us wanted it.

Things could have easily gone the other way for this forest. As our nation's population continues to grow, more and more of our green places are giving way to houses, roads, and stores. In a desperate effort to protect rural areas, most planning departments and environmental groups promote "infill" development instead of sprawl. Fill in areas in existing towns first, they suggest, by building on the oversized lots and in abandoned business spaces instead of sprawling out ever further. I belong to an environmental group that works hard for "smart growth"—keeping new building focused in the core—and in general favors infill development.

A developer had made plans for Oakland Forest. The lot once was part of Cornelius Vanderbilt's estate, but the estate had been sold off in pieces and a town had grown up around what was left. The thirty-acre parcel (ten open, twenty wooded) seemed perfectly suited for infill development. Infrastructure was already in place: roads, schools, police, fire, and water. How could smart-growth supporters argue against this one? The developer commissioned a survey and was on the waiting list for a "perc test."

The white, plastic pipes used to test drainage rates (percolation) are often the first physical indicators of impending development. I saw some this week in the middle of a recently harvested farm field. If it passes its perc test, I expect to see construction rather than farming going on in that field by this time next year. When the neighbors of Oakland Forest saw the pipes, they began paying attention. They questioned the development and slowed the permitting process.

RECENTLY, A FORESTER e-mailed me to comment on my apparent distaste for foresters. Ultimately, he reminded me, the choice of whether or not to log is the landowner's. True, I wrote back, but not all landowners understand the uniqueness of what they own, and not all foresters take the time to educate them. And then there is this conundrum: just because it's legal, and the landowner wants it done, does that mean it's the right thing to do?

One forester, Matt Largess, finally drew the line. In 1998, the developer of Oakland Forest hired him to decide which trees to cut and which to keep. Largess soon realized he was being asked to desecrate an ecologically intact old-growth forest. Unethically, perhaps, but oh-so-morally, Largess contacted scientists who could help him make the case for preservation. Then he contacted the Aquidneck Land Trust.

The land trust responded quickly to the threats, raising funds to buy the forest from the developer and opening it to the public. I thought it a nice touch that they left a few perc-test pipes in place as a sort of historical monument.

Meanwhile, Largess's world had been rocked. "I used to be a tree clearer until I found this forest, and then I changed completely," he said. "It's like being an alcoholic and going sober. Or being an atheist and becoming religious."

Some foresters, like Largess, change their attitudes abruptly; others never do and forever think of fiber production as a forest's primary role. Then there are the foresters who change gradually, and come to feel differently about forests at the end of their lives than they did when they were young. Gifford Pinchot, considered the father of U.S. forestry, experienced this sort of change. The first chief of the U.S. Forest Service from 1905 to 1910, he founded the Yale School of Forestry and literally wrote the book on forestry in 1914 with *Training of a Forester.* For most of his life, Pinchot opposed preservation, believed in market forces and efficiency, and believed that a forest's highest good was the wood it could produce for human use. It was not until the final, 1937 edition of his book that he admitted to other, perhaps less tangible benefits provided by forests. "Not all of us are able to give expression to our appreciation of forest beauty and mystery," he wrote, "but we feel it just the same. This 'good' which the forest offers so freely to all men cannot be measured in board feet and cords, in dollars and cents. It is immeasurable because it reaches and uplifts our inner selves."

Another forester who changed his opinion as he got older is Bill Whitmore. Already retired from his professor of forestry position when I met him, he was the first forester to stand behind my idea of setting aside "future old growth." In a letter to me after my first book was published, he wrote, "You are a real tree romantic, and so am I, but I came to that late in my career. My undergraduate degree was in forestry, which teaches pretty much that trees are a commodity."

An enlightened Whitmore testified before his state's representatives in support of a bill to protect Ohio's Mohican State Forest: "In my opinion, as a forester, intensive timber management and intensive recreational use are not compatible. We need the recreational attributes of this forest far more than the returns from logging." The Society of American Forests opposed the bill. Whitmore had been a member of the society for forty years, but bravely took a stand against the society on this occasion.

In the past two decades, some foresters have begun calling themselves *ecoforesters,* to distinguish themselves from industrial foresters. This is a positive sign, but so far I haven't met any foresters in the East who adhere strictly to ecoforestry principles. So far, what talk of sustainability I hear mostly has to do with the sustainability of wood fiber for human use.

If there are any foresters reading this, please recognize that you have choices. I know you love trees and understand more about them than anyone, I know your family may have been in this business for many generations, I know you need to pay your mortgage, but don't forget there are other generations coming behind you. Please do what you can to preserve our few remaining native forests that hold big, old trees and habitat for many species. Don't leave this job up to the tree huggers. After all, you will be invited to see forests we will never know about.

FROM THE TRAIL, through the serene forest of beech, oak, and maple, I could just barely see the backs of houses in the adjacent subdivision. How lucky the children who live here are, I thought. All children should have a healthy forest, prairie, or desert—or natural land of any sort—in their backyards (or at least within a short bicycle ride).

The concept of infill development is basically good, but it can be taken too far. To take an extreme example, consider New York City. Would it make sense to fill in Central Park to prevent some sprawl into Westchester? The plan to set aside Central Park was bold and forward thinking, and we all appreciate it now (although I'm sure some questioned it at the time). If we are going to live more densely, we also must increase the density of our parks.

Aldo Leopold observed that, "We can be ethical only in relation to something we can see, feel, understand, love, or otherwise have faith in." How are we going to raise the next generation to behave ethically toward our forests if they haven't any to relate to? The director of the Aquidneck Land Trust considers Oakland Forest a living classroom, where children can be touched by nature; perhaps those children will grow up to become the donors who save the next parcel of threatened land.

One difficulty with saving green space is that, as the land becomes more densely developed, it also becomes more valuable. When the last fragment of native woodland in an area is threatened with destruction, the price tag for protecting it is often beyond the fund-raising abilities of local conservation organizations.

The State of Maryland has a sensible solution to this problem: When property changes owners, half of one percent of the real estate transfer tax goes into a fund to preserve open space. As the value of real estate increases, so does the tax revenue, and therefore the ability to preserve land keeps pace with land values. In theory, this is a great program; in reality, it could work better. Some local governments apply for open-space funds to buy parking lots or playground equipment, or to create athletic fields that are mowed twice a week and sprayed with insecticides and herbicides, or, even worse, covered with artificial turf, and their applications are being funded. Meanwhile, I watch as neighborhood forests become fields and fields become housing developments.

Let us fill in with natural land first, and then consider how to build around it. Our green infrastructure needs to be valued as highly as the strength of our bridges if we are going to reverse this destructive spiral of not having, leading to not knowing, leading to not caring, leading to not having.

IN OAKLAND FOREST, the developer planned to build thirty-eight condominiums. If you were a town commissioner and looked at his plans, you might imagine the condominiums tucked into the wooded acreage and think the idea not so bad. You might think the community could live with that. And you might even fear that if you turned down his plans just because the forest was beautiful, he could sue you.

Time after time, I have looked at plans showing the smallish footprint of proposed buildings on a lot and my mind has fooled me by plopping them down onto the existing site like Dorothy's house plopped down on the Wicked Witch of the West. Experience has taught me the hard way that this mind trick has nothing to do with what actually happens. What actually happens, once the developer gets approval for development, is that heavy equipment comes in and regrades everything. Most site engineers like to start with something that looks like the surface of the moon. Unless there are regulations forbidding it, all native plants and most of the topsoil are scraped away. Holes and trenches are dug for foundations, storm water drains, water, sewer, and by the time they're done it looks nothing at all like the innocent development you imagined. Only now it is too late to do anything about it.

Once the buildings, parking lots, and roads are finished, whatever land is left over is seeded with grass or laid with sod, and nursery-grown plants such as Japanese hollies or Norway maples are planted to "beautify" the site. If any mayapples, turtles, frogs, or patent leather beetles lived on that land before, they don't live there any longer.

The largest, oldest native forest within fifty miles of my house was scraped away to build spec houses and condominiums. I'm sure you have such heartbreaking stories yourself. Now the market has collapsed and many of the units haven't sold. I'm tempted to think that's good, but it doesn't matter. It's too late to go back; it's too late for the trees.

THE SIGN ON this Rhode Island forest says, "It took tremendous effort and great generosity to save this forest. Now everybody can enjoy its beauty and experience what Aquidneck Island looked like prior to European settlement." I silently thanked them all for their effort and generosity. Rhode Island needs this little forest, I need this little forest, and the children who live in this neighborhood need this forest. Let's save more forests like this, if there are any left. If not, let us allow space for new ones.

We need natural land not just for beauty, although that is important, and not just as habitat for other species, although that is important, too. We need it not just to clean our air and our water, both vitally important. Research is beginning to show that we actually need natural places if we are to be mentally healthy humans.

Henry David Thoreau said we need natural land if we plan to raise poets and philosophers: "A town is saved, not more by the righteous men in it than by the woods and swamps that surround it. A township where one primitive forest waves above while another primitive forest rots below,— such a town is fitted to raise not only corn and potatoes, but poets and philosophers for the coming ages."

Each year, more and more children are diagnosed with attention deficit hyperactivity disorder or depression, and more children take prescription medications to treat those problems. We don't really understand if the conditions themselves are increasing or just being diagnosed more often, but there is growing evidence that time spent in nature alleviates the symptoms of these disorders. Adults, too, need nature. I am acutely aware of the healing power of nature in my own life, but I am a sample of one, with no control or recorded data. In the few scientific studies conducted on the subject, the evidence suggests that viewing natural scenes can lower stress levels and speed healing. Time in nature has also been correlated with increased creativity, ability to focus, and even spiritual epiphany. I don't doubt that the very state of our souls may be at risk if we show no respect for the natural world.

Oakland Forest is a success story. Every lot counts.

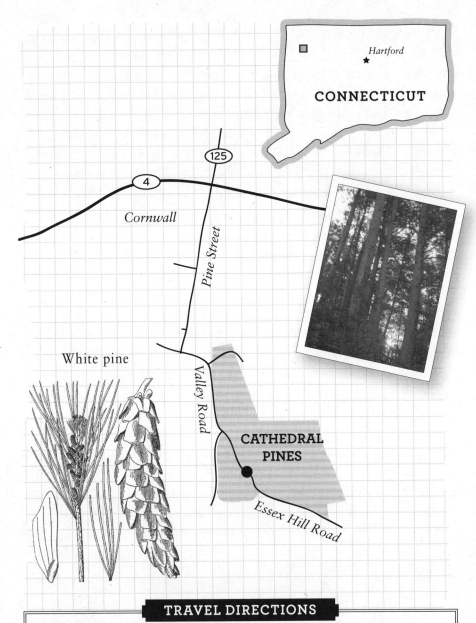

Hartford

CONNECTICUT

125

4

Cornwall

Pine Street

White pine

Valley Road

CATHEDRAL PINES

Essex Hill Road

TRAVEL DIRECTIONS

Northwestern part of state, Litchfield County. Closest town: Cornwall (not West Cornwall). In Cornwall, from the junction of Route 4 and Route 125, turn south onto Pine Street. After 0.3 miles, turn left onto Valley Road. After a sharp right bend in the road, bear left onto Essex Hill Road. In 0.2 miles you will see a blue blaze on a tall tree on the right side of the road, and across from that there will be a large boulder next to a two-car parking area marked with a sign.

Connecticut

CATHEDRAL PINES

Crows...Estimates of natural rotation...Gardens...Controls

I ENTERED THE GROVE on a very chilly early-fall morning. Right away, towering white pines and hemlocks surrounded me. The forest was very quiet; it was too cold for the insects to sing, and the dew-dampened duff on the ground muffled my footsteps. On the tops of the ridges, the shade was so dense that there was almost no undergrowth, just soft, brown forest floor. In the low depressions, where cool air gets trapped and the rainwater flows, ferns covered the forest floor. Crows cawed back and forth to one another, breaking the silence.

Crows are extremely smart and can recognize individual humans. Perhaps they knew the regulars in this forest and were warning each other about the presence of a stranger. Crows eat almost anything, including gypsy moth caterpillars, and I wondered what they were finding among the trees on this cool, still morning. Crows, like deer, roaches, robins, and coyotes, are among the few animals that benefit from our changes to the land. Where humans go, crows follow.

On my travels to various forests, I often saw crows standing along the shoulders of the roads. It took me a while to figure out what they were doing there, but I put it all together one dawn in Tennessee. The road passed through a vast forest where there had been a big moth hatch that morning.

As the moths fluttered across the road, I tried to swerve around them but wasn't always successful. In my rearview mirror, I could see the stunned insects tumble onto the road, and there a crow, patiently waiting. Our deadly cars have harmed many creatures, but crows—and vultures and a few others—have benefited.

THE CATHEDRAL PINES story started out with hope and foresight. It was one of the forests purposefully saved by a caring family. In 1883, during the logging boom, the Calhoun family bought and protected forty-two acres of forest. As everything around it was cut away, the family held fast to its towering trees. The Calhouns held it through multiple generations—for eighty-four years—before donating the land to the Nature Conservancy in 1967. At that time, the tract was considered the best old-growth forest in New England. It was dedicated as a National Natural Landmark in 1982 and seemed securely protected for all time. In fact, other old Connecticut forests were likely allowed to be logged during those years because this one was already protected. But in 1989, the unexpected happened; a storm blew over all but eight acres of Cathedral Pines.

Many, many natural events can destroy ancient forests: fires ignited by lightning strikes, tornadoes, landslides, ice storms, and you-name-it. The big, old trees are laid low, and the smallest saplings, offspring of the ancients, must grow for centuries before the forest looks the way it once did. The natural disturbances come more frequently in some places than in others. For instance, between 1620 and 1950, five different hurricanes hit parts of Massachusetts, but only one hurricane struck Vermont. By determining the average interval between disturbances and the average amount of forest destroyed by each, one can calculate the number of years a given forest is expected to survive before experiencing a natural stand-replacing event. This is called the *estimate of natural rotation*. For various Eastern forests, estimates of natural rotation due to fire range from seventy to three thousand years, and estimates due to wind, from eight hundred to twelve hundred years. Because these figures are averages, some spots within a region will be disturbed more frequently and others less frequently. The trees in Cathedral Pines had escaped disturbance for many years, but time was finally up for most of the stand. This would be a commonplace natural event if we had many old-growth forests, but when there is only one it becomes a tragedy—like dropping your basket of eggs.

FORESTERS CALLED IN after a disturbance event such as this often suggest "salvage logging." The big trees are very valuable and now very dead, they reason, so why not pull them out and sell them? In financial terms this makes sense, but not in ecological terms. The fallen trees contain a concentrated store of nutrients that will be used by a multitude of organisms, such as fungi, worms, insects, algae, and bacteria, if the trees are left on the ground. Those organisms will become food for small mammals, amphibians, reptiles, and insects. After the nutrients pass through those organisms, they are available to plants, so the fallen trees are indirectly feeding new trees. The fallen logs shade and protect seedlings lucky enough to spring up near them and nurse seeds that land on them. The rotted wood eventually becomes moisture-holding soil, which ensures a future healthy forest. Salvaging the fallen trees interrupts these natural patterns. Fortunately, ecologists working for the Nature Conservancy were aware of all this and decided the fallen trees should stay in the Cathedral Pines forest.

WRITER MICHAEL POLLAN (author of *Botany of Desire* and *Omnivore's Dilemma*) lived very close to Cathedral Pines when the blowdown happened. In his 1991 book *Second Nature,* he discussed the community's response in detail. Almost no one, including Pollan, agreed with the Nature Conservancy's decision to leave the trees. He argued that the forest wasn't a true *wilderness* anyway because of fire suppression, evidence of early logging, air pollution, and so on, so why not treat it as a *garden* instead? He feared that nature left to her own devices might create an "impoverished weed patch" where the giant pines used to stand, and suggested restoring the forest by burning the fallen pines and planting new ones.

But as I walked through the forest, I was glad it was owned by the Nature Conservancy, not Pollan or the township. Restoration is appropriate for places where human actions have created scars so deep that it is the only ethical action. Restore, please, the places where mountains were torn apart for coal, where the land was covered for decades by toxic asphalt, or

where we eliminated or poisoned the soil. But *here*, in this place with soil so healthy it springs back under your feet—in this place that, if not untouched by humans, is at least one of the most lightly touched—*here* we should stay out of nature's way.

In *No Man's Garden*, author Daniel Botkin noted, "Three great questions have occupied many philosophers, theologians, poets, and artists and, in modern times, scientists: What is the character of nature undisturbed by human influence? What is the influence of nature on people? What is the influence of people on nature?" We have few answers to the first two questions.

Soon, much too soon, I was out of the big, old trees and in a forest twenty years into recovery from an intense storm. There was more sunlight in the storm-damaged section. Many dead trees lay across the ground, but many small trees were growing up among them. Walking in the recovering forest was not as pleasant as walking through the old trees still standing, and I was disappointed I never got to see the beautiful grove it was before the storm, but it wasn't just the patch of honeysuckle and brambles Pollan had feared. The forest was healing, and I was glad to know that the saplings I saw hadn't been planted, weeded, or fertilized except by nature's hand.

Gardens are nice—I tend one myself—but we have turned almost the entire eastern United States into a garden, if you define a garden as land manipulated by humans according to human desires. Looking out my window, I see my lawn with its trees and flowers. Beyond that, I see a cornfield being manipulated at this very moment from the seat of a tractor. Beyond the field is the road, and on the other side of that a forest that was logged eighty years ago. I have a long vista from this window, but I cannot see a single spot that hasn't been purposefully and dramatically "gardened" by humans.

Why does it matter if a forest is natural or manipulated? Many people, even foresters, have never seen an eastern forest unmanipulated by humans, so it is difficult to convince them of what we have lost. There are aesthetic reasons of course—the beauty of an ancient forest is beyond comparison—but there are other reasons, too. The storm-damaged section of Cathedral Pines is not nearly as beautiful as the area where the big trees still stand, so if beauty were the only benchmark, then it might be better off as a garden. But as a scientist, I have been taught to have a control for all my experiments. If an experiment involves manipulation, the control is a section without manipulation. A control is a comparison, a way of showing what would have happened without your interference. Humans, one of the most recent species to evolve on this planet, have been busy experimenting over most of the land, but we have left very few controls. Even if an old-growth forest has burned or blown over and is no longer beautiful in human terms, it is still valuable as a control.

Controls enable us to study our planet's ecological workings, which we still don't fully understand, and are a baseline against which we can evaluate the impact of human activities. Controls preserve genetic diversity and can harbor species that have not benefited from our changes to the land. People searching for the last ivory-billed woodpeckers didn't expect to find them in the logged areas near town; they looked for them in the wilds of the cypress swamps.

There are some places we can, and should, manipulate, and there are places we should not. But it is difficult for most humans to accept limits. To Pollan I say, if Connecticut were still blessed with many acres of old-growth forest and one small forest in your town was destroyed in a storm, I wouldn't object to restoring it to the park-like place so many citizens enjoyed. But in reality, Connecticut has no sites of more than forty acres that researchers agree are old growth. The famous old-growth Colebrook Forest in North Colebrook was extensive and grand, but it was cut in 1912 and all we have left are a few photographs.

I'm glad Cathedral Pines was preserved, but in some ways it is now a symbol of our foolishness. We put all our eggs in one basket, and the basket blew over. That doesn't give us the right, however, to rush in and make it a garden. We need practice just letting things be—uncomfortable though that may make us. It takes courage to let things be. And, as Anne LaBastille described at the closing of her book *Woodswoman*, it takes an attitude of hope and trust toward the "ordered goodness of our earth" and its "gentle implacable push toward balance, regularity, homeostasis."

Living a life that trusts the earth onto which we have all been born will change not just the outer appearance of the landscape; it will also change our internal landscape. Estimates of natural rotation apply not just to forests, but to human generations, too. Being able to witness these cycles of life may enrich our understanding and acceptance of them. LaBastille spent many years living in the forest and had time to absorb its lessons. It taught her that "some trees get blown over by storms; some stars burn out; some people encounter crippling misfortunes of health or finances. But the forest remains; the skies keep twinkling; and human beings keep striving." She concluded her book with thoughts that arose one dark night as she floated in a small boat, surrounded by her beloved forest:

> Drifting about under the night heavens, I think and hope that I can weather the storms which will blow my way. And that these trials will give me depth and stature so that in old age I can be like my big white pines—dignified, lending beauty to the surroundings, and lifting their heads with strength and serenity to both sun and storms, snowflakes and swallows.

"And the tall shall be made low," it says in the Beatitudes of the Bible. The storms will always come. What matters is how we respond to them.

MASSACHUSETTS

• Springfield

Hop hornbeam

Trailhead

← To North Adams

2

MOHAWK TRAIL
STATE FOREST

To Charlemont,
I-91 →

TRAVEL DIRECTIONS

Northwestern part of state, Berkshire and Franklin Counties. Closest town: Charlemont. From Interstate 91, take exit 26 in Greenfield and follow Route 2 west for twenty-one miles. The park entrance will be clearly marked on the right. If you're coming from North Adams, take Route 2 east for 15.5 miles. The entrance will be on the left.

As you come in the main entrance, turn left toward the information booth. If no one is in the booth, pick up a trail map at the display board. Past the booth, where the road forks, bear right. At the next fork, make another right past a cabin and park near the picnic tables. You will see a gate to your left with a sign for the nature trail. Most of the old growth is along this trail and the Mohican-Mohawk trail. For detailed directions to specific old-growth trees, see *The Sierra Club Guide to the Ancient Forests of the Northeast*.

The park is open daily all year, and overnight between April and October. There are cabins for rent, camping spaces, restrooms, showers, and a swimming pool. For more information, see www.mass.gov/dcr.

Massachusetts

MOHAWK TRAIL STATE FOREST

*Gypsy moth caterpillars...Ruffled grouse...Bob Leverett...
Death comes to trees and humans*

I T WAS A perfect day. The sky was that clean, bright blue that burns its way into every cell of your brain. The cool, mostly calm air was disturbed only by an occasional gentle breeze. I was walking on a path the native people had used. These trees had been here so long that Native Americans had touched many of the same ones I was touching.

On days like this, in places like this, we are tempted to imagine that the forest we are experiencing is the same today as it was thousands of years ago. But no forest in eastern North America is truly "virgin." Contamination of our vast air and water systems reaches every place through acid rain, for example, or global warming. The Chestnut blight and the gypsy moth caterpillar are examples of a different sort. We rarely know when, where, or how a foreign invasive species was introduced, but we know those facts about the gypsy moth.

The story began here in Massachusetts in the mid-nineteenth century, when a twenty-five-year-old French immigrant named Leopold Trouvelot settled with his wife in the suburbs of Boston. He made his living painting portraits, but he was also fascinated by insects. He immediately started studying the caterpillars of his new continent. Particularly interested in caterpillars that produced silk for their cocoons, he began cultivating native

Polyphemus caterpillars, which pupate into large and beautiful moths with "eye spots" on their hind wings. When he was forty years old, Trouvelot published a paper in a respected scientific journal. In it he wrote:

> In 1860, after having tested the qualities of the cocoons of the different species of American silk worms, I endeavored to accumulate a large number of the cocoons of the Polyphemus moth, for the future propagation of this species. At first the undertaking seemed very simple; but who will ever know the difficulties, the hardships and discouragements which I encountered.

Today that passage seems prescient, but when he wrote it no one, including Trouvelot himself, had any idea of what was to come. The difficulties, hardships, and discouragements have multiplied greatly since then. He continued:

> By 1865 I came to be expert in cultivating them and in that year not less than a million could be seen feeding in the open air upon bushes covered with a net; five acres of woodland were swarming with caterpillar life.

He should have known better, but a few years later he returned from a trip to France with some gypsy-moth-caterpillar egg masses. He cultivated these new caterpillars on trees behind his house, as he had with the Polyphemus, and some of them escaped. Trouvelot understood the potential consequences of this accident and notified local entomologists, but they did nothing. How could they have imagined what would occur because a few foreign caterpillars escaped?

Although he closed his paper on Polyphemus with "to be continued...," Trouvelot stopped working with insects after the accidental release. He literally turned his sights toward the sky. Perhaps he had come to think of himself as too dangerous for this planet and wanted to do less harm by studying something untouchable—astronomical bodies.

Trouvelot put his art training to use drawing what he saw through Harvard University's telescope. In those days, the human eye was much more sensitive than the photographic plates available. He went on to produce more than seven thousand absolutely beautiful astronomical drawings and publish fifty more scientific papers, eventually joining Harvard's faculty as an astronomy professor. A crater on the moon was named in his honor, and he won a prestigious award from the French Academy of Sciences. He became somewhat famous, and was not yet infamous.

The year of the first gypsy moth outbreak on his street, 1882, Trouvelot moved back to France. I can't help thinking this wasn't a coincidence; he was only fifty-five and held an enviable academic position. Why would he have wanted to leave? The gypsy moths grew more problematic every year, and by 1889 an aggressive campaign had been initiated against them, including burning, egg scraping, and pesticide application. Eleven years later, the campaign ended in failure. Meanwhile, back in France, Trouvelot had died.

THE U.S. FOREST Service has produced an excellent animation for its website illustrating the spread of the gypsy moth. It begins with a white map on a white screen with state borders outlined in black. The gypsy moths first appear as a magenta dot in Massachusetts, which then spreads across the map like red wine spreading across a white carpet. As I write this, the stain stretches from Maine west to the Great Lakes and south to the Carolinas.

Not every forest within the reddish stain is plagued by gypsy moths every year. If the areas with intense infestations in any given year were shown as a darker color on the map, we would see the darker areas pulsating—appearing and disappearing. Just because gypsy moths have been a problem in a forest once doesn't mean they'll be a problem there again. If we were to examine the map on a finer scale, we'd see that some forests within the stain have had gypsy moth population explosions numerous times, while others have never been bothered.

The forest I was in suffered an outbreak of gypsy moth caterpillars in 1981, but they haven't been back since. Like most things in nature, we do not entirely understand what is happening. Why do caterpillar populations explode in some areas and not in others in any given year? Is it related to the spread of predators or parasites, or small-scale weather patterns? Who knows? Some interesting research has linked mice and gypsy moth populations with "masting" oak trees—that is, oaks that are producing many more acorns than usual in a given year. But this certainly doesn't explain all the variation.

On the gypsy moths' home ground in Asia, there lives a fungus deadly to the caterpillars. In 1910, early in the battle, this fungus was imported and released. To everyone's disappointment, the experiment failed. But then, seventy-nine years later, after everyone involved in the experiment was dead, the very same fungus caused a massive die-off of gypsy moth caterpillars in New England. It is impossible to say if the killer fungus came from the original introduction or some other, accidental introduction, or if the spores found their way here naturally, perhaps on air currents. More natural mysteries we cannot yet solve.

THIS FOREST IS known for its tall white pines, but there are also many leafy trees here, including oak, hop hornbeam, and big tooth aspen. These last two are favorite foods of the ruffed grouse, a strange bird more at home on the ground than in the sky. Grouse like to eat tree buds through the winter and early spring, and pollen-producing catkins in the late spring. In the summer, the fan-tailed birds turn to other foods, including caterpillars and amphibians. (One hunter found a live salamander on a bed of watercress in a ruffed grouse's stomach.) All of these foods are more abundant in an older forest, so when ancient forest acreage shrinks the grouse populations shrink, too. A famous example of this is a bird survey in Ohio in 1906. The survey found abundant grouse in one county before the forests were cut; after they were cut, grouse were no longer found there.

Many hikers, myself included, have been startled by an animal rushing out at them from the dense undergrowth along the side of a trail. The momentary fear is real, but once the heartbeat slows, knowing one has seen a grouse in the wild makes the fright more than worth it.

You are much more likely to hear a grouse than see one, especially during the spring courtship season. Like most male birds, the ruffed grouse emits sounds to claim its territory and attract females, but unlike most birds, it doesn't call vocally. Instead, it beats its wings against the air, generating low, slow, thumping pulsations that gradually speed up. The first time they hear it, most people don't realize the drumming is coming from a bird. As one writer put it in the colorful language of 1913, "it is the bird's best expression of its abounding vigor and virility, and signifies that the drummer is ready for love or war."

A male grouse always drums from the same exact spot, facing the same direction. He prefers the root end of a large, old, moss-covered tree that has

fallen naturally, a perch that enables him to see farther through the forest. He prefers a hardwood forest, too, for the same reason: With leaves off the trees in the early spring, he can spy potential mates—or predators—approaching. If you convert an old hardwood forest to a young pine plantation, you are converting it to a place without the sight or sounds of ruffed grouse.

Many states have enlisted the help of "citizen scientists" willing to survey for drumming sounds in the spring, an economical way to monitor the birds' population. Although the ruffed grouse has a wide range and its population is cyclical, it seems to be in decline overall as old-forest acreage shrinks and abundant deer graze away their protective cover.

ALTHOUGH I KNEW there were grouse here in this large forest with the structure and food they prefer, it was fall and the birds were quiet. I was looking for a small, unmarked trail that would lead me to the Jake Swamp Pine—the tallest tree in Massachusetts (that week, anyway, since such titles are constantly challenged). The narrow trail led me down into a hillside swale where I was surrounded by straight trunks. The trees' diameters were not notably impressive compared to what I have seen in other places, but the soaring heights they reached dazzled me. I found what must be the Jake Swamp Pine, marked by just a small white stone at its base.

We know about this tree and have a name for it because of Bob Leverett, a self-described "forest nut" and, I would argue, eastern old growth's most important living advocate. In 1996, he helped found the Eastern Native Tree Society, a network for forest nuts like us to champion trees and share information about old-growth forests. He is also executive director of Friends of the Mohawk Forest, so he has spent many, many hours in this forest.

Leverett named this tall white pine for Jake Swamp, a Mohawk chief who heads the Tree of Peace Society, which "emphasizes individual responsibility for one's actions, a deep personal relationship with the natural world, and the acknowledgment that all living things are blessings from the creator to be treated with sensitivity and respect."

Native Americans have lovely, lyrical terms for living beings. We are the *Two-Leggeds*, but we share the planet with the *Four-Leggeds*, the *Winged Ones*, and the *Water Beings*. Trees are the *Standing Ones* (or, sometimes, the *Standing People*). The Two-Leggeds and the Standing Ones have something in common, in that both are vertical and have the potential for being very long-lived—although trees can reach even further into the sky and live more centuries than we can. Perhaps this combination of commonality and exceptionality is why we are drawn to honor humans by naming trees after them, and to honor trees by naming humans after them (I think of Holly, Aspen, and others).

In September of 2002, along with a few volunteers, I tagged almost three thousand living trees in a Maryland forest near my home. Each tree was loosely circled with red yarn from which hung a metal tag with the name of a person killed on September 11, 2001. The tagging served a dual purpose: to memorialize the victims and to attempt to save a public forest from being clear-cut. Four years later, the forest was still standing, but as the trees grew the yarn had become tighter. Anything encircling a tree too tightly can cut off its "circulation" and kill it; how ironic it would be if we were the ones responsible for killing the trees! The yarn would have to be removed.

In September 2006, I went back into the forest with a pair of scissors. As I cut the yarn and removed the tags, I noticed that some of the trees—mostly smaller ones—had died. They hadn't died because of the yarn but because their time was up. Perhaps they were too shaded, infested by insects, or genetically weak. It made me think of the individuals whose names were on those tags. They had been dead for five years, and their families probably assumed that, if it weren't for the tragedy of that day, their loved one would still be alive. But in reality, a small portion of those victims would have died in the meantime from other causes. Even young ones.

In yesterday's newspaper, I read a story about a fourteen-year-old boy who went swimming in a warm, shallow pond in Arizona, where an amoeba that feeds on brain tissue splashed up his nose. A week later he complained of a headache, was taken to the hospital, and soon died. "Two weeks ago he was fine," his father was quoted as saying, "and now I'm here burying him."

Death can come at any time, for trees or for people. Many of us have mourned the death of a tree we were very familiar with, perhaps one we had planted on the lawn, but our experience of forest trees is usually much less personal. And the loss of one tree in a forest simply gives a younger tree standing nearby the chance to fill its fallen comrade's ecological niche.

I have argued in these pages for the welcome, and necessary, role of death in the forest, but in our complex human culture, mourning is a response to a niche that feels suddenly empty. Who could ever replace that particular person?

Because of my interest in native forests, I have gotten to know other people who have dedicated much of their lives to educating others and speaking out on behalf of the non-human inhabitants of the forest. Their research and their kindred spirits have been part of the fuel keeping my inner light glowing. Now, one after another, they are dying: Bill Whitmore, Bob DeGroot, Bob Zahner.

The last on my list of irreplaceable forest advocates who died in 2007 was Bruce Kershner. I never had the honor of meeting him, but I followed in many of his footsteps, walking the same trails and touching the same trees. He understood the old forests of the East better, perhaps, than anyone. Often his was the final determination in deciding if a forest was old growth or not, and if he said it was old growth, I was interested in visiting it. Just seven months after his death, Kershner was honored by New York State's passage of the "Bruce S. Kershner Old-Growth Forest Preservation and Protection Act," which protects all old-growth forests on state land in New York. He is one man who really made a difference. Although I never knew him personally, and cannot miss him in that way, I mourn the fact that I will never get to meet him, and that the world has lost one more important old-forest advocate.

Leverett has felt the sting of loss, too. Another of the ancient trees here he named the Jani Pine, in honor of his deceased wife, and recently he named another in memory of Kershner, his good friend and co-author.

As I hiked through this Massachusetts forest, I reminded myself that these men who loved forests understood the *Whole* of which the German poet Rainer Maria Rilke wrote. To a friend who had recently lost someone, Rilke wrote:

> All of our true relations, all of our penetrating experiences reach through the Whole, through life and death; we have to live in both, be intimately at home in both.... We are true and pure only in our willingness toward the whole.

In the forest, it is somewhat easier to accept the lessons of the Whole. But I still feel a space where each of these men stood, and pray there will be other special humans who rise up to fill the spaces they have left. The Persian poet Rumi said, "Days are sieves to filter spirit / reveal impurities, and too, / show the light of some who throw / their own shining into the universe." These special men have indeed thrown their shining into the universe. Now it is someone else's turn to shine.

WHEN THE TAGS came off the trees in the September 11th Memorial Forest, county officials announced that forty acres of it would be clear-cut. As bulldozers pushed roads through the forest, these officials tried to tell the reporter covering the story I cared about it only because it was in my backyard—as if that were something selfish. I hope someday more people will understand that when tree huggers work for the protection of a forest, we are not just working for our own pleasure. We care not just because it is our backyard; we care because it is the backyard of the world—including, if we are fortunate, ruffed grouse.

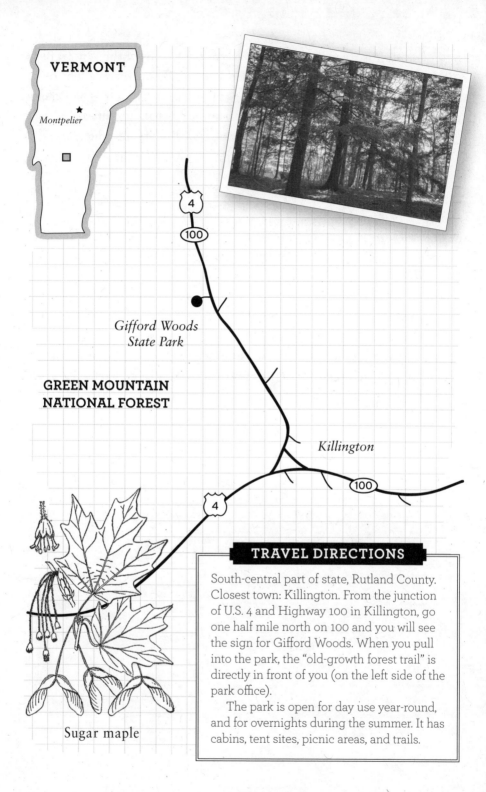

VERMONT

Montpelier

4

100

Gifford Woods
State Park

**GREEN MOUNTAIN
NATIONAL FOREST**

Killington

100

4

Sugar maple

TRAVEL DIRECTIONS

South-central part of state, Rutland County.
Closest town: Killington. From the junction
of U.S. 4 and Highway 100 in Killington, go
one half mile north on 100 and you will see
the sign for Gifford Woods. When you pull
into the park, the "old-growth forest trail" is
directly in front of you (on the left side of the
park office).

The park is open for day use year-round,
and for overnights during the summer. It has
cabins, tent sites, picnic areas, and trails.

Vermont

GIFFORD WOODS STATE PARK

Something wilder...Increment coring...Sugar maples...Slugs

THE BACK ROADS of Vermont looked like scenes from a picture postcard. A small bridge lifted me over a rocky stream; around the corner, I found a perfectly proportioned barn with a stone foundation. A horse grazed in the pasture, of course, and weeds bloomed along the fencerow. A bit further along I reached the store selling maple syrup, watering cans, homemade cookies, and anything else you might want. Then came the village, with its mix of architectural styles, the occasional perfect vegetable garden, and porches that looked like movie sets. But those apples in the barrel would get eaten, the broom would sweep, those boots would be worn, and those birds would really fly.

One more turn and I was there, Gifford Woods, advertised as "Vermont's best known old-growth northern hardwood stand, with many grand individual trees of sugar maple, beech, yellow birch, basswood, white ash, and hemlock."

The trail was shady, rocky, and ferny, and I saw a diverse range of species; but when I started down it, I discovered that it was a loop so small I could see people on the other side, even in the middle of a leafy summer. The trees were labeled, and there were stumps where dead trees had been removed. The trail covered one pitiful acre. Honestly.

I found myself wanting something wilder.

*   *   *

ACROSS THE ROAD from the park entrance was an unmanaged seven-acre patch of old growth. It had no trails, and the snags were still standing. I never escaped the sound of traffic, but on the other side of the road, I immediately felt *it*—that old-growth something I was missing on the manicured trail.

As I made my way carefully through the ferns and fallen wood, I wondered why this particular slice of forest got "saved." Not because of inaccessibility—it wasn't in a steep-sided ravine or far from a road. In fact, quite the opposite: it was in a particularly accessible spot for Vermont.

It wasn't protected by an owner who believed in preserving forest. The former owner, Walter Barrows, also operated a sawmill and logged thousands and thousands of acres in the surrounding area. It might have been saved because the large sugar maples were a source of syrup, but I like to imagine this particular forest was saved because Barrows felt *it,* too. He was willing and eager to make money logging, but he wanted one place where he could picnic with a friend—a lovely spot, easy to get to by wagon and with a water view. Beneath the shade of the big trees, they could watch the birds and the squirrels while enjoying their food. This was my own little movie, of course, and I wasn't quite sure whether to think of Barrows as a villain or a hero. Most likely he had shades of both, as we all do. The final test, I suppose, is that the forest still stands.

We know how old the trees are in Gifford Woods because they were studied intensively in 1964 by researchers who used increment corers to determine their ages. An increment corer is a long, thin, hollow metal tube that screws into the heart of a tree; it removes a narrow cylinder of wood in which the annual rings can be counted, starting with the first ring in the center. Researchers and foresters who use this technique will tell you it isn't harmful to the tree, and while I can understand why they would think that, I have read enough evidence to the contrary that I would never core a tree unless absolutely necessary. I would certainly need a reason beyond curiosity.

A cored tree never truly heals; it cannot grow new cells to fill the space. Instead, the tree forms a barrier of special cells around the injury in an attempt to halt further progression of the wound. In some species, such as the conifers, resinous sap quickly fills the holes and the coring seems to do no permanent harm, but in other species, the hole creates an entry point for fungal spores.

The outside of the hole may close, but inside, for the rest of its life, a tree will carry evidence of the damage. If the researcher returns in three years, the tree may look fine, but will he return in forty years? If he does, will he be able to locate the cored tree? If it has died after forty years—perhaps hundreds of years before it would have otherwise—who will write that research paper, or take responsibility for that tree's death?

Forty-three years after that study in Gifford Woods, I walked through the same forest wondering which of the dead trees I saw had died as the eventual result of someone's curiosity. I wondered which of the ancient ones held a small, inner wound. The sugar maples here were approaching three hundred years old, and one hemlock was well over four hundred.

Although I like to think Barrows saved this patch of forest for aesthetic reasons, most likely it was because of the sugar maples. By the early 1800s, two-thirds of all the farm families in Vermont participated in producing maple sugar or syrup. Much of the forest was being logged out in this era, but families would often leave a small patch of "sugarbush" uncut to provide them with this uniquely North American sweetener.

Most accounts say early settlers learned how to make maple syrup from the Native Americans, implying native people were involved in this activity since prehistoric times. Upon closer scrutiny, however, this story is suspect. Current scholarship on human utilization of the sap points to early French settlers in Canada. While it remains a mystery whether the French taught the natives or the other way around, whoever decided to tap the first maple tree likely learned it from the animals.

Birds called sapsuckers peck holes into numerous types of trees to obtain the slightly sweet sap. These birds have a good understanding of how sap flows: they always make new holes above old holes, because the holes block the downward flow of sap, and therefore the area directly above an old hole produces the largest flow.

Sapsuckers are most active during their nesting time. They catch insects, dip them in the sweet sap, and then carry the treats to their nestlings waiting in a tree cavity. Ruby-throated hummingbirds don't have beaks strong enough to make holes in the bark, but they often take advantage of the sapsuckers' work and sip from their holes. This source of nutrition is so important to the hummingbirds that it may be why their spring arrival closely matches that of the yellow-bellied sapsucker—often before any woodland flowers bloom.

Squirrels also like the sugar in the sap. In late winter, just before the sap starts to rise, they bite into the trunks of sugar maple trees, leaving behind a pair of small parallel grooves. The squirrels don't use the sap right away, but wait for it to drip down the tree and evaporate on the bark, leaving behind a sticky trail. They then return and lick the sugar from the bark.

Although tapping for syrup creates a wound, it is less harmful to a tree than coring. The tap goes in only a few inches, not to the center, and responsible syrup producers don't tap a tree until it measures more than thirty inches in circumference, and then limit themselves to three taps per tree. A good-sized tree will yield ten to twenty gallons of sap, which is cooked down to half a gallon of syrup. All the sugar in the sap was produced by the leaves the previous summer and stored in the roots over the winter. In late winter and early spring, the sugars are pushed back up to the buds to fuel the rapid expansion of new leaves and flowers. We are borrowing from this bank of solar energy when we sweeten our pancakes.

As maple sugar and syrup production became more popular, it moved south and became an important trade item for Native Americans. By the 1880s, though, cane sugar had become cheaper than maple sugar, and from that time on maple syrup became a specialty item, just one of many products produced on New England farms. The intense but short production period became, more than anything, a welcome way to bring families and tribes together at the end of a long winter.

So, MAYBE SYRUP saved this grove, but the trees had earned their retirement. I was glad to be in the *real* old growth, alone, moving slowly and quietly through the ferny forest. Then something slower and more silent than I could ever hope to be caught my attention. A tiny spotted slug was moving across the damp green moss. As I took the time to observe and appreciate it, I began to see just what a miracle it is for such a creature to survive. This slug was completely at my mercy; it could not run away, or sting me, or even retreat into a shell. Evolutionary biologists tell us that slugs evolved from snails; eliminating the shell was actually an evolutionary step forward. Our species took a similar leap toward vulnerability when we lost our fur.

This slug's vulnerability enabled me to begin to understand what its world was like. I could put my face just inches from its face and imagine a slow journey through cool moss. From that perspective, a logging truck or even the bottom of a boot would appear disastrous. I was becoming quite attached to the little slug and wondered what species it was—I had never seen one like it. One can memorize numerous features of a bird or a plant, and check the field guides to identify it back at home, but there's not much to memorize about a slug. Identification is usually made by preserving a specimen in formaldehyde or alcohol and bringing it to an expert in a laboratory who examines the breathing pore, the genital openings, and the folds of the intestines. I didn't have a jar of preservative with me, but even if I did, it would have been very difficult for me to put my new friend into it.

I later asked a park employee about the slug species, but he didn't know what it was either. There are thirty-two species of slugs in the United States. In the Pacific Northwest, a large yellow one, the banana slug, is an indicator of old-growth forests. We have no idea if there is an eastern old-growth-indicator slug species. Perhaps it is my little spotted friend.

I wish Barrows had left more of Vermont's original forest, but I am thankful he at least spared this grove. If slugs can be thankful, I'm sure they are, too.

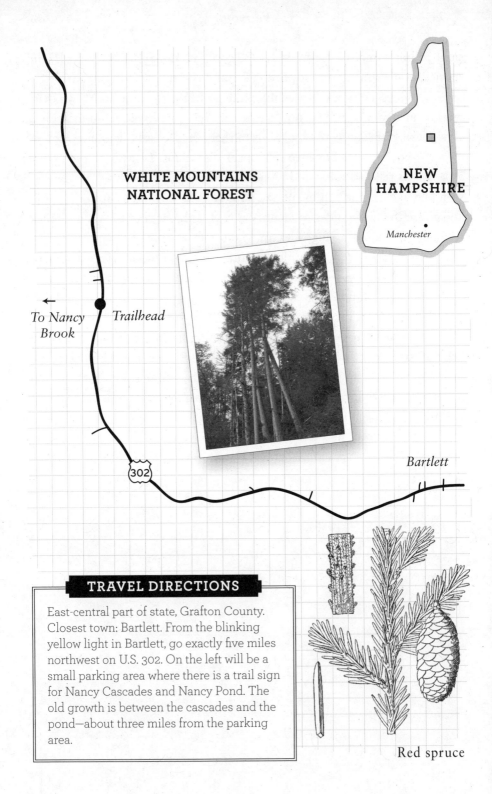

**WHITE MOUNTAINS
NATIONAL FOREST**

**NEW
HAMPSHIRE**

Manchester

To Nancy
Brook

Trailhead

302

Bartlett

TRAVEL DIRECTIONS

East-central part of state, Grafton County.
Closest town: Bartlett. From the blinking
yellow light in Bartlett, go exactly five miles
northwest on U.S. 302. On the left will be a
small parking area where there is a trail sign
for Nancy Cascades and Nancy Pond. The
old growth is between the cascades and the
pond—about three miles from the parking
area.

Red spruce

New Hampshire

Nancy Brook Natural Area, White Mountains National Forest

Red spruce...The hero's journey...The need for eco-reserves

THE TRAIL TO the old growth in New Hampshire is not for the faint of heart or knee—it is uphill and rocky. Many old-growth forests have escaped logging through guardianship or legislation; this one survived because it was so difficult to get to, then and now. At mile two-and-a-half, you are rewarded with a waterfall, Nancy Cascades, which is so shady, cool, and lovely it makes you want to go no further. But if you want to get to the old growth you must, and then the trail gets even steeper and rockier.

Every forest is unique, but what makes this one especially so is that the oldest trees are the red spruce, evergreens with short needles attached to the twigs singly in all directions, unlike hemlocks. There are many slight variations in the evergreen palette, and when you become sensitive to them, you can see that red spruce needles take their place on the yellow-green end of the spectrum. Another way to identify an evergreen is to shake hands with it; hemlock and fir are soft, but spruce will make you say "ouch."

If you are seeking a stroll through huge trees, this is not the place. Considering all the effort it takes to get here, the trees are not impressively large; I can almost get my arms around them. Tree size, though, is not always an indicator of age. When conditions are not ideal for red spruce, they grow very, very slowly. Some trees increase their stem diameter by less than a third of an inch in ten years, and a four- to five-foot-tall tree might be fifty years old. The trees here are truly ancient—some have been cored and found to be more than four hundred years old—but high on this hillside the wind is harsh and drying, the soil thin and rocky, and the growing season just a blip in the long, cold year. Nearby, on top of Mount Washington, where conditions are even more extreme, some old-growth trees are only knee high! Persistence, not size, is their strong suit.

And nature's challenges have been compounded by human-created challenges. All along the eastern Appalachian mountain chain, from New England to Georgia, growth rates have declined in high-elevation red spruce since the 1960s, and the consensus is that air pollution is to blame. Today this seems sadly ironic; as I swoon with pleasure at the clean, green scent they release into the air, they suffer from burned needles caused by vapors emitted by our machines.

SOME OF MY friends cannot imagine why I travel so far to see ancient forests, but Nancy, who has studied mythology for years, says I am on a quest, a hero's journey. As I packed for this trip, she urged me to take her copy of *The Hero with a Thousand Faces*, by Joseph Campbell, who studied the mythological hero's journey from the differing perspectives of many cultures worldwide. This is not light reading, but one line resonated with me: "The passage of the mythological hero may be overground, incidentally; fundamentally it is inward—into depths where obscure resistances are overcome, and long lost, forgotten powers are revivified, to be made available for the transfiguration of the world."

Am I on a quest to transfigure the world? As I read, I began to see the parallels my friend had seen. "The usual person," Campbell wrote, "is more than content, he is even proud, to remain within the indicated bounds, and popular belief gives him every reason to fear so much as the first step into the unexplored." But I was not content to remain within bounds. I had heard the call and wanted to experience the ancient forests firsthand. My question was as much about how to grow old myself as it was about how trees grow old. In the ancient forests, I sensed an authenticity missing in the younger, disturbed plots. Could the forests teach me lessons about human life, I wondered? Do old trees hold clues for how best to become old humans?

For a journey of this sort, one must first separate and become detached from typical worldly activities, a transfiguration Campbell calls both a dying and a birth. My formal leave of absence from my teaching job and my informal leave from my gardens, my housekeeping, and my usual volunteering were deliberate, necessary measures. Of course, we are all on a hero's journey of sorts, but this year in particular I sensed all the strands coming together: self-confidence, physical health, economic means, openness to adventure, a deep love for the planet, a mature understanding of how the planet functions, despair over how we are changing it, and a desire to make a difference.

My initial anger at the destruction of our forests had begun to manifest as a respect for the individuals who have cared enough to save what is left, an awareness of how many others care, and a renewed sense of hope for a better future for our forests and the many creatures that live in them.

WHAT IS HAPPENING in New Hampshire is a great example of what could and should be happening in every state. In 1901, a group of committed citizens formed the Society for the Protection of New Hampshire Forests to try to curb the destructive logging. Membership swelled, donations grew, and now the group boasts ten thousand members and owns more than forty thousand acres, with conservation easements on many more. The society's original vision was that logging would continue in a responsible, sustainable manner. In 2001, however, the trustees recognized that even sustainable logging has long-term effects. So little old, unlogged forest remains, they reasoned, that the responsible thing to do is create more of it. Consequently, they created a management category called *eco-reserve*. "This designation," said Mike Smith, chairman of the trustees, "means that these lands will always stay primitive and wild, free of roads, timber harvesting, or other human intervention, except for that necessary to manage hiking trails and other public recreational use. Over time, these forests will develop old-growth characteristics that are virtually absent from the New Hampshire landscape after centuries of intensive land use. Old forests are important to wildlife, preservation of biological diversity, and to people."

As of this writing, they have classified more than six thousand acres as eco-reserves and expect to eventually designate 30 percent of all their holdings. There is at least one eco-reserve in each of New Hampshire's counties, and all are open to the public. "The hope is that three hundred years from now, all Forest Society eco-reserves will contain old-growth forest structures," said Peter Ellis, the Society's forest ecologist.

Future old-growth forests: I love that. Why can't we do this throughout the forested states of our nation? At least one in every county, all open to the public; seeds of hope sprinkled throughout our land.

Good work is being done in many places, as in New Hampshire, but elsewhere long-term forest protection has not been a priority. The sheer bureaucracy required to form an organization often overwhelms people who care. Still, I dream of the birth of a network that would recognize or create publicly accessible old-growth or future old-growth reserves throughout the country. To be sure that no areas are forgotten and everybody can visit one, there should be at least one in *every county*. In some counties, such reserves already exist and merely need to be recognized, but direct support, funding, or mandates may be needed in others.

This may seem too ambitious and unlikely, but our federal government has supported such ecologically necessary and forward-thinking measures before. In the late 1800s, a small group of reformers recognized that our natural resources were being exploited and endangered, and they introduced bills in Congress to protect the nation's forests. Congress passed the Forest Reserve Act in 1891 authorizing the creation of forest reserves, the forerunner of the National Forest System. I am forever grateful for the foresight, courage, and hard work it took to make that happen.

At first it might seem the reserves I have in mind could simply be carved from the national forests, but seven states do not have any national forests, and in the states that do, not every county contains national forest land. My vision requires a different sort of program.

The U.S. Department of Agriculture's Healthy Forests Reserve Program was signed into law in 2003, but as of now it is poorly funded and little known. In 2006, only landowners in Maine, Arkansas, and Mississippi were eligible for the program. Its goals—enhancing forest ecosystems, promoting the recovery of endangered species, and improving biodiversity—might seem to perfectly mesh with my vision of an old-growth network, but a closer look reveals its shortcomings: only private or tribal land is eligible for enrollment, and public access is not required.

National Natural Landmarks, another innovative federal program, "aims to encourage and support voluntary preservation of sites that illustrate the geological and ecological history of the United States, and to strengthen the public's appreciation of America's natural heritage based on the premise that the job of protecting the nation's natural heritage is everyone's responsibility." Unlike the National Forest System or the Healthy Forests Reserve Program, both in the Department of Agriculture, this program is in the Department of the Interior, which alone should give it an advantage. After all, if you are viewing trees as a crop, you are unlikely to leave them alone. No landowner-ship category is excluded, which sounds great, but only two new landmarks were named between 1989 and 2009. And, unfortunately, sites declared National Natural Landmarks are not required to be accessible to anyone else except the wealthy people who own them. How can that be right?

Everyone, young and old, needs to see and experience these places. We have plenty of "green" spaces, such as farms or parks, but few where nature reigns. How will we really know our planet if we never see it in its natural, unmanipulated condition, in its "suchness," as the Buddhists might say?

We need something else: a network. This is the vision that grew out of my journeys. Perhaps quest *is* the right word.

ON THE STEEPEST part of the hillside, surrounded by ancient red spruce and yellow birch, I sat on a rock in the middle of the narrow trail to breathe the delicious air and take a few notes. I hadn't seen any other hikers all day and so assumed I wouldn't be in anyone's way, but after a few minutes, I heard the *tap-tap* of metal hiking poles on rock. I looked up to see a woman my age approaching from above. When I stood to let her pass, a conversation quickly started. Her husband arrived behind her and joined in. They had traveled from Washington State to enjoy the rocky trails and early fall colors of the deciduous trees in New Hampshire. In fewer than ten minutes, I learned that this stranger I met high on an otherwise deserted mountain path had written a book on mythology, complete with a chapter on the hero's journey.

My friend Nancy tells me that once the call has been heard and the journey begun, signs and helpers will appear.

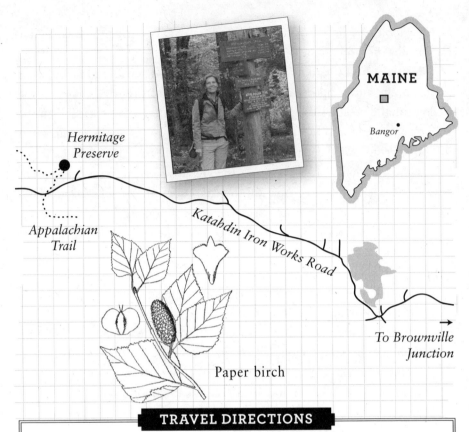

Hermitage
Preserve

Appalachian
Trail

Katahdin Iron Works Road

MAINE

Bangor

To Brownville
Junction

Paper birch

TRAVEL DIRECTIONS

Central part of the state, Piscataquis County. Closest town: Brownville Junction. From the town of Milo, take Route 11 north for twelve miles. This will take you through the hamlet of Brownville Junction, where you will see a sign for Katahdin Iron Works on the left. If you are coming from Millinocket, take Route 11 south for twenty-five miles to the entrance gate on the right. After you turn off 11 toward Katahdin Iron Works, go seven miles on the gravel road. There will be a checkpoint (open 6:00 a.m. to 9:00 p.m.) where you pay the entrance fee. Although the Nature Conservancy property is free and open to the public, you must cross timber company property to get there, and you will be charged for this access. I recommend purchasing the trail map available at the checkpoint.

Travel another seven miles on a gravel logging road to the trailhead. Be sure you have plenty of gas and a good spare tire. Watch out for the logging trucks. There is a short trail to the Pleasant River from the parking area. You must cross a wide but shallow river filled with slippery rocks to get to the Hermitage Preserve. The Gulf Hagas trail continues from there. Because of the slippery stream crossing and the steep ledges along the trail, I recommend this hike for adults only. There are good camping spots all through the Katahdin Iron Works Jo-Mary forest, but no camping is allowed on the Gulf Hagas trail.

Maine

HERMITAGE PRESERVE, GULF HAGAS

*Appalachian Trail…Roxanne Quimby…Baxter State Park…
Howland Forest*

*I*T WAS SEPTEMBER in Maine, and if that brings to mind blue skies, cool breezes, and yellow maple leaves, you could have almost been there with me as I stood on a bed of soft needles and tilted my head far back to see the tops of the tall, tall white pines.

Although I had my socks and boots back on, my toes were still cool and damp from crossing the river barefoot. In 1892 an immigrant built a cabin, Thoreauvian style, here on a bank of the wide, shallow river under tall white pines that sang in the breeze. Just a short walk away was a lovely, twisting waterfall. Campbell Young was happy to live alone in these woods like a hermit. His cabin is gone now, but the pines still stand—some of the few ancient trees in a vast working landscape. The Nature Conservancy bought the land under the big pines in 1967, a sparkling jewel in a sea of timberland.

The 2,170-mile Appalachian Trail that runs from Georgia to Maine twists and turns its last hundred miles through this area, ending at the top of Mount Katahdin. Most people trying to hike the whole trail in one year start in Georgia with the first blush of spring and walk north with true spring following closely behind. At some point in the journey, spring catches up and becomes summer, and by the time they make it to Maine, summer has turned to fall. Of the estimated sixteen hundred people who start the hike each year, only a few hundred make it this far. This section is called the Hundred-Mile Wilderness and is the most remote section of the trail. There are no stores or post offices where supplies can be picked up; what you enter with is all you will have. Although it is called a wilderness because it is remote from the conveniences of civilization, the timber companies that own this land log to within a few hundred feet of the trail. The Appalachian Trail has been nick-named "the long green tunnel" because it is surrounded by forest, but only a minuscule fraction of the tunnel passes through old growth.

While crossing the river, I met a through-hiker. It had taken him months to get to this spot, and it had taken me many hours of driving, but we could see almost all of the Hermitage Preserve while standing in one spot. These few acres couldn't really be considered a *forest*, but the towering trees gave us an idea of what the surrounding forest used to look like.

Although the hiker had seen very little old-growth forest, he had seen millions of trees in the past few months. As we hiked together we talked trees, discussing how some seem to live long and well even under poor con-ditions and others die young even though they landed as seeds in seemingly good locations. We were speaking of trees, but I was thinking the same was true for people: how some, seemingly blessed at birth, lived short or painful lives, while others, born into difficult circumstances, outlived or outloved the majority as if some special light shone on them. Nothing is certain in this life, for humans or trees.

The trail was a delight of waterfalls and fallen leaves, chipmunks and clean air. Although we were soon out of the old growth, we were still sur-rounded by forest. Here in the North, needle-leaved trees dominate—be-sides the white pines, there are red spruce and hemlocks. Broadleaf birches and maples give the forest its fall color, but many other broadleaf species, such as oak, sweet gum, and sassafras, are missing from this forest; the growing season here is too brief for them. If I were to continue traveling north, out of the U.S. even, I would see fewer and fewer deciduous trees un-til I was in an entirely evergreen forest, the great Boreal Forest of the North.

MAINE HAS A particularly interesting arboreal history. In the state's ear-ly years, the government granted or sold vast tracks of old-growth forest in plots measured not in acres but in miles. Thirty-six-square-mile plots were typical, and most became the property of investment groups—men who lived elsewhere, in civilized cities, but directed local loggers to cut and sell in their name. As Thoreau noted, "The mission of men there seems to be, like so many busy demons, to drive the forest out of all the country, from every solitary beaver-swamp and mountain-side, as soon as possible."

Things haven't changed all that much. As corporations finish logging their land today, they sell it to other investment partnerships willing to hold it for longer as part of a diversified portfolio. Pension-fund holding companies, in particular, are fond of these long-term investments, and you can be sure they plan to cut the forest again eventually.

Throughout Maine, acre after acre, mile after mile, the big trees have all been logged out. Where did they go? The answers are myriad. Some uses spring quickly to mind—ship masts, barn timbers, railroad ties—but most were put to much less dignified uses. Giant, ancient trees were cut into little tiny pieces to make all sorts of things; Thoreau mentions shingles and matches, but we should not forget shoe pegs, tongue depressors, and pencils. Many stately old trees were burned for heat or in the steam engines of trains and ships.

Not far from this trail is an old iron furnace where ore was heated to extract metal. Hundreds of men were employed just to cut timber for the furnace, which burned fifty cords at a time. It operated from 1843 until 1890 and incinerated *twenty thousand* cords of wood *each year.*

And then there were the many acres burned for the sole purpose of clearing farm fields. Thoreau writes of traveling through Maine and coming across "more than a hundred acres of heavy timber, which had just been felled and burnt over, and was still smoking...and no man be warmed by it."

IN MAINE, EVERYTHING seems to happen on a large scale. First it was all covered in trees, and then almost all the trees were cut. Between 1998 and 2003, five and a half million acres traded hands: big deals, involving big money, carried out in big boardrooms far from the forest. In 2003, with a pocket full of money, Roxanne Quimby joined the game.

Quimby got rich by starting Burt's Bees. She was living in a cabin with no plumbing, trying to earn money by buying and selling at yard sales. She started making skin-care products in her kitchen, then expanded the business to an unused cabin, and finally moved into real production space. Her products were pure and her marketing savvy. Eventually a New York investment group noticed and bought the business. Suddenly she had 175 million dollars.

Quimby started using her money to buy cut-over timberland. In the same year she sold her business, she paid more than nineteen million dollars for about forty thousand acres of forest land. She could think of nothing she'd rather do with her money than save some of Maine's forests from being cut yet again.

"I'm interested in creating wilderness to allow natural processes to evolve, and where human impacts are as minimal as possible," she said in response to questions about her intentions. Many people would be pleased to hear their new neighbor say that, but not the Mainers I met.

When I stopped in a convenience store on my way to Gulf Hagas, I saw a pile of bumper stickers on the counter that said "No Roxanne," with a red circle and a slash through her name. The guy behind the counter practically started spitting when I asked why he didn't like what she was doing. Seems that when timber companies own the land, local folks can do whatever they want there. Many of the locals lease "camps"; they can drive in on the logging roads, hunt whatever is legal, and cut firewood. If you're a logger or a truck driver, even your paycheck comes from the timber company.

Now some rich woman wanted to close some of the logging roads, raise the rents, and halt the killing and cutting, and the locals were mad as hell about that. Her response was gutsy: "Irving [the former owner] didn't give me this land. I didn't inherit it. I didn't win the lottery. I sweated and worked for years and earned the privilege of being the steward."

But she doesn't want to stay the steward forever. Her dream is that the property she purchases will someday become part of a new national park that would wrap around Baxter State Park, providing even more habitat for birds and beasts. The forests would be allowed to recover.

"As I get into the second half of my life," Quimby said, "I ask myself, 'What have I left behind?' and, 'What is my legacy?'" She finds inspiration in the legacy of Baxter State Park's founder, Percy Baxter.

Baxter came from a wealthy family and was active in Maine politics in the early 1900s. He was also a student of history and knew that timber

barons had gotten rich from what rightfully belonged to the citizens of the state. Baxter lived in the worst possible era for anyone who loved forests. The virgin timber had mostly all been cut, and the fresh scars covered the land. Whatever original forest was left was falling quickly. Baxter longed to preserve some of it as a sanctuary for "wild beasts and birds," as well as for the benefit of the people. He set his sights on Maine's most famous mountain, Mount Katahdin.

At a speech he gave in 1921, Baxter asked, "Shall any great timberland or paper-making corporation, or group of such corporations, themselves the owners of millions of acres of Maine forests, say to the People of this State, 'You shall not have Mount Katahdin, either as a memorial of your past or as a heritage for your future'?"

But indeed, the corporations did say that, and even his political influence didn't help. Time after time, Baxter introduced bills to purchase Katahdin as a state park, and time after time, they were defeated.

So he did it the old-fashioned, American way—with private capital. Af-ter he retired from politics, he started buying land and donating it to the state. By the time he died, he had purchased and donated more than two hundred thousand acres for Baxter State Park, acquiring the last parcel when he was eighty-seven years old. Like Quimby, Baxter wanted the land to be "forever wild" and didn't allow hunting in the park.

William O. Douglas was a Supreme Court justice for thirty-six years, from 1939 to 1975. He was probably the last true naturalist to serve on our nation's highest court and the only one to hike the entire Appalachian Trail. He famously argued that trees and other natural resources should have le-gal standing and we should be able to sue for their preservation. About Baxter State Park, he remarked, "No cutting of trees. No killing of animals or birds. No roads. This is the kind of wilderness for which men pray."

It's also the kind of wilderness that makes some locals fighting mad. I'm sure there were some who hated Baxter in his time too, but today he is con-sidered a visionary and a hero, and hundreds of thousands of people visit his park each year.

YESTERDAY, I TOOK some environmental economics students on a forest tour, describing to them what an old-growth forest would look like. One of the students asked about the relationship between forests and carbon dioxide. "How important are the forests in lowering carbon dioxide levels and reducing the rate of climate change?" Another asked, "Do older forests sequester more carbon than young forests?" Good questions. To answer them, we need instruments that measure carbon dioxide—fairly easy to ob-tain—and forests of varying ages on which to install research plots. I shared with the students the story of one particular research plot in Maine where some of their questions were being answered.

IN THE 1980s, the Environmental Protection Agency initiated the Moun-tain Cloud Chemistry Project. Research stations were set up in forests in the mountains of North Carolina, Virginia, New York, and Maine, and the federal government helped pay for research instruments. These sites would be monitored for air pollutants, such as ozone, nitrogen oxides, and sulfur oxides; the rain would be analyzed for acidity and pollutants; and trees in select plots would be measured and monitored. By comparing results across a wide geographic area, perhaps we could better understand how human actions were affecting forests.

The Maine research site was established at Howland Forest, a 550-acre parcel of mature forest owned by International Paper. In 1986, IP declared it a research forest and allowed access to government agencies and universities. Soon, monitoring equipment was installed and measurements began.

By this time, the scientific community recognized that not only were air pollution and acid rain threatening our forests, but the rise in atmospheric carbon dioxide had intricate links to our forest ecosystems as well. NASA's Atmospheric Sciences research group set up equipment to measure carbon gases as part of its Forest Ecosystem Dynamics study. Researchers from the University of Maine, the University of New Hampshire, and the Woods Hole Research Center started to work in Howland Forest, and the list of government agencies and universities involved in research there continued to grow. Data was shared between teams, and the synergy and complexity of their models was unprecedented in the world. Among other lessons, their research has taught us that forests are the most important carbon sink on land, that the increase in atmospheric carbon is causing forests to grow faster than they used to grow; and that old-growth forests continue to sequester carbon by storing most of it in the soil.

Howland Forest may be the best example of old-growth forest in Maine, but as an important study plot containing expensive scientific instruments, it isn't open to the public.

Although researchers have been allowed to use it for two decades, Howland Forest was recently threatened by logging. International Paper sold its forests to an investment company, GMO Renewable Resources, and the new ownership was under no obligation to allow research to continue. In fact, the most valuable wood they had was in this old-growth forest. The chief executive officer of the investment company, a former Harvard economics major, has given instructions to "maximize the profits." The numbers in the portfolio are paramount, and sometimes the profits from threatening destruction are pretty good. The new owners made a deal: give us a million dollars and we won't log your precious old-growth research forest.

It's not fair—it's like blackmail—but what could the researchers and forest lovers do except come up with the money? Quimby's foundation has donated to this cause, too.

HOLLY HUGHES IS a Howland Forest researcher, but she wasn't spending her weekend researching, hiking, or even cleaning her house. She was spending it at an agricultural fair, educating the public about what was happening to Howland Forest and hoping to raise contributions to save it. That's where I met her. She's the one who told me about the Hermitage at Gulf Hagas, and the little bit of old growth there open to the public.

I HAD A lovely day in the northern forest and a nice visit with the through-hiker. But when I look at a map of Maine and see its vastness, and remember that it was covered with old-growth forest at the dawning of this nation and now only a minuscule fraction is left to enjoy...when I see what the combination of commerce and apathy have done to our landscape...well, I hope we are capable of better.

I will let William O. Douglas close this chapter, as he closed his book *My Wilderness: East to Katahdin*:

> Those who value the woods in terms of dollars will always be pitted against those who love wilderness for itself. If we are to survive, we must make Katahdin the symbol of our struggle for independence from the machine that promises to enslave us. We must multiply the Baxter Parks a thousandfold in order to accommodate our burgeoning population. We must provide enough wilderness areas so that, no matter how dense our population, man—though apartment born—may attend the great school of the outdoors, and come to know the joy of walking in the woods, alone and unafraid. Once he experiences that joy he will be restless to return over and over again to discover the never-ending glories of God's wilderness and perhaps solve some of its mysteries. Before long he will cease to enter our wild precincts as a predator. He will come with reverence.

Epilogue

Y JOURNEYS TO old growth for this book have ended, but in
some ways my relationship with old growth has just begun. I
now know what it is like to be in the heart of a forest unmanaged by humans. Time after time, in the depths of the forest, I was surprised by the experience of beauty. Author and poet Frederick Turner said,
"The experience of beauty is a recognition of the deepest tendency or theme
of the universe as a whole."

If the universe has a direction, I can think of none better than toward
the beautiful. Nature writer Susan Zwinger, who also traveled alone in her
truck, wrote, "I believe that our salvation as a species will come through
the revival of the sense of beauty, our wanting it above all else; through it a
vital need to preserve nature arrives." As we develop our sense of beauty, I
believe we will come to prefer old growth to gross income.

Some people I have met feel threatened by that idea. They say I am un-
realistic. "Don't you live in a wood-framed house, burn wood for heat, and
print your words on tree fiber?" Well, yes, I do, and I plan to continue doing
so. I can accept that some percentage of our forests will be cleared and developed, whether for farming or for building, and that some percentage will
be managed for timber resources. But I cannot accept that those uses should

add up to 99 percent, as they do now in most eastern states. I am just asking for some balance, for some places where forests can grow old.

NOW THAT I have been to at least one old-growth forest in every state east of the Mississippi River (perhaps a record of some sort), I am frequently asked what my favorites are. Choosing an order would be impossible, but my top four are Cook Forest in Pennsylvania, the Porcupine Mountains in Michigan, Sipsey Wilderness in Alabama, and Congaree National Park in South Carolina. These are the places I keep urging others to visit so they, too, will see and understand what our land aspires to be, and what it can perhaps be again in more places, given enough time. When I think about what these four hold in common, besides their old-growth status, I see that they each cover vast acreage. In these expanses, many tree communities can exist, and many animal communities can find the food and shelter they require—and of course, the two are related. Although the smaller bits of old growth are just as lovely when one is sitting in their midst, they do not—cannot—function ecologically in the same way as a large expanse of forest.

The struggle to preserve our oldest forests is far from over, but there is good news along with the bad. The land trust movement is growing as more and more landowners decide to protect their property for the benefit of future generations and to preserve habitat for the many other life forms that live with us. Foresters are waking up to what is happening. The Nature Conservancy continues to bid on any old-growth remnants that come up for sale, thanks to the generosity of its donors.

Many people do care. I meet them every day. They give me hope that what I dream really is possible: we will so love and appreciate old-growth forests that we will not only stop the cutting of those that remain, but also be moved to create future old-growth forests—places that have been cut over in the past, but where we have the foresight to say, "No, not again." This could be our generation's unique legacy: more old growth instead of less. If we could do it, we would be the first generation in recorded history to do so.

I was encouraged when I learned recently that a proposal had been put forward to create an Old-Growth National Park, which would link many existing old-growth forests in California, Oregon, and Washington and bring them under federal protection.

I have started working toward my dream of an old-growth forest network. I invite you to be a part of that quest. Please contact me via www. amongtheancient.com, and we'll see what we can do together.

RECENTLY, I WAS invited to see a massive tree just ten miles from my office. I was thrilled to recognize the patterns of an old-growth forest: large trees of many different species, standing snags, downed logs in varying stages of decomposition, an undulating forest floor, a deep layer of litter and duff, the songs of forest birds, the feeling of joy, the presence of beauty.

The absentee landowner was convinced to sell the forest to the Nature Conservancy, and they awarded me a grant to study it; my science calls me back. Since my travels ended, I have been spending my days in the local forests with students from the university. Together we are recording tree species, sizes, and spacing. We are using statistics, measurements in centimeters, and computer spreadsheets to describe these special places of dappled light. Satellites help us keep track of our plot locations. The students have learned the Latin names of the trees.

But I haven't forgotten what I learned about beauty; that, too, I have subjected to scientific examination. After testing hundreds of university students, I learned that knowledge makes little difference in what we perceive as "beautiful" in a forest. What seems to matter most is the age of the trees: the older they are, the more beautiful they are. Well, how about that?

THESE LINES BY poet T. S. Eliot are familiar, but now I hear them in a new way:

> We shall not cease from exploration
> And the end of all our exploring
> Will be to arrive where we started
> And know the place for the first time.
> Through the unknown, unremembered gate
> When the last of the earth left to discover
> Is that which was the beginning;

To know this place, our planetary home, entirely is an impossible task. But there are some places we can go and some things we can learn during our time here that will make our experience of life richer. These places and this knowledge bring a sense of connection often lacking in our everyday lives. We can go there. We can put our brief lives in perspective. We can be surrounded by beauty and mystery. We can get to old growth. I'll see you there.

Other Forests of Interest

Not all of these forests are open to the public without making prior arrangements.

ALABAMA: Flomaton Natural Area

CONNECTICUT: Sage's Ravine

DELAWARE: Flint Woods Preserve

FLORIDA: Eglin Air Force Base Natural Areas

GEORGIA: Coleman River Trail, Chattahoochee National Forest

ILLINOIS: Spitler Woods State Natural Area

INDIANA: Rocky Hollow, Falls Canyon Nature Preserve

KENTUCKY: Lilley Cornett Woods

MAINE: Big Reed Preserve

MARYLAND: Crabtree Creek Woods, Potomac/Garrett State Forest

MASSACHUSETTS: Ice Glen

MICHIGAN: Hartwick Pines State Park

MISSISSIPPI: Sky Lake Wildlife Management Area, Leroy Percy State Park

NEW HAMPSHIRE: Tamworth Big Pines

NEW JERSEY: Hutcheson Memorial Forest

NEW YORK: Five Ponds Wilderness, Adirondacks

NORTH CAROLINA: Cataloochee Valley, Great Smoky Mountains National Park

OHIO: Dysart Woods

PENNSYLVANIA: Snyder-Middleswarth Natural Area

RHODE ISLAND: Crandall Swamp

SOUTH CAROLINA: Francis Beidler Forest

TENNESSEE: Albright Grove, Great Smoky Mountains National Park

VERMONT: Camel's Hump State Forest

VIRGINIA: Cypress Bridge along Nottoway River

WEST VIRGINIA: Gaudineer Scenic Area

WISCONSIN: Wyalusing State Park

Notes

EPIGRAPH

Rilke lines: Rainer Maria Rilke, "Orpheus. Eurydice. Hermes," *Neue gedichte* (*New Poems*) (1907), lines 75-81, trans. Joan Maloof.

PREFACE

The maps of the virgin forest area came from: W. B. Greeley, "The Relation of Geography to Timber Supply," *Economic Geography* 1, no. 1 (1925): 1-14.

For definitions of old growth, see: Maurice Schwartz, "Ninety-eight (Yes, 98) (Alleged) Definitions of Old Growth Forests!" http://www. nativetreesociety.org/oldgrowth/ninetyeight.htm. This list was originally prepared by the Food and Agriculture Organization of the United Nations, Forestry Division; and John Davis, *Eastern Old-growth Forests: Prospects for Rediscovery and Recovery* (Washington, DC: Island Press, 1996), xi; and Bruce Kershner and Robert T. Leverett, *The Sierra Club Guide to the Ancient Forests of the Northeast* (San Francisco: Sierra Club Books, 2004).

For information on the amount of old growth left, see: Mary Byrd Davis, ed., *Eastern Old-growth Forests: Prospects for Rediscovery and Recovery*

(Washington, DC: Island Press, 1996), 31.

For a western forest viewpoint on our inability to agree on what old growth is, how much exists, or how much existed in the past, see: Mickey Ross, "Old Growth: Failures of the Past and Hope for the Future," *Old Growth in a New World* (Washington, DC: Island Press, 2009), 158-167.

ALABAMA

Date of visit: October 12-13, 2007

For Gosse quote, see: Philip Henry Gosse, *Letters from Alabama: Chiefly Relating to Natural History* (1859; repr. Tuscaloosa: University of Alabama Press, 1993), 117-118.

For Rumi quote, see: Coleman Barks, *The Essential Rumi* (New Jersey: Castle Books, 1997), 36.

TENNESSEE

Date of visit: August 16, 2007

For information on the heat wave, see: B. Rucker, "Scorching Temps in South, Midwest Kill 37," *The Daily Times* (Salisbury, MD), August 18, 2007.

For Muir quote, see: John Muir, *A Thousand-Mile Walk to the Gulf* (Boston: Houghton Mifflin, 1916), 38.

For information on yellow buckeye trees, see: Edward Clebsch and Richard T. Busing, "Secondary Succession, Gap Dynamics, and Community Structure in a Southern Appalachian Cove Forest," *Ecology* 70 (1989): 728-735; and the *Silvics Manual* available online at http://na.fs.fed.us/spfo/silvics_manual/volume_2/aesculus/octandra.htm. Age estimates courtesy of Neil Pederson, Eastern Kentucky University, pers. comm. with author, August, 21, 2007.

For Douglas quote, see: William O. Douglas, *My Wilderness: East to Katahdin* (New York: Doubleday, 1961), 161.

Natural History Notes

The white snakeroot flowers are *Eupatorium rugosum*.
The buckeyes are *Aeseulus octandra*.

North Carolina

Date of visit: August 16, 2007

For Faulkner quote, see: William Faulkner, "The Bear," in *Go Down, Moses* (New York: Random House, 1942; New York: Vintage Books, 1973). For green burial quote, see: Woodland Services website, site updated August 7, 2007, accessed August 23, 2007, http://www.eternalforest.org. For information on basal area in the forest, see: Henry Oosting and P. Bordeau, "Virgin Hemlock Forest Segregates in the Joyce Kilmer Memorial Forest of Western North Carolina," *Botanical Gazette* 116 (1955): 340-359.

For information about Ravenel's Woods, see: Robert Zahner, *The Mountain at the End of the Trail* (Highlands, NC: privately printed, 1994), 72-73; and Henry Oosting and W. D. Billings, "Edapho-Vegetational Relation's in Ravenel's Woods, A Virgin Hemlock Forest near Highlands, North Carolina," *American Midland Naturalist* 22 (1939): 333-350.

South Carolina

Date of visit: October 26, 2007

For Hampton quotes, see: Harry Hampton, *Woods and Waters and Some Asides* (Columbia: State Printing, 1979), 294.

Florida

Date of visit: December 3, 2007

For Wilson quotes, see: Edward O. Wilson, *Naturalist* (Washington, DC: Island Press, 1994), 268-281.

For Cushing quote, see: Frank Cushing, "Exploration of Ancient Key Dwellers' Remains on the Gulf Coast of Florida," *Proceedings of the American Philosophical Society* 35 (1896): 329-448.

Natural History Notes

The lignumvitae tree is *Guaiacum sanctum*.
The Florida purple wing butterfly is *Eunica tatila*.
The poisonwood tree is *Metopium toxiferum*.
The family of the poisonwood and poison ivy is Anacardiaceae.
The gumbo limbo is *Bursea simaruba*.

GEORGIA
Date of visit: May 19, 2009

For information on longleaf pine forests, including amount left, biodiversity, and dependence on fire, see: Lawrence S. Earley, *Looking for Longleaf* (Chapel Hill: University of North Carolina Press, 2004).

For information on locations of old-growth longleaf pine, see: John S. Kush, "Remnant Old-Growth Longleaf Pine (*Pinus palustris* Mill.) Savannas and Forests of the Southeastern USA: Status and Threats," *Natural Areas Journal* 24, no.2 (2004): 141-149.

For more on the history of the Moody family and the forest, see: Janisse Ray, ed., *Moody Forest* (Baxley, GA: Wildfire Press, 2007).

The quote from Rachel Carson is from: Rachel Carson and Linda Lear, *Lost Woods: Discovered Writing of Rachel Carson* (Boston: Beacon Press, 1998), 159.

For information on sight in the worm lizard, see: Carl Eigenmann, *Cave Vertebrates of America: A Study in Degenerative Evolution* (Washington, DC: Carnegie Institution, 1909).

Natural History Notes
The longleaf pine is *Pinus palustris*.
The wiregrass is *Andropogon spp.*
The candyroot is *Polygala nana*.
The Queen's-delight is *Stillingia sylvatica*.
The cat bells are *Baptisia perfoliata*.
The finger rot is *Cnidoscolus urens*.
The skullcap is *Scutellaria sp.*
The red-cockaded woodpecker is *Picoides borealis*.
The rare black rove beetle is *Lordithon niger*.
The tumbling flower beetle is in the family Mordellidae.
The Florida worm lizard is *Rhineura floridana*.

Travel Notes
Once you turn off Route 1, most of the roads are red clay; they can get very slippery after a rain. Also, be prepared for mosquitoes.

Mississippi
Date of visit: October 11, 2007

For quotes about the scenic area, see: GORP website, "National Parks-National Forests, Bienville," accessed October 15, 2007, http://gorp.away.com/gorp/resource/us_national_forest/ms_missi.htm; and "The Bienville Pines Scenic Area, Management Plan of the Bienville National Forest," (unpublished, 1986).

For information on the history of Bienville Pines, see: Ray Connaro, "The Beginning: Recollections and Comments," (Mississippi Forest Service, unknown year, also available from the Forest History Society).

Natural History Notes
The loblolly pine is *Pinus taeda.*
The shortleaf pine is *Pinus echinata.*

Virginia
Date of visit: July 30, 2006

For information on nettles, see: Niklas Janz, Klas Nyblom, and Soren Nylin, "Evolutionary Dynamics of Host-Plant Specialization: A Case Study of the Tribe Nymphalini," *Evolution* 55 (2001): 783-796.

Natural History Notes
Wineberries are *Rubus phoenicolasius.*
Wood-nettles are *Laportea canadensis.*

Travel Notes
I suggest going in late July or early August when the wineberries are ripe and the water in the creek is low.

West Virginia
Date of visit: June 26, 2007

For information on spider mating, see: R. L. Gering, "Structure and Function of the Genitalia in Some American Agelenid Spiders," *Smithsonian Miscellaneous Collections* 121 (1953): ii-84, quotes from 47, 55, 60,

63; and Mirjam D. Papke, Susan E. Riechert, and Stefan Schulz, "An Airborne Female Pheromone Associated with Male Attraction and Courtship in a Desert Spider," *Animal Behaviour* 61 (2001): 877-886; and Fred Singer, Susan E. Riechert, Hongfa Xu, Anthony W. Morris, Jeanette Hale, and Noureddine Maher, "Analysis of Courtship Success in the Funnel-Web Spider *Agelenopsis aperta*," *Behaviour* 137 (2000): 93-117; and Elizabeth Becker, Susan E. Riechert, and Fred Singer, "Male Induction of Female Quiescence/Catalepsis During Courtship in the Spider *Agelenopsis aperta*," *Behaviour* 142 (2005): 57-70.

For Emerson quote, see: Ralph Waldo Emerson, *The American Scholar: Self-Reliance, Compensation* (New York: American Book, 1911), 90.

For Luoma quote, see: Jon R. Luoma, *The Hidden Forest* (Corvallis: Oregon State University Press, 1999), 209.

For information on fern feeding caterpillars, see: T. E. Ruehlmann, R. W. Matthews, and J. R. Matthews, "Roles for Structural and Temporal Shelter-Changing by Fern-Feeding Lepidopteran Larvae," *Oecologia* 75 (1988): 228-232; and Martha R. Weiss, "Good Housekeeping: Why do Shelter-Dwelling Caterpillars Fling their Frass?" *Ecology Letters* 6 (2003): 361-370.

For Marsh quote on hydrology, see: George Perkins Marsh, *Man and Nature* (New York: Charles Scribner, 1864), 172.

For the history of logging in the east, see: Roy B. Clarkson, *Tumult on the Mountains* (Parsons, WV: McClain Printing, 1964; repr. 1997); and Pete Gerrell, *Old Trees: The Illustrated History of Logging the Virgin Timber in the Southeastern United States* (Crawfordville, FL: SYP Publishing, 2000).

Natural History Notes
The spider is probably an *Agelenopsis* in the family Agelenidae.
The fern with the ball is *Dryopteris intermedia*.
The green caterpillar is *Herpetogramma*.

Travel Notes
Bring a picnic—there's a nice shelter—or eat at the local restaurant just across the street from the parking area. The closest campground is Horseshoe Recreation Area, about ten miles away (but I was not able to find it). There are also campsites and a lodge at Blackwater Falls State Park, just a bit further south. To the north are private campgrounds along the Cheat River.

DELAWARE

Date of visit: August 7, 2006

For quote from Peter Pan, see: James Matthew Barrie, *Peter Pan and Wendy* (New York Scribner, 1953), 215.

For quotes about the James Branch, see: Ed Lewandowski, "Canoeing the James Branch," *Outdoor Delaware* (1998): 4-8.

For information about dragonflies, see: Philip S. Corbet, *Dragonflies: Behavior and Ecology* (Ithaca, NY: Comstock, 1999).

For quotes about shooting birds, see: John James Audubon, *Ornithological Biography* (Edinburgh: Adam and Charles Black, 1831), 136; and John Burroughs, *Wake-Robin* (Boston: Houghton Mifflin, 1913), 45.

Natural History Notes
The darners were probably in the genus *Anax* or *Aeshna*.

MARYLAND

Date of visit: May 22, 2008

For information on Oxalis reproduction, see: Marie Jasieniuk and M. Lechowicz, "Spatial and Temporal Variation in Chasmogamy and Cleistogamy in *Oxalis montana* (Oxalidaceae)," *American Journal of Botany* 74, no. 11 (1987): 1672-1680.

For information on the history of Maryland's state forests, see: Fred W. Besley, *The Forests of Maryland* (Annapolis: Advertiser-Republican, 1916), 25; and "Hundreds of Majestic Oaks in Garrett Fall Prey to Ax," *The Sun* (Baltimore), September 14, 1940; and Eugene P. Parker, "When Forests Trumped Parks: the Maryland Experience, 1906-1950," *Maryland Historical Magazine* 101, no. 2 (2006): 203-224.

NEW JERSEY

Date of visit: July 24, 2007

For quote about Saddler's Woods, see: D. Yarrow, "MacArthur Heritage Forest," *New York Old-Growth Forest Association newsletter*, April 2, 2002.

For the history of Saddler's Woods, see: The website of the Saddler's

Woods Conservation Association, "History," accessed August 6, 2007, http://www.saddlerswoods.org.

Pennsylvania

Date of visit: June 28-29, 2007

For Leopold quote, see: Aldo Leopold, *A Sand County Almanac* (New York: Ballantine Books, 1949, repr. 1966), 262.

For the story of the Chestnut blight, see: Susan Freinkel, *The Perfect Tree: The Life, Death and Rebirth of the American Chestnut* (Berkeley: University of California Press, 2007).

For information about spiral grain, see: J. Maddern Harris, *Spiral Grain and Wave Phenomena in Wood Formation* (Berlin: Springer-Verlag, 1989).

For the history of Cook Forest, see: Arthur E. Cook, *The Cook Forest: An Island in Time* (Helena, MT: Falcon, 1997).

For quote on the economic value of wild places, see: Paul Richards, "The Return of NREPA: Thinking Big in the Northern Rockies," *CounterPunch*, April 21/22, 2007, http://www.counterpunch.org/richards04212007.html.

For information on bacteria in and on humans, see: Alexandra Goho, "Our Microbes, Ourselves," *Science News* 171 (2007): 314-315.

For information on leaf and human blood bacteria,see: Pers. comm., Mark Holland, Salisbury University, Salisbury, MD.

For philosophical discussion of serious beauty, see: Ronald Hepburn, "Trivial and Serious in Aesthetic Appreciation of Nature," in *Landscape, Natural Beauty, and the Arts*, Salim Kemal and Ivan Gaskell, eds. (Cambridge: Cambridge University Press, 1993).

Kentucky

Date of visit: August 15, 2007

For information on magnolias, see: Hiroshi Azuma, José G. Garcia-Franco, Victor Rico-Gray, and Leonard Thien, "Molecular Phylogeny of the Magnoliaceae: the Biography of Tropical and Temperate Disjunctions," *American Journal of Botany* 88 (2001): 2,275-2,285.

For information on refugia and tree migration, see: Hazel R. Delcourt, *Forests in Peril* (Blacksburg, VA: McDonald and Woodward, 2002); and Louis R.

Iverson, Anantha M. Prasad, Betsy J. Hale, and Elaine K. Sutherland, *Atlas of Current and Potential Future Distribution of Common Trees of the Eastern United States,* Gen. Tech. Rep. NE-265, (Radnor, PA: U.S. Department of Agriculture, Forest Service, Northeastern Research Station, 1999).

For information about Braun's Kentucky forest, see: E. Lucy Braun, "The Forest of Lynn Fork of Leatherwood," *Nature Magazine* (1936): 237-238; and Marcia M. Bonta, ed., *American Women Afield* (Texas A & M University Press, College Station, TX: 1995).

For information on rock tripe growth rates, see: B. Fink, "The Rate of Growth and Ecesis in Lichens," *Mycologia* 9 (1917): 138-158.

Natural History Notes
The fraser magnolia is *Magnolia fraseri.*
The mushroom that grows on magnolia cones is *Strobilurus conigenoides.*
The swamp magnolia is *Magnolia virginiana.*
The smooth rock tripe lichen is *Umbilicaria mammulata.*

Travel Notes
The trail is open sunrise to sunset. There is an elegant new bathhouse near the pool at the true start of the trail. No camping is allowed at the trailhead, but there are a number of parks with camping areas within a twenty-mile radius. There are motels in Harlan.

ILLINOIS
Date of visit: September 6, 2007
For butterfly information, see: Jacalyn Loyd Goetz, "Zebra Swallowtail," Johnson County K-State Research and Extension Master Gardener, http://www.oznet.ksu.edu/johnson/hort/Butterfly/ZebraSwallowtail.htm

For the Silvics manual, see: Russell M. Burns, and Barbara H. Honkala, tech. coords., *Silvics of North America: 1. Conifers; 2. Hardwoods*, Agriculture Handbook 654, (Washington, DC: U.S. Department of Agriculture, Forest Service, 1990).

Doctor who claims pawpaws can cure cancer: Jerry McLaughlin.

For information on patent leather beetles, see: A. S. Pearse, M. Patterson, J. Rankin, and G. W. Wharton, "The Ecology of *Passalus cornutus fabricus*, a Beetle which Lives in Rotting Logs," *Ecological Monographs* 6 (1936): 455-490; and I. E. Gray, "Observations on the Life History of the Horned Passalus," *American Midland Naturalist* 35 (1946): 728-746; and Ning Zhang, Sung-Oui Suh, and Meredith Blackwell, "Microorganisms in the Gut of Beetles: Evidence from Molecular Cloning," *Journal of Invertebrate Pathology* 84 (2003): 226-233.

Natural History Notes
The beautiful spicebush swallowtail is *Papilio troilus*.
The tiny wormlike nematode is *Chondronema passali*.

Travel Notes
Although camping is available at the park, I urge you to stay at the Inn at New Harmony, Indiana, about twenty miles away across the Wabash River.

Indiana
Date of visit: September 5, 2007
    For Wendell Berry line, see: Wendell Berry, "The Country of Marriage," stanza 4, *The Country of Marriage* (New York: Harcourt Brace Jovanovich, 1975), 7.
    For information on the songs of insects, see: Lang Elliot and Wil Hershberger, *The Songs of Insects* (Boston: Houghton Mifflin, 2007).

Travel notes
I recommend a stop to see the remarkable lobby of the West Baden Springs Hotel (www.frenchlick.com), eleven miles from the forest.

Ohio
Date of visit: June 28, 2007
    For information on Naess, see: Arne Naess, *Life's Philosophy: Reason and Feeling in a Deeper World* (Athens: The University of Georgia Press, 2002).
    For Antler poem quote, see: Elizabeth Roberts and Elias Amidon, eds., *Earth Prayers from Around the World* (San Francisco: Harper Collins, 1991), 316.

For information on mayapple rust, see: H. H. Whetzel, H. S. Jackson, and E. B. Mains, "The Composite Life History of *Puccinia podophylli* Schw.," *Journal of Agricultural Research* 30 (1925): 65-79.

For Braun quotes, see: E. Lucy Braun, *The Woody Plants of Ohio* (Columbus: Ohio State University Press, 1961).

Natural History Notes

The mayapple is *Podophyllum peltatum.*

Mayapple rust is *Puccinia podophylli.*

Travel Notes

The nearby town of Kidron is the heart of Amish country. Please be respectful to those traveling by horse and buggy. On Thursdays between 10:00 a.m. and 2:30 p.m., there is a fascinating livestock auction worth planning your trip around. There is nowhere to camp in this county, unless you're interested in an asphalt-covered RV park. The Royal Star Inn just south of Orrville has received good reviews.

WISCONSIN

Date of visit: July 14-15, 2007

The biblical reference to Balm-of-Gilead is *Jeremiah* 8:22.

For information about the uses of balsam poplar, see: Earl J. S. Rook, "*Populus balsamifera,*" updated March 4, 2006, http://rook.org/earl/bwca/nature/trees/populusbal.html.

For quote about the old growth, see: The website of the National Park Service, "Apostle Islands National Lakeshore—The Island Forest," http://nps.gov/apis/old_grow.htm.

For Buber quote, see: Martin Buber, *I and Thou,* trans. Ronald Gregor Smith (New York: Scribner's, 1923; repr. 1958), 7.

Travel Notes

Justice Bay has a beautiful beach with terracotta sand and smooth, round stones in a variety of colors. At one end of the beach are sea caves, which you can paddle through and enjoy the rippling, reflected sunlight on the cave's ceilings.

MICHIGAN
Date of visit: July 15-17, 2007

For Thoreau quote, see: Henry David Thoreau, *The Maine Woods* (Princeton: Princeton University Press, 1974).

For information on the green spider, see: M. Aiken and F. A. Coyle, "Habitat Distribution, Life History and Behavior of Tetragnatha Spider Species in the Great Smoky Mountains National Park," *Journal of Arachnology* 28 (2000): 97-106.

For information on the bird feeding study, see: Robert T. Mitchell, "Consumption of Spruce Budworms by Birds in a Maine Spruce-Fir Forest," *Journal of Forestry* 50 (1952): 387-389.

For information on Blackburnian warblers, see: J. Christopher Haney and Charles P. Schaadt, "Functional Roles of Eastern Old Growth in Promoting Forest Bird Diversity," in *Eastern Old-Growth Forests* (Washington, DC: Island Press, 1996), 76-88; and Robert H. MacArthur, "Population Ecology of Some Warblers of Northeastern Coniferous Forests," *Ecology* 39 (1958): 599-619; and V. P. Wystrach, "General Note: Ashton Blackburne's Place in American Ornithology," *Auk* 92 (1975): 607-610.

For information on Phoebes, see: Steven R. Hill and J. Edward Gates, "Nesting Ecology and Microhabitat of the Eastern Phoebe in the Central Appalachians," *American Midland Naturalist* 120 (1988): 313-324.

For the Rilke quote, see: Rainer Maria Rilke, "Everything Beckons to Us," *Possibility of Being* (New York: New Directions, 1977).

Natural History Notes
The bluebead lily is *Clintonia borealis.*
The small green spider discovered on the hemlock trees is *Tetragnatha viridis.*

NEW YORK
Date of visit: July 25, 2007

For the history of Manhattan, see: The website of Old and Sold, "The White Man Arrives," accessed July 29, 2007, orig. pub. in *Manhattan And New York City History* (n.p., 1930s), http://www.oldandsold.com/articles14/new-york-2.shtml.

Searching for remaining natural bits of Manhattan: Nick Paumgarten, "The Mannahatta Project," *The New Yorker* (October 1, 2007): 44-50.

For quote on sound of nature, see: Jane Kay, "Lifelong Listener Fears the Sound of Nature's Silence; He has Recorded Call of the Wild for Decades, but Worries Earth's Music will Soon be Lost," *San Francisco Chronicle*, May 20, 2007.

For information about the Adirondack forest preserve, see: The website of the New York State Department of Environmental Conservation, "Adirondack Forest Preserve," http://dec.ny.gov/lands/5263.html.

Natural History Notes
Ginkgo is *Ginkgo biloba*.
The red-tailed hawk is *Buteo jamaicensis*.

RHODE ISLAND

Date of visit: September 25, 2007

For Thoreau quotes, see: Henry David Thoreau, "Walking" in *The Natural History Essays*, R. Sattelmeyer, ed. (Salt Lake City: Peregrine Smith Books, 1980), 117.

For Pinchot quotes and information, see: Gifford Pinchot, *The Training of a Forester* (Philadelphia: Lippencott, 1937), 14; and Char Miller, "A Reconstruction of Gifford Pinchot's *Training of a Forester*, 1914-37," *Forest & Conservation History* 38 (1994): 7-15.

For Largess quotes, see: Carol Stocker, "Old-Growth, Grand Specimens Drive Big-Tree Hunters," *Boston Globe*, November 17, 2005.

For information on the principles of ecoforestry, see: Alan Drenson and Duncan Taylor, eds., *Ecoforestry* (Gabrioloa Island, BC: New Society Publishers, 1997), 274.

For the healing power of nature, see: Richard Louv, *Last Child in the Woods: Saving our Children from Nature-Deficit Disorder* (Chapel Hill: Algonquin Books of Chapel Hill, 2005); and Rachel Kaplan and Stephen Kaplan, *The Experience of Nature: A Psychological Perspective* (Cambridge: Cambridge University Press, 1989).

CONNECTICUT

Date of visit: September 18, 2007

For information on crows, see: John M. Marzluff and Tony Angell, *In the Company of Crows and Ravens* (New Haven: Yale University Press, 2005).

For information on natural forest disturbance, see: Gorgon G. Whitney, *From Coastal Wilderness to Fruited Plain* (Cambridge: Cambridge University Press, 1994), 73-74.

For Pollan quotes, see: Michael Pollan, *Second Nature: A Gardener's Education* (New York: Dell, 1991), 209-238.

For Botkin quote, see: Daniel Botkin, *No Man's Garden: Thoreau and a New Vision for Civilization and Nature* (Washington, DC: Island Press, 2001), 9.

For LaBastille quote, see: Anne LaBastille, *Woodswoman* (New York: Dutton, 1978), 276-277.

MASSACHUSETTS

Date of visit: September 18, 2007

For information on Trouvelot and gypsy moths, see: Leopold Trouvelot, "The American Silk Worm," *American Naturalist* 1 (1867): 30-38; and the website of the U.S. Forest Service, "E. Leopold Trouvelot, Perpetrator of our Problem," last modified October 29, 2003, by Sandy Liebhold, accessed August 10, 2007, http://fs.fed.us/ne/morgantown/4557/gmoth/trouvelot/; and "Map of Gypsy Moth Spread," http://fs.fed.us/ne/morgantown/4557/gmoth/atlas/quar1a.gif.

For the quote about grouse drumming, see: Edward Howe Forbush, *Useful Birds and their Protection: Containing Brief Descriptions of the More Common and Useful Species of Massachusetts, with Accounts of their Food Habits, and a Chapter on the Means of Attracting and Protecting Birds* (Boston: Wright and Potter, 1913).

For information about the grouse survey, see: W. F. Henninger, "A Preliminary List of the Birds of Seneca County, Ohio," *Wilson Bulletin* 18, no. 2 (1906): 47-60.

For additional information about grouse, including stomach contents, see: Don L. Johnson, *Grouse & Woodcock: A Gunner's Guide* (Iola, WI: Krause Publications, 1995).

For quote from bereaved father, see: Chris Kahn, "6 Die from Brain-Eating Amoeba in Lakes," Associated Press Release, Phoenix, AZ, September 29, 2007.

For information on New York State's old-growth bill, see: The website of the Environmental News Service, "Old-Growth Forests in New York State Protected by Law," September 8, 2008, http://ens-newswire.com/ens/sep2008/2008-09-08-092.html.

For Rilke quote, see: Ulrich Baer, ed., *Letters on Life: New Prose Translations/Rainer Maria Rilke* (New York: The Modern Library, 2006), 114.

For Rumi poem, see: John Moyne and Coleman Barks, *Unseen Rain: Quatrains of Rumi* (Watsonville, CA: Threshold Books, 1986), 4.

Natural History Notes
The gypsy moth is *Lymantria dispair.*
The ruffed grouse is *Bonasa umbellus.*

VERMONT
Date of visit: July 5, 2006
For quote about Gifford Woods, see: "Gifford Woods State Park," in website of Vermont Forest, Parks and Recreation, http://vtstateparks.com/htm/gifford.cfm.

For information on aging trees in Gifford Woods, see: F. H. Bormann and M. F. Buell, "Old-Age Stand of Hemlock-Northern Hardwood Forest in Central Vermont," *Bulletin of the Torrey Botanical Club* 91, no. 6 (1964): 451-65.

For information on the effects of increment coring, see: Dieter Eckstein and Dirk Dujesiefken, "Long-Term Effects in Trees Due to Increment Borings," *Dendrochronologia* 16-17, (1998-1999): 205-211.

For information about the history of maple syrup, see: Gordon Whitney and Mariana Upmeyer, "Sweet Trees, Sour Circumstances: the Long Search for Sustainability in the North American Maple Products Industry," *Forest Ecology and Management* 200 (2004): 313-333.

For information on sapsuckers', hummingbirds', and squirrels' utilization of sugar maple sap, see: Laurie Eberhart, "Use and Selection of Sap Trees by Yellow-Bellied Sapsuckers," *The Auk* 117, no.1 (2000): 41-51; and Richard S. Miller and Robert W. Nero, "Hummingbird-Sapsucker

Associations in Northern Climates," *Canadian Journal of Zoology* 61 (1983): 1,540-1,546; and Bernard Heinrich, "Maple Sugaring by Red Squirrels," *Journal of Mammology* 73, no. 1 (1992): 51-54.

Natural History Notes
The yellow-bellied sapsucker is *Sphyrapicus varius*.
The slug might have been *Pallifera dorsalis*.

Travel Notes
This is one bit of old growth that two-year-olds and great-grandparents can enjoy together. If you want to explore the other side of the road, you will need hiking boots and strong ankles. For the sake of all living things and the scientists that have research projects going on there, please be extremely conscious of where you are stepping and do not go with a large group.

NEW HAMPSHIRE
Date of visit: September 19, 2007
For readings on mythology and the hero's journey, see: Joseph Campbell, *The Hero with a Thousand Faces* (1949; Princeton: Princeton University Press, 1972), 29, 78; and Robert Eisner, *The Road to Daulis: Psychoanalysis, Psychology, and Classical Mythology* (Syracuse: Syracuse University Press, 1987).

For information on the Society for the Protection of New Hampshire Forests, see: P. Ellis, "Forest Society Establishes New 'Natural Areas' on Mount Monadnock," Forest Society press release, August 11, 2004; and P. Ellis, "Fostering a Biological Legacy," *Forest Notes* (Fall/Winter 2006): 26-28.

For quote by Douglas, see: William O. Douglas, *My Wilderness: East to Katahdin* (New York: Doubleday, 1961), 212.

For information on red spruce, see: Arthur C. Hart, "Red Spruce (Picea rubens Sarg.)" in *Silvics of Forest Trees of the United States* (Washington, DC: U.S. Department of Agriculture, *Agriculture Handbook* 271, 1965), 305-310.

Travel Notes
There is no camping on the trail or at the parking area. There are many places to stay nearby, including the pricey Notchland Inn, which is practically

next door to the trail. Camping is available at the Dry River Campground in Crawford Notch State Park from mid-May until early October. Call 603-374-2272.

MAINE

Date of visit: September 24, 2007

For information on Roxanne Quimby, see: P. Austin, "Roxanne Quimby Purchases High Priority 24,000 Acre Township East of Baxter Park," *Maine Environmental News,* November 24, 2003.

For quotes by Douglas, see: William O. Douglas, *My Wilderness: East to Katahdin* (New York: Doubleday, 1961), 178, 282, 290.

For information on Percy Baxter, see: C. Bolte and N. Rolde, "The Man who Loved Wilderness," *American Heritage* 29 (1978): 48-55.

For quotes by Thoreau, see: Henry David Thoreau, *The Maine Woods* (Princeton: Princeton University Press, 1974), 6, 70.

For information on the Howland forest, see: The website of the Northeast Wilderness Trust, "Conservation Initiatives," accessed October 21, 2007, http://newilderesstrust.org/article/articleview/13624.

EPILOGUE

For quotes on beauty, see: Fredrick Turner, "An Evolutionary/Chaotic Theory of Beauty and Meaning," *Journal of Social and Evolutionary Systems* 19, no. 2 (1996): 103-125; and Susan Zwinger, *Stalking the Ice Dragon* (Tucson: The University of Arizona Press, 1991), 49.

For poem by Eliot, see: T. S. Eliot, "Four Quartets," number 4, *Little Gidding* (London: Faber and Faber, 1942).

ACKNOWLEDGEMENTS

For known locations of old growth, see: Mary Byrd Davis, ed., *Old Growth in the East: A Survey,* rev. ed. 2003. The revised edition has not been published in hard copy; it is available only as a disk or a download from Appalachia–Science in the Public Interest, Mount Vernon, KY.

Gifford Woods State Park, Vermont

Acknowledgments

I T IS CUSTOMARY to give thanks to one's partner at the end of the acknowledgments, but I must thank my husband, Rick Maloof, first and foremost. Rick was there when the dream of getting to old growth was born, and he supported my vision from beginning to end. Rick, my deepest thanks.

My entire family has been very supportive, and many of my friends have shown genuine interest in my work, and genuine understanding when I was so often unavailable. Extra special thanks go to Alyssa Maloof, Elizabeth Cooper, Carolyn Kearns, David McDaniel, Kaye and Lloyd Byrd, Matthew Cimino, Alexandra Pratt, Nancy Mitchell, James Hatley, Michael Lewis, and Tom Horton.

In the community of old-growth-forest lovers, I would like to acknowledge the work of Mary Byrd Davis and Robert Leverett. If any single person deserves credit for gathering what is known of eastern old growth into one document, it would be Davis. She published the first edition of *Old Growth in the East: A Survey* in 1993. That spark fanned the flame of interest in eastern old growth, and so many new reports came in that Davis created a revised edition in 2003. I used that document as a reference to find ancient forests. Her work—and Leverett's—tracking what little is left made my explorations much easier.

Grateful thanks go to Salisbury University for allowing me to take leave during the 2007 fall semester so I could travel to the forests. Special thanks to Tom Jones and Mark Holland, my provost and department chair, respectively, at that time. My colleagues have shown interest in and support for this project. As usual, the Salisbury University library staff has been cheerful and helpful.

During the writing of this book, I was awarded a brief residency in the H. J. Andrews Forest by the Spring Creek Project at Oregon State University, enabling me to spend some time in beautiful western old growth while assembling the manuscript.

Thanks for accommodations and conversations go to Barbara and Jon Boone, Bill Gehron, and Jane Owens, who has since passed.

Thanks to the many rangers, naturalists, and folks at information desks who patiently answered my questions. I did not always get names, but we are fortunate to have so many wonderful people working in and around our old-growth forests.

A number of people have been kind enough to read earlier versions of a few of these essays and comment on them. Thanks go to Ryan Taylor, Robert Eisner, Colin Johnson, Bill Jacks, Amy Kamble, and three anonymous readers. Of course, any errors remaining on these pages are entirely mine.

Finally, I offer my heartfelt gratitude to anyone who has, in any way, worked to protect a forest.

Index

Ruka Press is committed to preserving ancient forests and natural resources. We elected to print this title on 100% post consumer recycled paper, processed chlorine free. As a result, for this printing, we have saved:

24 Trees (40' tall and 6-8" diameter)
8 Million BTUs of Total Energy
2,305 Pounds of Greenhouse Gases
11,101 Gallons of Wastewater
674 Pounds of Solid Waste

Ruka Press made this paper choice because our printer, Thomson-Shore, Inc., is a member of Green Press Initiative, a nonprofit program dedicated to supporting authors, publishers, and suppliers in their efforts to reduce their use of fiber obtained from endangered forests.

For more information, visit www.greenpressinitiative.org

Environmental impact estimates were made using the Environmental Defense Paper Calculator. For more information visit: www.papercalculator.org.